BLUE GUIDE

Tunisia

Amanda Hinton

D0581511

A & C Black
London

W W Norton
New York

First edition 1996

Published by A & C Black (Publishers) Limited
35 Bedford Row, London WC1R 4JH

A CIP catalogue record of this book is available from the British Library.

ISBN 0–7136–4105–3

Published in the United States of America by
WW Norton and Company, Inc
500 Fifth Avenue, New York, NY 10110

Published simultaneously in Canada by
Penguin Books Canada Limited
2801 John Street, Markham, Ontario L3R 1B4

ISBN 0–393–31419–7 USA

The author and the publishers have done their best to ensure the accuracy of all the
information in Blue Guide Tunisia; however, they can accept no responsibility for any
loss, injury or inconvenience sustained by any traveller as a result of information or
advice contained in the guide.

Amanda Hinton was educated in France and in the UK, and has spent the last 10 years
living, teaching and travelling in the Mediterranean. She has also written many guide
books on Turkey and Italy.

Maps and plans © A & C Black, drawn by Robert Smith
Illustrations © Beatrix Blake 1996

The publishers invite readers to write in with comments, suggestions and corrections for
the next edition of the Blue Guide. Writers of the best letters will be awarded a free Blue
Guide of their choice.

Printed and bound in Great Britain by Butler & Tanner Ltd, Frome and London

THE BLUE GUIDES

Albania
Austria
Belgium and Luxembourg
China
Cyprus
Czech and Slovak Republics
Denmark
Egypt

FRANCE
France
Paris and Versailles
Burgundy
Loire Valley
Midi-Pyrénées
Normandy
South West France
Corsica

GERMANY
Berlin and Eastern Germany
Western Germany

GREECE
Greece
Athens and environs
Crete

HOLLAND
Holland
Amsterdam

Hungary
Ireland

ITALY
Northern Italy
Southern Italy
Florence
Rome and environs
Sicily
Tuscany
Umbria
Venice

Jerusalem
Jordan
Malta and Gozo
Mexico
Morocco
Moscow and St Petersburg
Portugal

SPAIN
Spain
Barcelona
Madrid

Sweden
Switzerland

TURKEY
Turkey
Istanbul

Tunisia

UK
England
Scotland
Wales
London
Museums and Galleries
   of London
Oxford and Cambridge
Country Houses of England
Gardens of England
Literary Britain and Ireland
Victorian Architecture in Britain
Churches and Chapels of
   Northern England
Churches and Chapels of
   Southern England
Channel Islands

USA
New York
Museums and Galleries of New York
Boston and Cambridge

Acholla Tower

PREFACE

Tunisia, with its long summer season and many beach resorts, is a popular tourist destination, with travel companies offering extremely good value holiday and flight packages from Britain and continental Europe to the major east coast seaside resorts, such as Hammamet. Many tourists venture only short distances from their resort, leaving much of the country relatively unspoilt and free from mass tourism. On the more remote north coast the beaches are almost deserted, while small market towns inland bustle with local life and colour. In city medinas, if you take just a few steps off the beaten track, you can find yourself wandering along narrow whitewashed streets, past brilliant blue doors, with not another tourist in sight; while the sheer scale of the ancient cities left by the Romans means that coach parties are simply swallowed up, allowing space and peace to contemplate the history and atmosphere of Tunisia's splendid archaeological attractions.

Up to the present, Tunisia has preserved and cared for its cultural and historical monuments but has done little to make them accessible to the independent traveller. Many archaeological sites are without identifying maps or signs, and tourist offices often do not have town plans or useful information about the area. I hope Blue Guide Tunisia will enable travellers to find their way around and pursue their own interests, without being obliged to pay a local guide or join a tour group. I also hope to make a visit to Tunisia more meaningful and memorable by providing historical and cultural background material and insights into the country.

The book is organised into ten chapters, each covering a geographical region of the country, and divided into a total of 31 routes. Excursions and diversions are described within horizontal lines within the main body of the text. Historical background information and 'asides' are presented as indented text. The routes interlink and can be followed consecutively, or joined to create a personal itinerary. The comprehensive index at the back of the book will enable the readers to make their own travel plans. Descriptions of each route and approximate distances are given in italic type at the beginning of each route. Road directions are described in detail for those who have their own means of transport, and information is provided on public transport for those who do not.

CONTENTS

Background Information

I Tunis and Ancient Carthage

II The Northern Coast

III Mejerda Valley and Hills

IV Cap Bon Peninsula

V The Steppe

VI Gafsa and the Chott

Maps and plans

PRACTICAL INFORMATION

Planning your trip

Climate

The best time to visit Tunisia is spring, during the brilliant flowering season, when the temperature is warm but not as searingly hot as it can be in the summer. The average temperature during March, April and May is a comfortable 16°C in Tunis and 20.1°C in Tozeur.

During the three months of winter, from December to February, the average temperature in Tunis is 11.6°C; in the south at Tozeur it is marginally cooler at 11.4°C; however, throughout the southern desert regions the temperature drops dramatically at night, often to below zero. The coldest part of the country is the centre, where the average winter temperature is 6.1°C, and snow often falls at the higher altitudes in the Khroumerie mountains and in the region between El Kef and Kasserine.

The summer lasts for roughly four months with an average temperature in Tunis of 25.1°C and in Tozeur of 30.5°C. This may not seem dramatically hot until one remembers that actual daytime temperatures can be considerably higher than the seasonal averages and that temperatures during the day in the south are frequently over 40°C. The summer is also the driest season with very little rainfall in any part of the country and often drought conditions during June, July and August. During spring and autumn it remains dry in the south, but is slightly wetter in Tunis, where there is rain for an average of seven days a month. The wettest months are December and January, with an average of 12 rainy days a month in Tunis, and just two days in Tozeur.

Passports and formalities

For UK, Canadian and US citizens a valid passport is all that is needed to enter Tunisia. This automatically permits a stay of up to three months, or four months in the case of US citizens. A stay of longer than three months requires an extension; this is a long bureaucratic process which involves proving that you have the means to support yourself. An easier alternative is to leave the country temporarily, either by crossing the border into Algeria, or by taking a ferry to Sicily, and getting another three months' stay automatically stamped in your passport as you re-enter. Citizens of Australia and New Zealand need to apply for a visa from their local Tunisian consulate before leaving their country of residence. Queries about visa requirements can be addressed to the Tunisian Embassy in the **UK** at 29 Princes Gate, London SW7 1QG, tel. (0181) 584 8117. In the **US**, 1515 Massachusetts Avenue NW, Washington DC 20005, tel. 862 1860; fax 862 1858. In **Canada**, 515 Rue O'Connor, Ottawa, Ontario, K1S 3PG, tel. 237 0330, 237 0332, 237 0338, fax 237 7939. The embassy in Japan is responsible for **Australia** 18–8 1 Chome Wakaba, Shinjuku-Ku, Tokyo 160, tel. 335 34 111, 335 34 112, fax 322 54 387.

Customs' regulations permit you to take the following into Tunisia: 1 litre of spirits; 2 litres of wine; 400 cigarettes or 100 cigars or 500g tobacco; 1 litre of toilet water; two cameras; 20 rolls of film; one video camera; 20 reels of video film; one portable radio; sports equipment.

National tourist boards

The Tunisian National Tourist Boards, ONTT (Office National de Tourisme Tunisienne), have offices in most towns throughout Tunisia. They produce a limited range of publications, many of which are often not available in the language of your choice, if at all, and provide limited local information. However, most offices hold a list of accommodation, and may be willing to help you book a room. In the **UK**, general literature and accommodation information can be obtained from: Tunisian National Tourist Board, 77a Wigmore Street, London W1H 9LJ, tel. (0171) 224 5561. In the **US** and **Canada** the Tunisian National Tourist Office is in their respective embassies (see previous page for addresses), and also in Montreal at 1125 Bd. de Maisonneuve Ouest, Montreal, Quebec M3A 3B6, tel. 985 0928, 985 2565, fax 985 2588.

Travel agents

It is worth asking your local travel agent about bargain packages to Tunisia, for, even if you do not use the accommodation throughout your holiday, it can at least provide a starting point for more adventurous travelling. Some of the major tour operators in Tunisia are listed below, but for a comprehensive list of companies contact the Tunisian National Tourist Board.

Tunisian Travel Bureau, 304 Old Brompton Road, London SW5 9JF, tel. (0171) 373 4411.
Panorama Holidays, 29 Queens Road, Brighton BN1 3YN, tel. (1273) 206531.
Cosmos Air, Tourama House, 17 Homesdale Road, Bromley, Kent BR2 9LX, tel. (0161) 4805799.

You may be interested in taking a special interest package holiday. These are offered by the following companies.
Art and archaeology tours:
Martin Randall Travel, 10 Barley Mow Passage, Chiswick, London W4 4PH, tel. (0181) 7423355.
Prospect Art Tours Ltd, 454–458 Chiswick High Road, London W4 5TT, tel. (0181) 9952151.

Birdwatching holidays:
Branta Holidays, 7 Wingfield Street, London W1V 3TE, tel. (0171) 635 5812.

Golf holidays:
Select World Golf, 31 Haven Road, Canford Cliffs, Poole BH13 7LE, tel. (01202) 701881.
Panorama Holidays, 29 Queens Road, Brighton BN1 3YN, tel. (01275) 206531.
Golf International, Bridge House, Orchard Lane, Huntingdon PE18 6QT, tel. (01480) 433000.

The tour company Panorama (see address above) also organises tours of Second World War battlefields and cemeteries.

Disabled travellers
Facilities for disabled travellers in Tunisia are virtually non-existent, making a visit to the country something of a challenge, though certainly not impossible. Pavements and road surfaces generally leave much to be desired, and traffic in the narrow streets is often hazardous. There are few public conveniences designed for wheelchairs, although you will probably find facilities in a good hotel or restaurant. Hotels usually have ground floor accommodation, but you should book in advance, particularly during peak season, and state your requirements. Ramps for wheelchair access are sometimes provided in major museums and archaeological sites.

Getting to Tunisia

By air
British Airways scheduled flights to Tunis depart from Heathrow on Mondays, Wednesdays and Thursdays (reservations tel. (0181) 897 4000). Tunis Air scheduled flights to Tunis depart from Heathrow on Sundays, Tuesdays and Fridays (tel. (0171) 734 7644). The flight, which takes just over 2½hours, costs around £150 for an Apex fare and £400 for an open return.

Charter flights to Monastir and Jerba, as well as to Tunis, operate from Gatwick, Luton, Bristol, Newcastle, Glasgow, Stansted, Birmingham and Manchester. Cheap flights often under £100 (particularly out of season), can be found in the travel pages of the Sunday newspapers and *Time Out*. Alternatively the Tunisian National Tourist Board has addresses of companies operating charter flights. The disadvantage of travelling by charter is that the planes are cramped and schedules are subject to late alterations, both of time and destination.

Travellers from the US and Canada need to change at Rome or Paris, as there are no direct flights to Tunisia. An alternative is to change at London, from where there are some of the cheapest flights on offer to Tunisia.

By train
Combining a rail trip through Europe with a ferry to Tunisia from France or Italy might make a good holiday, but it is not the most economical or the swiftest way to get there. From London Victoria it is over 48 hours by train to Trapani in Sicily, which is the nearest port to Tunis. The return rail ticket costs around £200, although if you are under 26 or over 65 you may be eligible for a bargain ticket, such as Inter Rail which is available for 2 weeks or 1 month, at different prices depending on choice of route through Europe. This ticket is not available for use in Tunisia itself. For further details about rail travel, contact the British Rail Travel Centre, Victoria Station, London SW1V 1JY tel. (0171) 834 2345.

By bus

Eurolines coaches, which can be booked from any National Express ticket office, offer fares that are a little more expensive than rail fares although travel time is a little shorter.

By car

Overland travel to Tunisia is not economical either of time or money, but travelling by your own means of transport at least offers you some independence, and the cost of putting your vehicle on the ferry can be offset against the costs that would be incurred by hiring a car in Tunisia. Before you set out, check that you have your documents in order: logbook, driving licence (preferably an International Driving Licence too), and a Green Card which will cover you in Europe, but does not usually include Tunisia. Temporary third-party insurance cover can be taken out at the Tunisian border. If you are travelling by camper, caravan, or with a trailer, you will need a 'Carnet de Passage en Douane', details of which can be obtained from the AA or RAC. You are also advised to make a duplicate inventory of your vehicle's contents and value as this may be requested at the border. It will be returned to you on your departure.

By ferry

Approaching Tunis across the water is the most romantic way to arrive in Tunisia, and by booking a cabin on the overnight ferry you can arrive feeling quite refreshed. There are ferry crossings from Marseilles, Genoa, Naples and Trapani.

The ferry from Marseilles can be booked in the UK through Southern Ferries Ltd, 179 Piccadilly, London W1V 9DB, tel. (0171) 491 4988. The crossing takes 24 hours. A return ticket costs around £150 ($225) for a passenger, and £260 ($390) for a car.

The ferries from Cagliari (Sardinia) and Trapani (Sicily) can be booked in the UK through Serena Holidays, 40–42 Kenway Road, London SW5 ORA, tel. (0171) 373 6548. The crossing from Cagliari takes 22 hours and costs around £120 ($180) return for a passenger, and £150 ($225) for a car. From Trapani the crossing takes around eight hours and costs approximately £110 ($165) return for a passenger, and £150 ($225) for a car.

Reservations on the crossings from Genoa and Naples can only be made through booking offices in Italy. The Genoa crossing, which takes 24 hours, is run by the Compagnie Tunisienne de Navigation (CTN) (010) 8301893 and Tirrenia Navigazione, Stazione Marittima, Ponte Colombo, Genoa, tel. (010) 258041. The Naples crossing, which takes 22 hours, is run by Tirrenia Navigazione, Sezione Marittima Molo Angioino, Naples, tel. (081) 7201513.

During the summer season there are three crossings a week by hydrofoil from Trapani to Kelibia which takes just three hours. To make a booking, contact Linea Laura, Alilauro, Via Ammiraglio Staiti, Trapani, Sicily, tel. (0923) 24073.

Arriving in Tunisia

Most people will fly into Carthage International Airport, which is 6km from the city of Tunis. Take the No. 35 shuttle bus to Avenue Habib Bourguiba, the centre of town and where most accommodation is located, or hire a metered taxi, which should cost around 5D.

If you arrive by ship you will dock at La Goulette; take the TGM train from the port to the last stop on the line, the Tunis Nord station, which is at the eastern end of Avenue Habib Bourguiba, the city's main artery. It is a ten minute walk from here along Avenue Habib Bourguiba to the city centre. On the way you will pass the tourist office, just after the flyover on your right, where you might want to call in for accommodation listings, a city plan, and a map of the medina.

Accommodation

If you want to book accommodation in advance, contact Medward Travel, 304 Old Brompton Road, London SW5 9JF, tel. (0171) 373 4411. For budget accommodation, contact Aeroscope, Scope House, Hospital Road, Moreton-in-Marsh GL56 0BQ, tel. (01608) 650103.

If you have not booked accommodation in advance, the local tourist office will provide you with a list of hotels which will guide you on prices and facilities, and provide addresses and telephone numbers. When you arrive at a hotel it is a good idea to ask to see a room before booking, particularly in the lower category accommodation, as the reception area is often not very representative of the actual standard of the rooms. Once you have decided to stay, you must fill in a form for police records. In some hotels the management will undertake this on your behalf. The form is quite straightforward, requiring your name, passport number, passport expiry date, where you are travelling from and to, and the length of your stay. The hotel reception will also ask to keep your passport until you check out.

Tunisian accommodation ranges from very basic to luxury class hotels. The recommendations given in this guide are generally in three categories, with prices as follows for a double room:

Expensive – upwards of 40D
Reasonable – 20–40D
Cheap – 3–20D

Hotels are classified by local authorities into five categories: luxury 4-star, 4-star, 3-star, 2-star and 1-star, but the standards are not consistent. The cheapest accommodation, which is non-classified, is rough and ready, and you would be well advised to inspect the toilets and washing facilities. It is probably worth paying that bit extra for something in the reasonable category—1- and 2-star hotels—which will guarantee you a clean and comfortable bed, and often an annexed bathroom, albeit with unreliable plumbing. For real western comfort you need to look at the hotels in the expensive category (3-star and upwards). Four-star hotels are guaranteed to have air-conditioning (a serious consideration in the hot summer months) and often have swimming pools and other sports facilities, as well as restaurants and boutiques, although out of season some of these may be closed.

Camping is not very popular in Tunisia and there are no more than ten official campsites, all of which are located near the major tourist resorts.

Restaurants

The standard of restaurant food in Tunisia is mediocre. Service is prompt and locals seem to down their food as quickly as possible, usually while watching the ubiquitous television. The best selection of food is to be found in the tourist centres where many restaurants serve fixed rate tourist menus; these often include western-style food, although this is no guarantee of quality. In less-visited towns the choice of food, especially in the evenings, can be very limited. The good thing about Tunisian restaurants is that they are not expensive. A meal for two can cost as little as 5D, even in tourist resorts.

If you like to drink wine or beer with your meal, you will have to go to a licensed restaurant, where your bill will be in the region of 20D for a meal for two. Seafood restaurants, where the fish is often sold by weight, serve some of the best quality meals and are generally licensed, but they can be expensive. A cheaper alternative can be found in the licensed bars where hot meals and snacks are served to soak up the beer which the almost exclusively male clientele consumes.

Wherever you decide to eat, always check the prices beforehand, and if possible have a look at the food first to check that it is fresh.

Food and Drink

The most characteristic flavour of Tunisian food is that of **harissa**, a chilli, oil and garlic paste that is extremely widely used in Tunisian cooking, and may be served with bread as a starter. The staple food, however, is **couscous**, an onomatopoeic word, which sounds like the hissing of the steam in the couscousier when it is being cooked. It was originally a Berber dish, which was eaten with preserved butter and accompanied with soured milk, but it is now eaten with a wide variety of different sauces throughout the Maghreb. In Tunisia the large mound of couscous is usually served with a robust lamb sauce, set on fire by the addition of varying amounts of *harissa*.

Brik is also a very common dish. It is made from thin sheets of pastry filled with raw egg, and a variety of other things, most commonly tuna, green coriander, cumin, *harissa*, salt and pepper. It is assembled on the spot, immediately deep fried, and served hot and crispy.

Other common dishes are **mechoui**, the Tunisian version of mixed grill, usually lamb and sausage, and **mechouia**, a salad of diced tomato, peppers, egg and tuna fish.

Dairy products do not play a large part in the Tunisian diet, although you will find imported as well as locally produced camembert in some supermarkets. Cakes, French-style *pâtisseries*, and Arab sweets based on honey, almonds, dates and pistachios are very popular. Seasonal fresh fruit is usually of excellent quality and very fresh, and local varieties, such as white apricots, are well worth looking out for. Dates are sold from stalls at the side of the road in many towns throughout the year, but fresh ones come on to the market in September.

Although Tunisia is an Islamic country alcohol is available, though less so in the south of the country, where sales are resticted to specially licensed and often well hidden shops. Alcohol is not sold on Fridays, or during religious events, such as the month of Ramadan, when it is removed from the shelves of supermarkets, all bars are closed, and restaurants serve soft drinks only.

The selection of **alcoholic drinks** is fairly limited. Beer, sold in small bottles or very small cans, is a fizzy light ale called *Celtia*, which can be refreshing when served cold. Local wine is drunk young and has a fairly high alcohol content (around 11–12 per cent). *Mornag*, the most common label, comes in rosé and red. Muscat de Kelibia, a white muscatel with a distinctive taste, is more refined than most Tunisian wines and is good with fish or as an aperitif. Other labels that are well reputed include Tyna Rouge, Magon Rouge, Coteaux d'Utique Rouge, Vieux Thibar Rosé, Thibar Rouge and Rosé, and Coteaux de Carthage Blanc. *Laghmi*, a form of palm wine, is brewed and sold in palmeries, but is only consumed locally. Spirits are also available, both local and imported from France, and there are some interesting locally produced liqueurs, including *Boukle*, which is made from figs.

Non-alcoholic drinks include all the normal fizzy drinks, Coca-Cola, 7-Up etc., and are supplemented by cordials which are often served at coffee and cake shops from special chilled containers. *Citronata*, a lemon drink, is particularly refreshing. Tea, black and strong, is drunk from small glasses, as is mint tea, while coffee is drunk both in the French style, long and milky, and in the Turkish style, black with thick grouts at the bottom of the cup. Tap water is chlorinated and therefore drinkable, but it does not taste very nice and it is much better to buy and drink bottled mineral water.

Travelling around Tunisia

By rail

The rail network in Tunisia covers some 2000km. The main lines run from Tunis along the north coast, through Bizerte and Tabarka; and from Tunis along the east coast through Hammamet, Sousse and Sfax. A third major line cuts diagonally across the north part of the country from Tunis through Beja and Jendouba to Ghardimao. A minor line connects Sousse, Kairouan, Sbeitla, Kasserine and Redeyef, close to the Algerian border.

The railway is operated by SNCFT (Société Nationale de Chemins de Fer Tunisiens) and is reasonably punctual and efficient. Fares are low, even for first-class tickets; these need to be booked in advance, but it is worth the effort as travelling second class can be cramped and uncomfortable. Timetables are posted in all railway stations and are published in the newspaper, *La Presse*, where any alterations will also be indicated.

By bus

Travel by bus is slightly cheaper than by rail, and the network is much larger, but has the disadvantage of not operating on a fixed timetable: most buses simply depart when they are full. Both local and nationwide buses are operated by SNTRI (Société Nationale de Transport Rural et Interurbain), which has its headquarters at Ave Mohammed V, Tunis, tel. (01) 784433. The network connects all major towns and cities with Tunis, as well as interconnecting 22 regional capitals. The 68 inter-urban lines are run by 200 coaches, half of which are air-conditioned. Local buses, which connect regional capitals with outlying villages, are run by private companies and SRT (Société Régionale de Transport), which often operates the services within cities, too. Tickets for urban buses are sold from kiosks and newspaper stands and need to be stamped in the machine at the back of the bus when boarding. Tickets for rural and inter-urban buses are sold from ticket offices at the bus station.

A system of shared taxis, *louages*, usually operate from, or nearby, bus stations, and are a good alternative if you have just missed a bus. *Louages* are privately owned cars, often beaten-up Peugeots, converted to provide maximum seat capacity. Fares are slightly higher than buses, but the system is very flexible and you can be picked up and put down anywhere along the route. *Louages* leave when they have sufficient passengers and fill up to capacity en route, which can make a journey rather squashed, hot and uncomfortable in summer.

By taxi

There are two types of taxi in Tunisia: *bébés taxis*, which are usually red, carry a maximum of three passengers, and are only allowed to circulate within a given zone; and *grands taxis*, which carry a maximum of four passengers and are free to circulate where they want. The *bébés taxis* tend to be cheaper than the *grands taxis*. The majority of taxis are fitted with meters, but most taxi drivers tend not to use them; therefore, at the outset of your journey either ask for the meter to be turned on or agree upon a price. You will be charged 50 per cent extra after dark, and will have to pay a supplement for heavy baggage. If you take a taxi outside its usual territory, you will be expected to pay for its return journey, whether or not you use it.

By car

Tunisia has a road network that covers some 20,000km. The roads are reasonably maintained and the great majority have decent asphalt surfaces. There are two main classifications: GP (Grand Parcours), which is a major asphalt road, and MC (Moyenne Communication), a secondary road which is usually asphalt, but sometimes surfaced with sand and stone. There is also one toll-free motorway, which runs from Tunis to Hammamet. All the roads are numbered; its category and number are marked on milestones at the roadside.

Car hire in Tunisia is fairly expensive and you can expect to pay around £300 ($450) per week. Avis, Europcar and Hertz all operate in Tunisia and can be booked through your local office or travel agent before leaving home; if the car is included in a fly-drive package you may be eligible for a discount. Addresses of car hire companies in Tunisia can be obtained from the Tunisian

National Tourist Board and include a number of smaller local hire companies which offer slightly discounted rates. In order to hire a car you need a full driving licence and must be over 21 years old.

Petrol stations are found along the major roads, but you should make sure you have a full tank before setting out on minor roads, particularly in the desert regions of the south. Petrol is available in super and normal grades, but it is of lower quality than in Europe, and if you are bringing your own car, you would be well advised to fit a petrol filter to avoid problems with dirty fuel. Petrol is slightly cheaper than in Europe, and costs around 900M per litre.

Driving is on the right and road signs and driving regulations follow the international conventions. The speed limit is 120km/h on major roads outside urban areas, and 50km/h inside, with the exception of the Island of Jerba where the maximum speed limit anywhere is 70km/h. Road hazards include pot-holes, sand drifts across the road which make the surface slippery, vendors at the roadside who lunge at your car offering their wares, and vehicles travelling at night without lights. Traffic police are very vigilant and there are numerous checkpoints along the roads, particularly in the southern regions. Cars are flagged down for routine checks, and fines are issued for speeding and other road offences. Many motorists slow down to about 30km/h when passing a police checkpoint, irrespective of the actual speed limit, so be prepared for cars to break sharply in front of you when approaching a parked police car.

If you are planning to drive in the desert regions, always carry plenty of water. Allow a minimum of 5 litres per person per day and three times the capacity of your car radiator. Always consult the local national guard, usually passed on a town's outskirts, about road conditions before setting out on a journey, and inform him of your departure and intended route. Stop at each guard post you pass on your way and inform the guard of your destination. Remember that people have died in the desert after straying just a short distance off their route and losing their way, or encountering mechanical problems. For further information on motoring in Tunisia, contact the automobile club in Tunis: National Automobile Club Tunisien, 29 Avenue Habib Bourguiba, Tunis; tel. (01) 241176.

Should you need legal assistance in the case of an accident or breakdown, apply to the following address: Diplomat Assistance, 12 Rue de Hollande, Tunis; tel. (01) 248303.

Maps

The Tunisian National Tourist Board issues a free 1:800,000 road map of Tunisia, but it does not show recent road developments, such as the new motorway from Tunis to Hammamet. Indeed very few maps do, but the Michelin Algeria Tunisia (No. 972) 1:1,000,000 map shows a good amount of detail, including an enlargement of the area around Tunis (scale 1:500,000). Other maps on the market include the Kummerly & Frey 1:1,000,000 map of Tunisia, which has an enlargement of the Island of Jerba (scale 1:250,000). Hallwag has also produced a 1:1,000,000 map, while Freytag & Berndt have produced a 1:800,000 scale map, including details of Jerba, Carthage and Tunis.

General information

Currency regulations

There are no restrictions on the amount of foreign currency you can take in or out of Tunisia, but the amount should be recorded on a form at Customs and kept until your departure, along with receipts for any money changes made in Tunisia. Do not overestimate the amount of foreign currency you need to change as you can only reconvert up to 100 dinars or 30 per cent of the total amount of currency exchanged that you have receipts for.

Money

The Tunisian dinar (D) is divided into 1000 millimes (M). Dinar notes come in denominations of 1, 5, 10 and 20; dinar coins come in nominations of 1 and 5. Millimes come in coins of 500, 100, 50, 10, and 5. In 1995 £1 was exchanged for 1.48D.

American Express, Access, Mastercard and Visa credit cards are accepted at major hotels and restaurants and some of the larger souvenir shops, but are not as widely used as in Europe.

Both traveller cheques and Eurocheques are accepted at banks with exchange facilities, but remember to have your passport with you for identification.

It is a good idea to have some dinars on you before you arrive, preferably in small denominations, to pay for transport or refreshments on arrival. Due to the restrictions on export and import of the dinar, you may have to book currency in advance from your local *bureau de change*. Exchange rates are published in the French language newspapers in Tunisia and can be found by looking under '*Cours des Devises*'.

Opening hours

Shops open from 08.00 to 12.00 in the morning, and from 15.00 until 18.00 in the afternoon; in summer, the shops open and close up to an hour later in the afternoon. Shops and businesses are closed on Sundays and many also close on Saturday afternoons.

The **banks'** opening hours vary according to the season. From 16 September to 30 June, banks are open Monday–Thursday, 08.00–11.00 and 14.00–16.15, and Friday, 08.00–11.00 and 13.00–15.15. From 1 July to 15 September, the opening times are Monday–Friday, 08.00–11.00. The only variation from this pattern is during the month of Ramadan when banks are open Monday–Friday, 08.00–11.30 and 13.00–14.30.

The opening times of **museums** and **archaeological sites** also depend on the season. During the summer season, which runs from 1 April to 30 September, opening times are usually 09.00–16.30. During the winter season, which runs from 1 October to 31 March, opening times are 09.00–12.00 and 14.00–17.30. Museums and archaeological sites are closed on Mondays and public holidays. Most museums and archaeological sites charge an entry fee and also a fee for taking photographs and using video equipment. Flashes and tripods are generally forbidden.

Although some of the best and most important monuments in Tunisia are **mosques**, these are not open to non-Muslims, although visitors are usually allowed to enter the outer courtyard of some of the larger mosques between 08.00–11.00.

Public holidays

Tunisia's secular national holidays are as follows:

1 January	New Year's Day
18 January	Anniversary of the Revolution
20 March	Independence Anniversary
9 April	Martyrs' Day
1 May	International Labour Day
2 June	Youth Day
25 July	Republic Day
3 August	President Bourguiba's Birthday
13 August	Women's Day
3 September	Anniversary of Foundation of Destour Party
15–16 October	Liberation Day

The dates of religious holidays change each year as the Islamic calendar is lunar, and is 11 days shorter than the solar calendar. The date for the commencement of the major holidays is determined by the sighting of the new moon. The first holiday in the Islamic year is *Muharram*, the Islamic New Year's Day. The next is a two-day celebration after the end of the holy fasting month of Ramadan, which is known as *Aid Es Saghir*. Forty days later is the important festival of *Aid El Kebir*, which celebrates Abraham's sacrifice of a ram in place of his son Isaac. During this festival, most families who can afford it slaughter a sheep and gather for a celebratory meal together, which means that the streets can be both bloody and crowded. The final religious holiday is the *Mouloud*, which celebrates the birthday of the Prophet Mohammed.

Health

No special health precautions are needed for Tunisia, and health risks can generally be avoided by taking a few sensible precautions. Firstly, avoid drinking tap water, particularly in the southern regions, and avoid drinks mixed with ice if the water is of doubtful quality. Secondly, do not eat fruit without either peeling or washing it. Thirdly, make sure that all your inoculations are up to date. Chemists are generally well stocked and have antidotes for snake and insect bites and are able and willing to treat most minor ailments. More serious problems should be taken to the nearest hospital, the addresses and telephone numbers of which are included where available in the information sections for each city in the main text of the book. As the European system of reciprocal health care does not cover visitors to Tunisia, it is sensible to take out medical insurance before you leave.

Useful addresses

All embassies and consulates are to be found in Tunis at the following addresses:

UK, 5 Place de la Victoire, tel. (01) 245100.
US, 144 Avenue de la Liberté, tel. (01) 282566.
Canada, 3 Rue Didon, tel. (01) 286577.

Crime

There is less crime in Tunisia than in many parts of Europe, but sensible precautions, such as keeping your money in a safe place and never leaving anything visible in a parked car, should still be taken. Should you be involved in any crime incident, go to the nearest police station where you will be asked to make a report.

Sporting and leisure activities

All major hotels in coastal resorts have sports facilities, including tennis, wind-surfing and sailing. In recent years Tunisia has developed several well-appointed golf courses, amongst the best of which are: the Soukra Country Club, between Tunis and Carthage; the Kantaoui Golf Course, which is north of Sousse; the El Achab Golf Course at Monastir; and the Hammamet Golf Course. Horse-riding is also becoming increasingly popular: for information, contact the Horse-riding Centre of Soukra, 15km from Tunis. Hunting is restricted, but hunting parties are organised by the Club de la Chasse at Rades. For information on sub-aqua diving and fishing, contact the International Nautical Centre of Tunisia, 22 Rue de Medine, Tunis, tel. (01) 282209.

Major hotels often have discos and provide floor shows in their restaurants, and there are also nightclubs in the major cities. In Tunis there is a theatre which shows classic productions. There are no more than perhaps 20 cinemas in the whole country. During the summer, films, which are often in French with Arabic subtitles, are screened outside.

Telephone and postal services

The Tunisian post office is known as the PTT (Poste Téléphone Télégraphe); offices are located in the centre of most towns and cities. They offer a full range of postal services, but telephones are often situated in a nearby building. Telephone cubicles can also be found in lock-up shops (small shops without windows or doors which are locked up at night by pulling a metal shutter across), known as taxi-phone, along most high streets. There is generally an attendant on duty to provide change; one dinar coins are needed to make international calls; these can be dialled direct, using the prefixes given below, from most telephones. You will find it is cheaper to make calls from public telephones than from your hotel.

International code	00	US	1
Britain	44	Canada	1

Area codes for Tunisia are as follows:

Tunis, Ariana, Ben Arous	01	Gafsa, Tozeur, Sidi Bouzid	06
Nabeul, Bizerte, Zaghouan	02	Kairouan, Kasserine	07
Sousse, Monastir, Mahdia	03	El Kef, Beja, Jendouba	08
Sfax	04	Mobile telephones nationwide	09
Gabès, Kebili, Medenine, Tataouine	05		

If you need stamps, you do not have to go to the post office unless your mail is overweight, as tobacconists and newspaper kiosks sell them. Letterboxes are yellow, similar to ones in France. At the post office there is a separate box for overseas mail.

Newspapers

There are three Tunisian newspapers published in French: *La Presse*, *L'Action* and *Le Temps*. British and American newspapers are available in Tunis and other major cities. They are generally one or two days out of date and are sold at fixed international rates.

Public toilets

Public toilets are found in museums, at places of interest, and at garages and cafés. Most towns also have a public toilet, although these are generally not very clean. Continental footpad-style toilets are common, and toilet paper is rarely supplied. A tip of 100–200M should be left if there is an attendant.

Local customs

Tunisia is an Islamic country and a level of sensitivity and respect for Islamic values is advisable. Dress tends to be discreet, and although headscarves are not worn by all women, both men and women generally cover their arms and legs and tend not to wear revealing clothing. Alcohol, although it is very common in the seaside towns of the centre and north of the country, is always drunk inside a bar and not on the street. Shoes should be removed when entering religious buildings, and also upon entering someone's house. Whatever impression is formed from the above advice, it should be said that Tunisians are very friendly and tolerant. Tunisia is one of the more progressive countries in the Islamic world and foreigners are often not expected to conform to conservative local values.

Women travelling alone

It is generally inadvisable for women to travel alone in Tunisia. However, if you do, you are well-advised not to hitch-hike, or wander about in the evenings unaccompanied, unless you are prepared for the consequences. Should you find yourself in difficulty, do not hesitate to turn to a local person for help.

HISTORY OF TUNISIA

Origins

Although the earliest traces of man in North Africa—stone axes found in El Kef, Metlaoui and Gafsa—date back 250,000 years, evidence of a complex culture is not found until 40,000 years ago. Curious shrine-like structures, possibly built by Neanderthal man, composed of balls of stone arranged in pyramids in the basins of springs, have been found at El Guettar. The first ancient burials, dating from 14,000 years ago, have been found on Tunisia's northern shores. They belong to Cro-Magnon man, who buried his dead in a crouching position.

In the south, a quite separate culture, known as **Capsian**, which was limited to the inland high plains and may have been Negroid in origin, came into existence about 8000 years ago. At the most famous site, **Gafsa** (Capsa), heaps of snail shells—25m by 25m and 3m deep—have been found; an accumulation, archaeologists have worked out, of about 2500 years. Flint tools, rock sculptures and decorated ostrich eggs dating from 7000 BC were also found at the site, as were stone figurines and engraved stones from 5000 BC. Capsian burials and cemeteries, such as that at Doukanet el Khoutifa, were also discovered. Red ochre was found on the bones of the dead, and one skull had two small holes bored in it to allow it to be hung up, suggesting that the Capsians practised ancestor worship and performed religious or magic ceremonies for their dead.

Descendants of the Capsian began herding sheep and goats and cultivating grain crops, enabling them to establish more developed settlements from 5000 BC onwards. The cultivation of land required the clearance of trees and finely polished stone axes have been found near settlements of this period. There is also evidence that obsidian, a stone very suited to the production of high quality stone tools, was imported from Mediterranean islands, indicating that sea trade was already in existence. At Pantellaria, 60km east of Cap Bon, all the artefacts found are made from obsidian.

The **neolithic** period arrived late in Tunisia, around 3000 BC. Archaeological evidence tells us quite a lot about neolithic man's diet, which included, sorghum, millet, barley, beans, peas, turnips, almonds, figs, grapes, and dates. The early chamber tombs found in mountainous areas of Tunisia date from 2000 BC and consist of large cists covered by a stone capstone. These sepulchres, *djouala*, were later attributed by the Berbers to a race of giants, while in actual fact they were erected by their ancestors, and were modelled on similar burial chambers discovered in Sardinia. The oldest type are approached by an unroofed passage in a circular mound, an example of which can be seen at Henchir el Hadjar near Enfidaville. Later tombs, such as those at Elles, have multiple chambers, the walls formed of piled up slabs, the floor paved, with a roof of large horizontal slabs. Funerary objects, including bronze jewellery, cornelian beads, ostrich eggshells, flint arrowheads and pottery, were placed in the tombs with the dead. The pottery vessels, with their flat bases, which from the Bronze Age onwards accompanied the body, resemble traditional Berber pottery, but like the tombs had their origin in Sardinia. Among the many bones found in such tombs, which were used by the tribe over many centuries, were those of animal offerings. It is interesting to note that these were mostly goat and sheep, but never pig.

Up until this point the Sahara had been a fairly fertile area, but c 2000 BC the region dried up and became isolated apart from Berber tribes who lived in settlements of huts, and reared sheep and goats. They also maintained some agriculture and lived independently in Tunisia up until the arrival of the Romans. The next important moment in Tunisian history, however, was not until the first millennium BC when the Phoenicians arrived by sea.

The arrival of the Phoenicians

The Phoenicians came from Tyre in the Lebanon and were the ancestors of the Carthaginians. In about 1000 BC they established a series of anchoring points along the North African coast as part of their marine trading network. Each 35km apart, these anchorages linked Tyre with the southern coast of Spain, where the Phoenicians were engaged in the trading of metals, principally silver and tin. Along the 5500km route there must have been more than 100 such anchorages, where the sailors, or rowers, were able to rest and stock up with supplies. Some of these anchorages developed into permanent settlements, the first recorded in Tunisia being Sousse, Utica and Bizerte c 12C BC. According to tradition, **Carthage**, which was to become the capital of a federation of the settlements along the Tunisian coast, was founded in 814 BC by Dido, also known as Elissa, who was daughter of the King of Tyre. She fled here to escape from her brother, who, in his ambition to win his father's throne, had killed her husband. However, archaeologists believe that Carthage was founded about 100 years later.

By 6C BC Carthage had become the leading power in the western Mediterranean and had colonised the islands off its coast, including Sardinia, Corsica and the Balearics, and was well-established on Sicily. Carthage's dominance was challenged, however, by the emerging power of the Greek city states, and many bloody battles were fought over territory and influence. Being challenged in the Mediterranean, Carthage sent king Hanno, who was known as the Navigator, on a voyage of discovery in the early 5C BC. He travelled through the Straits of Gibraltar and down the West African coast to Sierra Leone with 60 ships, to found new settlements and to develop potential trade routes. All we know of his discoveries is that he brought back news of strange animals, such as hippos and crocodiles.

Carthage, with her import of food from Sicily threatened by the Greeks, set about developing her own agriculture, and the fertile land in North Tunisia, especially beside the Medjerda river, began to produce an abundance of fruit, vegetables and cereals. Such was the Carthaginians' skill that land considered unfarmable today was made productive. The Romans later had the treatise on agriculture, which was written by the founder of the Magonid dynasty, Majo, translated into Latin; as a result, after the destruction of Carthage, subsequent generations believed that it was Rome, not Carthage, which had invented techniques such as the grafting of fruit trees on to wild rootstocks.

The Carthaginian army

The Carthaginian army was initially largely composed of mercenaries; later troops were levied from the Carthaginian territories. Foot soldiers carried spears and swords, and were armoured in the Greek fashion, with helmets, leg greaves and a bossed shield. The nobility were mounted; they wore black and white crests on their helmets and carried short swords and javelins. 'Libyan' cavalry and infantry were used early on but were later replaced by Spanish troops. The infantry fought in phalanx formation; they were strengthened by javelin throwers who had partially shaved heads and wore ostrich feathers.

Cavalry from Numidia formed a very important part of the army. They were armed with daggers and javelins and carried small round shields. Their mounts were the local small horse; they were organised in squadrons of 64 men but fought in a looser, more mobile formation than the infantry.

Spanish infantry could be identified by their white tunics with crimson borders, and their iron armour and weapons (short swords and javelins). Spanish cavalry carried wooden shields and long spears and swords. There were also specialist sling-throwers who came from the Balearic Islands off Spain; Gauls, who always bore the brunt of the casualties, were used as infantry; they wore plaid trousers and perhaps a cloak, and carried short iron swords.

Elephants, principally the African forest elephant, which stood up to 3m tall, were put in a line across the front of the army, about 30m apart. They were unpredictable and could cause as much damage to the Carthaginian army as to the enemy, if they got out of control. Riders were equipped with mallets and spikes to kill those elephants that panicked. The whole army was kept supplied by a wagon train pulled by Spanish oxen.

Roman history

The first treaty between Rome and Carthage was signed in 510 BC. The treaty was a cautious act of diplomacy designed to protect the interests of the two cities and to reduce the chances of conflict between them. For 250 years the two cities watched each other growing in strength, before finally being drawn into battle by events in Sicily.

The First Punic War: 264–242 BC

When Campanian mercenaries in Sicily seized Messina (Messana) in 259 BC, the ruler of Syracuse asked Carthage for help. The mercenaries called on Rome to assist them and by so doing brought the two powers into direct conflict. Carthage lost control of most of Sicily but nonetheless managed to impress Rome with the exploits of her navy. Rome immediately built a navy to match; her ships were equipped with the '*corvus*', a large gangplank 10 metres long and 1.5 metres wide, which was attached to the prow of the vessel and could be lowered onto the enemy boat, where a large spike anchored it to the deck. This gave the inexperienced Roman navy a distinct advantage as it rendered the fast-moving Carthaginian boats immobile, thus allowing the Roman marines to fight a 'land' battle at sea. The Roman navy gradually took control of the Mediterranean and was able to launch an invasion of Africa with 40,000 troops in 256 BC. However, Rome delayed the offensive for the winter, thus allowing Carthage to raise an army which soundly defeated the Romans.

Despite her defeat, Rome continued to wage war against the two remaining Carthaginian towns in Sicily, Trapani (Drepana) and Lilybaeun. At first, the Romans were unsuccessful. They lost their fleet at Trapani, when Publius Claudius, ignoring the augur of chickens which refused to eat (he threw them into the sea to 'let them drink' instead), attacked the Carthaginian fleet at anchor. This was only a temporary setback and Carthage was forced to sue for peace and their General, **Hamilcar**, returned to Africa in 242 BC. Carthage was made to pay Rome compensation of 2200 talents for the next ten years, which left the city with no money to maintain a mercenary army. The army rose in rebellion which was put down by Hamilcar; this provoked civil war, the embers of which were not extinguished until 238 BC.

Between the wars: Carthage moves to Spain

Having been forced out of Sicily, Hamilcar turned his attention to Spain. After marching along the North African coast accompanied by his fleet, Hamilcar crossed the Straits of Gibraltar and spent the last nine years of his life fighting the inland tribes of Spain into submission. Hamilcar was succeeded by his sons, Hasdrubal, and then eight years later, in 221 BC, by **Hannibal**, by which time the Iberian peninsula had been tamed. The success of the Carthaginians in Spain had not gone unnoticed by Rome, and a northern boundary along the Ebro river was created to prevent further expansion. In 219 BC Hannibal was forced to march north to the city of Saguntum, which although it lay south of the Ebro had been seized by Rome. After an eight-month siege, and a badly wounded thigh, Hannibal took the city, the population committing mass suicide. Rome demanded that Hannibal surrender; at a meeting between Hannibal and the Roman embassy the representative held out the fold in his toga, proclaimed that it contained either peace or war, and asked the Carthaginians which was it to be. Hannibal's reply was 'whatever pleases you'. The Roman answer was unequivocal: 'War then'.

The Second Punic War: 218–202 BC

Hannibal decided to seize the initiative and attack Italy. He crossed the Ebro in mid-July with a force of around 30,000 foot soldiers and 10,000 horses. Over the next 12 years Hannibal ravaged the country, defeating four major Roman armies.

Unable to defeat Hannibal at home, Rome focused her efforts on Sicily and Spain. New Carthage was taken and Hannibal's brother Hasdrubal, who commanded the Carthaginian forces in Spain, was forced to withdraw. He escaped to Italy with his army, marching over the Alps in 207 BC, only to be defeated and killed in northern Italy.

After his conquest of Spain, the Roman general **Scipio** returned to Rome in 205 BC where he was elected consul. Scipio gathered support for his plan to take the war to Africa and in 204 BC sailed with 30,000 men in 440 boats from Sicily to Cap Farina, just north of Utica. Scipio was then joined by Masinissa, one of two important Numidian chiefs, and laid siege to Utica for 40 days before the arrival of Carthaginian forces. Scipio withdrew a couple of miles to a well-defended peninsula for the winter; afterwards, he entered into negotiations with the Carthaginians, drawing up a treaty whereby Hannibal would leave Italy in return for Roman troops leaving Africa. Suddenly, Scipio made a surprise attack on Carthaginian forces and resumed the siege of Utica, later defeating the Carthaginian army at Souk el Kremis on the Medjerda (Bagradas) river. Hannibal was immediately recalled from Italy and peace negotiations were again set in motion, only to be broken by Scipio, who ravaged the Bagradas valley, forcing Hannibal to march against him with only limited forces. The two armies met at Zama, where Hannibal unleashed his elephants; but they were repulsed by concerted trumpet calls from the Roman forces. The fighting was fierce and prolonged, and it was not until Masinissa's Numidian cavalry swept in behind Hannibal's troops, attacking his army from the rear, that the Romans could claim victory.

His army shattered, Hannibal retreated to Carthage and a peace treaty was ratified, which left Rome in control of most of the Carthaginian hinterland. Hannibal introduced financial reforms which helped put Carthage back on her feet, before the threat of extradition to Rome forced him to flee in 195 BC. While Hannibal languished in exile, Carthage was recovering from the defeat it had suffered at the hands of Scipio. Scipio, able to dictate the peace terms, had dug a trench limiting Carthaginian territory from Tabarka (Thabraca) to Tyna (Thaenae) just south of Sfax, giving all land beyond that to the Numidian King Masinissa. Forbidden from engaging in any military exercise, even in self-defence, Carthage was unable to prevent the Numidians from encroaching on their territory. The Carthaginians' pleas to Rome went unanswered, and finally, when the Numidians absorbed an area of land at Souk el Khemis in 154 BC, Carthage felt obliged to act on her own behalf. In contravention of the treaty, Carthage raised an army, but in 150 BC was defeated by Masinissa's forces, raising the worrying spectre for Rome of a very powerful potential new enemy in Africa.

The Third Punic War: 149–146 BC

To solve this dilemma, Rome decided to destroy Carthage once and for all; at the same time the Romans planned to secure the African coast near Sicily by annexing part of the Numidian territories as a province of Rome. When Cato the Elder, just before he died in 149 BC, held out the figs to the Senate and proclaimed: '*Delenda est Carthago*' ('Carthage must be destroyed'), he was commenting not only on the richness of the province and thus its power, but also on its close proximity to Rome (the figs were still fresh). Rome dispatched a large army, some 84,000 strong, to Utica, which had joined forces with Rome, along with the cities of Sousse (Hadrumetum), Lamta (Leptis), Rass Dimass (Thapsus) near Moknine, and Ras Botria (Acholla) just south of Ksour Essaf. In the face of such opposition, the Carthaginians sued for peace but were given impossible terms. The Romans ordered that the Carthaginians should abandon their city and resettle at least 8¾ miles (approximately) inland from the coast. They took up their arms again, unable to contemplate abandoning their city completely, preferring to die in battle. The siege lasted three whole years and ended with the massacre of the inhabitants of Carthage. The few survivors were sold into slavery. The Romans then razed the city to the ground and put salt upon the ruins as a curse. Carthage was no more.

The Roman foothold in Africa

From the Roman governor's residence at Utica, Rome pursued an initial policy of containment in Africa, with the territory within the original '*fossa regia*' (the ditch dug by Scipio in 202 BC), being divided up as spoils of war among those who had assisted Rome in her struggle with Carthage.

Rome's ally, the Numidian King Masinissa, was succeeded by his son Micipsa. His rule was challenged by Jugurtha, the illegitimate son of one of his brothers, who was popular and very able on the battlefield, and Micipsa was forced to make him his joint heir along with his two sons. When Micipsa died in 118 BC, Jugurtha murdered one of his sons, defeated the other (Adherbal) on the battlefield, and took the throne. Rome did not move against Jugurtha, despite Adherbal's pleas, until 112 BC, when the usurper attacked a town sheltering Adherbal and killed several Roman citizens. After six years of war, Jugurtha was betrayed and captured and Gauda, his half-brother, assumed the throne.

Rome's civil war in Africa: Julius Caesar 47–46 BC

The Roman civil war, which was based on the conflict between Pompey and Casesar, which arose from Caesar's superiority to Pompey in terms of power and glory (Pompey felt eclipsed by Caesar) entered one of its final phases in North Africa, when **Julius Caesar** pursued Pompey's followers, who had fled to Utica in order to join up with Pompey's sons Gnaeus and Sextus and the King of Numidia, Juba. Caesar landed in Sousse (Hadrumetum), in 47 BC; here, he rested for a day before marching on to Monastir (Ruspina) where he was greeted by friendly crowds. Caesar was harassed by the Numidian cavalry and his foraging parties were attacked, when Scipio Aemilianus, who was elected consul, afraid to meet him in battle, camped 3km outside Monastir. On the 26 January, Caesar broke camp and headed south to Uzita, near Jemmel. After several weeks he marched south in search of new supplies, camping at Aggar, just north of Ksour Essaf; he was followed here by Scipio and Juba, who camped at nearby Bourjine (Tegea). After a skirmish near Kheniss (Zeta), where he witnessed the Pompeian tactics, Caesar spent some time retraining his troops. He then marched to attack one of Scipio's main bases at Thapsus on Cape Dimass, which was defended by the Moknine marsh, its only access along a narrow corridor of land. He camped round the walls and laid siege to the town. Scipio prepared for battle but was charged by Caesar before he had even finished addressing his troops. His soldiers panicked and were trampled by their own elephants. 10,000 Pompeians were killed. After the battle Caesar undertook mopping up operations in the rest of the province, taking Thapsus, El Jem (Thysdra), Uzita and Hadrumetum. He then destroyed the remnants of the Pompeian forces at Utica, where Scipio's cavalry had retired after their defeat, storming the town and massacring its inhabitants. King Juba, the last Pompeian ally, was killed in a duel; Caesar took the opportunity to incorporate his kingdom into Roman Africa, before returning to Rome in July 46 BC.

The Roman conquest of Africa: 46 BC–AD 37

With Roman Africa now three times the size it had been, Caesar set about securing it by settling veterans and the landless of Rome on the territory, but had little time to pursue any further plans before he was murdered in 44 BC. Augustus, Caesar's successor, gained control of the whole province in 36 BC and continued Caesar's policy, even refounding the city of Carthage. In 27 BC, Carthage became the seat of the proconsul, who governed the province for the Senate, to whom Augustus had ceded Africa. Thus the name of the African province became 'Africa Proconsularis'. The proconsul was the commander of the Third Augustan Legion, which Augustus gave the province to ensure its security and stability. As well as patrolling the province, the legion also undertook major engineering works, especially the construction of roads. The first one was built in AD 14, and ran from Gabes (Tacapae) to the legion's base at Haidra (Ammaedara), just north of the mountains of Tebessa on the Algerian/Tunisian border, a distance of more than 260km. Its construction was the trigger for the uprising of the Musulamii tribe in AD 17, across whose transhumance routes it ran. The tribe's leader, Tacfarinas, led a skilled guerrilla campaign against the Roman force, which, unused to such tactics, was unable to overcome him, and it was not until he was captured and killed some seven years later that the tribes were subdued. These troubles persuaded the next emperor, Caligula, that the Senate's control of the army in Africa was less than effective, and he passed control of the legion from the civilian proconsul to a military legate. Partly as a result, the first three centuries AD were by and large peaceful and prosperous times for the province. It was a time of great civil engineering projects and agricultural and urban expansion.

The development of Roman Africa: AD 37–439

After completing their first road, the legion set about constructing a complete network that criss-crossed Africa. Over the next 200 years they built some 20,000km of unpaved road, all marked with milestones, as well as one stone-surfaced road from Carthage to Haidra (Ammaedara). The legion was also responsible for the construction of the massive aqueducts that were built to provide water for the growing urban population. The aqueduct built to supply Carthage stretched all the way from Zaghouan and was 132km long. Port facilities were also improved to help the ports cope with the growing amount of agricultural produce which was being exported to Italy from the province, and the Island of Jerba was linked to the mainland by a causeway.

Africa Proconsularis became the breadbasket of the Roman Empire, exporting over half a million tonnes of grain a year. Italy relied on this supply, as the country was unable to grow enough to support herself, and did much to encourage the development of uncultivated areas of land. In the second century, the cultivation of olives was stimulated and within a decade or two Africa Proconsularis was also producing huge amounts of olive oil, a vital commodity in the ancient world, where it was the major source of lighting fuel, as well as being extensively used in cooking and washing.

By the third century, there were more than 200 Roman cities in the northern part of Tunisia alone, many of them nestled in the rich agricultural land either side of the Medjerda valley. Some of these cities were purpose-built sites for veterans and other new settlers, while others had grown up around the nucleus of an inland tribal town like Dougga (Thugga), or coastal Carthaginian settlements like Carthage itself. The purpose-built cities were based on the Roman town plan: two main roads passed through the town at right-angles to one another, meeting at the forum in the centre. The forum thus formed the hub of the city, and was surrounded by the town hall (curia), courts (basilica), shops and bars. Surrounding the forum were temples and streets which contained both houses and shops, laid out on a regular grid pattern. Where existing towns were incorporated into a growing Roman one, the pattern was less simple, as earlier developments and topography often made it impossible for the builders to follow the regular grid pattern, giving rise to sprawling cities, strung out along the hill-tops, like Dougga. Most cities, at least by today's standards, had fairly small populations, averaging around 10,000–15,000, and were classified as either 'colonia', 'municipium' or 'civitates' (a decree by the emperor often changed a town's status from one classification to another). The 'colonia' enjoyed both Roman-style civic government and full citizen status, while the 'municipium' had Roman civic institutions but limited citizenship rights, and the 'civitates' had neither.

The peace was broken in 238 when Gordian, Proconsul of Africa, was persuaded by the citizens of El Jem (Thysdrus) (who were in rebellion against the heavy taxes imposed by the newly proclaimed emperor Maximinus), to proclaim himself emperor. Even though the Senate in Rome was in favour of the usurpation, the legate of the Augustan Third Legion and the Governor of Numidia, Capellianus, remained loyal to Maximinus and waged war on Gordian. Gordian I ruled jointly with his son Gordian II (who reigned for just 21 days), and it was he who met Capellianus in battle, where he was defeated and killed. On hearing the news, his father killed himself and Capellianus rampaged through Africa Proconsularis killing all who had been loyal to the Gordians.

In Africa, as in the rest of the late Roman Empire, the number of Christian converts was growing, and persecution had already begun. Under Septimius Severus (193–211) Carthage had witnessed the martydom of Perpetua, who was thrown to wild animals before having her throat cut. The persecution of Christians re-emerged in the middle of the century when Cyprian, Bishop of Carthage, had the misfortune to be persecuted by three emperors; the first, Decius, merely exiled him to Korba (Curubis) on Cap Bon, just north of Nabeul, in 250; the last, Valentian, was less tolerant and had Cyprian beheaded in 258. It was as a result of similar persecutions at the beginning of the 4C, under the Emperor Diocletian, when Christianity had already become the popular religion of the poor, that a split in the Church occurred. Rival clergy were set up in opposition to those who had not stood firm in the face of persecution, under the leadership of Donatus, the rival Bishop of Carthage. So serious were the consequences that the Emperor Constantine (306–337) intervened—acting to protect Rome's supply of grain and oil as much as through his beliefs. After hearings, Constantine ruled in favour of the Catholics (those who obeyed the Emperor), and when the Donatists failed to back down he ordered the confiscation of their property and had the army put many of them to death. As a result of their persecution by the state, the Donatists gained widespread popular support. However, the persecution continued until 411, when Emperor Honorius made an attempt to resolve the split. A conference was organised in Carthage in which 570 bishops, half from each camp, debated the issue, the Catholic side led by St Augustine. The Catholics won, and Honorius made Donatism a criminal offence later that year.

Augustine of Hippo (354–430)

Aurelius Augustinius, one of the four Doctors of the Church, made important contributions to philosophy and theology through his writing, dwelling upon such themes as grace, sin and free will. He also contributed to the arguments of his own time, especially to the Donatist controversy. Apart from five years, he lived in North Africa all his life and was Bishop of Hippo for the last 34. His writings, especially the *Confessions*, have exerted a powerful influence on later thinkers, particularly Aquinas, Petrarch, Luther, Pascal, Kierkegaard and more recently Wittgenstein.

Augustine's mother, Monica, had a Berber name; she gave birth to Augustine in a hill town called Thagaste in the province of Numidia Consularis, which is now in East Algeria. His father, Patricius, was a farmer and belonged to the middle classes. Augustine was educated in Carthage, owing to the financial assistance he received from a wealthy neighbour, Romaniarius. Although he was taught Greek at school Augustine never mastered the language, and throughout his life he was always more comfortable with Latin.

When he was 17, Augustine fell in love with a Carthaginian girl. They lived together for 13 years and had a son.

Augustine's father had been a pagan and his mother a Christian, but while in Carthage Augustine became attracted to the Manichee sect, an ultra-ascetic sect which regarded the lower half of the body as the work of the devil. There were two levels in the sect; Augustine belonged to the lower of the two which allowed sexual activity but only at certain times of the month. Members of the sect ate a lot of melons and cucumbers which were regarded as having a good proportion of the god's goodness, which had been shattered by the forces of evil.

Augustine remained loyal to Manicheism for ten years while teaching rhetoric and literature at Carthage and in Rome. In 384 he was offered a post as Professor of Rhetoric in Milan. There, he gave up reading sceptical philosophy and was converted to Neo-Platonism. At this time Augustine's mother sent his common-law wife back to Carthage. This dealt Augustine a 'blow which crushed my heart to bleeding'. Augustine's mother then schemed for him to marry a young heiress. Whilst engaged to her he also had an affair with another woman. Aware of the problem that his sexual appetite caused him Augustine prayed for release from his desires and for celibacy, though he added the clause 'but not yet'.

In Milan Augustine's health slowly began to deteriorate and in 386 he decided to give up teaching and break off his engagement. He made the decision to be baptised as a Christian and moved to Cassiciacum near Como where he was baptised at Easter c 387. He described coming to the Christian faith as 'coming into harbour after a stormy passage'. His former beliefs were not abandoned but assimilated into the new faith and he described Christianity as 'Platonism for the masses'. He believed that God was perfection and that man's nature fails to live up to God's intentions, but he also believed that although God was supreme, he transcended the gulf between himself and man, bringing knowledge, life and humility to men. At the same time Augustine clung to the Manichee belief that the physical aspect of life must be avoided to comprehend the mystical transendence of God. But by 387, with the completion of his book on free will, *De Libero Arbitrio*, he felt that it was the weakness of man's soul not his body that led to evil. He decided to return to Africa, but on the journey his mother died and was buried at Ostia, the port of Rome. Augustine returned to Africa and founded a small monastic community with his pupil Alypius and his friends. It was the first Latin monastic order in Africa, and lasted two and a half years. Augustine's book, *The Teacher*, which derived from his discussions of this period, was dedicated to his son, Adeodatus, whose death at the age of 17 devastated him. In the book he makes it clear that for him the word of God as found in the Bible is figurative and metaphorical and not intended to be interpreted as fact. Indeed, his commentary on Genesis (401) was approved of by the radical Galileo some years later. Augustine also indicates that awareness of the subconscious was already in existence 1500 years before Freud: 'You can know something which you are not aware that you know.' In his writings he set down paradoxes, such as 'It is better to find God by not finding him'; he also made observations, such as the following one about babies: 'If infants do no injury, it is for lack of strength, not for lack of will'.

Augustine's next book was dedicated to Romaniarius, who had helped him finance his schooling when he was a student. It was called *On True Religion* and argued against Manicheism, to which Augustine had converted Romaniarius and from which he now converted him to Christian Catholicism. In 391 he made a visit to Hippo Regius and was forcibly ordained there by the congregation. For the rest of his life he lived in a monastery in the church gardens. He also established a nunnery, the head of which was his widowed sister. In 397 Augustine was appointed joint Bishop of Hippo Regius, and began to write one of his most famous books, *Confessions*, which was in part an autobiographical account, the form of which was analagous to the philosophical idea of the creation, fall and conversion.

It was a dangerous time for the Catholic clergy as priests and bishops were frequently attacked and sometimes killed as Donatist Christians. As he was adviser to Aurelius, Bishop of Carthage, he was inevitably drawn into the dispute between Catholics and Donatists. He acted as spokesman for the Catholic Church at a joint conference in Carthage in 411, where

570 Catholic and Donatist bishops battled it out. Here, he met his arch-rival Petilian, the Donatist Bishop of Constantine, for the first time. Although he was against violence, Augustine argued in favour of the repressive measures that were taken against the break-away Donastist church.

Augustine's active social conscience is seen in the radical actions of his church, for example, the freeing of a boatload of slaves from a vessel in the harbour at Hippo Regius. His most famous work was *City of God* which he started at the age of 59, three years after the fall of Rome, and completed when he was 72. It was in part prompted by the belief that the abandoning of the old gods and their temples and sacrifices had brought about the catastrophe that had befallen Rome at the hands of the 'Barbarians'. He argued that the people themselves were responsible for Rome's fall, and commented that the state was better at suppressing vice than it was at stimulating virtue. The book was partly political theory and partly a philosphy of history which described a divine pattern in the events of the world. In the last years of his life Augustine reviewed his achievements and failures; he had written 93 works and hundreds of letters and sermons. He died during the Vandals' siege of Hippo Regius in 430.

Vandal history

The Vandal invasion of Africa: 439–534

A power struggle between two Roman generals, Aëtius and Boniface under the boy emperor Valentinian III led to an alliance being forged between the **Vandals** in Spain and the general Boniface in Africa Proconsularis. Boniface had been the victim of intrigue by his rival Aëtius who had poisoned the court in Ravenna against him, but by the time the defamation of character had been discovered it was too late. In 429 the Vandals invaded and Boniface was defeated in battle; he retreated to Hippo Regius, where he was put under siege. The emperor sought help from Constantinople, which dispatched a fleet to bolster the Roman army led by Boniface. The joint force marched on the Vandals but it was defeated and Boniface returned to the court at Ravenna. The Vandals continued their conquest of Africa, making Hippo Regius their first capital; after taking Carthage in 439, they relocated their capital there, bringing to an end over 500 years of Roman domination of Africa.

Far from destroying everything in sight as their name might suggest, the Vandals adopted the customs of Africa Proconsularis, even learning Latin. They threw out the Roman landlords and reaped the benefits of the corn and oil harvests, living lives of indulgence and luxury, a ruling élite, comprising only 5 per cent of the population. From their base in Carthage they plundered the west Mediterranean, occupying Sardinia and Corsica and raiding Sicily. In 455 the Vandal king Genseric even invaded Italy to loot Rome, returning home with ships piled high with riches.

After this time, however, the Vandals' fortunes began to wane: the Berber kingdoms on the borders began to cause increasing problems, and the imposition of Arian Christianity, which held that Christ was not consubstantial with God, on the population caused the fragile empire to fragment. In 530, ostensibly to avenge the murder of the half Roman, half Vandal king,

Hilderic, the Byzantine Eastern Roman Empire under Justinian thought it time to intervene.

Byzantine history

In 533, some 500 ships carrying an army of 16,000 men and 6000 horses, set sail from Constantinople for Africa, led by Justinian's best general, **Count Belisarius**. The army landed at Rass Kaboudia, near Ksour Essaf; they met with no opposition, as the Vandal king, Gelimer, was at Bulla Regia, 300km away. Belisarius marched his army north along the coast, careful to win favour with the population by keeping his mercenary troops in check, only stopping briefly near Hammamet to plunder the luxurious Vandal villas there, before defeating Gelimer outside Carthage. Gelimer retreated with the remainder of his force to Bulla Regia while Belisarius took Carthage. The two met again in battle; this time the defeated Gelimer abandoned all hope of recovering his empire and retreated to a lonely Moorish villlage on a mountaintop near Hippo Regius. From here he was eventually taken to Asia Minor, to live at estates there magnanimously granted him by Justinian.

Early Byzantine rule in Africa was uneasy; almost as soon as Belisarius had gone there were tribal uprisings and an insurrection in the Byzantine army. Belisarius was forced to return to quell the tribes and discipline the army rebels; after this, the Byzantine forces fortified the towns with crenellated walls 3 metres thick and eight metres high; many of them built with masonry plundered from Roman buildings. But as well as building forts, they also built baths at Carthage and numerous churches and cathedrals, many of which were adorned with mosaic paving.

In 543 there was another inter tribal uprising, this time in the southern part of modern Tunisia which was known then as Byzacena. The Byzantine army won the first encounter, but being denied the chance to plunder, the mercenaries refused to fight a second engagement, and the army was defeated. Civil war broke out, and after another Byzantine defeat, this time at the hands of the Louata tribe at Le Kef (Sicca Veneria), the country was ravaged by marauding armies. Justinian sent his general John Troglita to restore order. Troglita fought back the enemies from the walls of Carthage, finally defeating them in a battle in the Byzacena province in 548, which restored peace to the country for the next 15 years.

An uprising in 579 was followed by brief periods of peace and prosperity. The final blow to the Byzantine empire came in the reign of the Orthodox emperor, Constans II (641–668), when the exarch of the African provinces, the Catholic, Gregory, declared himself emperor in 646. He did not try to take the throne in Constantinople but proclaimed Africa's independence. However, the following year his lands were invaded by Muslim Arab raiders, who were to sweep Christianity, and the Byzantines with it, out of Africa for ever.

The Life of Mohammed, the Prophet

Mohammed, whose name means 'highly praised', was born in 570. His family belonged to the Quraysh and were aristocractic Meccans, but both parents died during Mohammed's first years. As a youth he did odd jobs tending sheep and selling goods, and became agent to Khadija, a wealthy businesswoman, travelling north to Syria which was then Byzantine Christian. When he was 25, Khadija married Mohammed, even though she was 40 and had been twice married already. They had three sons and four daughters; all the sons died in childbirth and only one daughter outlived him and had descendants. He was faithful to Khadija for the next 25 years until her death.

Mohammed retired to a cave in the mountain of Hira to meditate. In 610, while he was asleep in the cave, an angel appeared and told him to read. Distressed Mohammed tried to commit suicide, but the angel intervened and identified himself as Gabriel. A second revelation ordered him to begin work, to 'rise and warn' the people, and Mohammed began preaching in Mecca in 613, teaching that Allah was the one true God, that the rich must share their wealth with the poor, and that God would judge all men. However, the Quraysh received him with hostility and he was stoned and beaten. A group of his followers went to Christian Abyssinia to escape persecution, where despite the Meccans' efforts to have them thrown out, they were allowed to stay.

In September 622 he travelled to Yathrib where a group of pilgrims offered their protection. Mohammed organised his new religion from Yathrib, where he began to wield increasing religious and political authority; the city was to become known as 'Medina'. Mohammed attempted to court favour with the small but influential Jewish community in Medina by adopting some of their practices, including that of facing Jerusalem during prayer, but although a few converted, the majority rejected his claims and he was forced to seek his followers among the Arab community. What are now traditional Islamic practices originated in this period; the muezzin's call to prayer which was first uttered by the Abyssinian, Bilal; the Ramadan fast, and Mecca as the direction in which to pray.

Conflict developed as the Muslims of Medina began attacking and robbing the richly laden caravans that passed the town bound for Mecca. A battle ensued in which the Muslims triumphed, although greatly outnumbered. The Meccans arrived soon afterwards with an even greater army and defeated but did not destroy the Muslims at Medina; two years later, in 627, they returned to finish the task. Mohammed prepared for the assault, and successfully defended the community, and the Meccans returned to Mecca. The Jews of Medina had been approached by the Meccans to attack the Muslims from within the city. Even though they had not done so, after the siege was lifted 600 of them were beheaded. The following year, Mohammed took his faithful on a pilgrimage to Mecca, but on the way they were threatened by Meccan horsemen. He negotiated a peace treaty which gave provision for an annual pilgrimage to Mecca; this was implemented the following year when Mohammed led 2000 Muslims there. Unfortunately, the pilgrimage was marred by violence, which prompted Mohammed to return the following year with a 10,000-strong force to storm the city and destroy the idols in the Kaaba shrine.

Having secured his power base in Mecca Mohammed turned his attention to spreading the new faith throughout the Arabian peninsula. When, in 633, at the age of 63, Mohammed became ill and died, he left behind him a ten-year-old religion which in a very short space of time was to become one of the most widespread and powerful in the world. Islam arrived in that part of Africa now known as Tunisia just 14 years after Mohammed's death.

The five pillars of Islam

Central to the Muslim religion are the Five Pillars of Islam: faith, prayer, almsgiving, fasting and pilgrimage.

Faith: 'La ilaha illa Allah; Mohammed rasul Allah' ('there is no God but Allah, and Mohammed is his Prophet') is the basic profession of faith and is supported by three other beliefs, namely that the Koran is the word of God, that Angels act as the instruments of God's will, and that there is a final judgement day.

Prayer: There are two types of prayer: *du'a* (inner prayer) and *salut* (ritual prayer). *Salut*, which involves a series of movements known as '*raka*', takes place five times daily: just after dawn; just after noon; late afternoon; after sunset; and after nightfall. The call to prayer, apart from that in the morning which adds 'prayer is better than sleep', is as follows:

God is Great
I testify there is no God but Allah
I testify that Mohammed is the Messenger of Allah
Come to prayer
Come to salvation
God is most great
There is no God but Allah.

There must be one ablution a day to make the prayers valid; this involves washing the face, hands and arms up to the elbows, feet to ankles, and hair.

Almsgiving: donation of a part of what is owned or earned.

Fasting: this takes place during the month of Ramadan, which recalls when the Koran was first revealed. The Koran is believed to have been revealed to Mohammed in stages over a period of 20 years. The revelations were brought to him by the angel Gabriel. The fast is only broken at sunset each day before being resumed at sunrise the following morning.

Pilgrimage: the annual pilgrimage (hajj) to Mecca is prescribed to all Muslims, at least once in a lifetime, provided they have the means.

Islamic history

Arab conquest: 647–800

When Caliph Uthman ordered raids of Byzantine Africa in 647, forces led by Abdullah Ibn Saad managed to defeat Gregory at Sbeitla. However, after looting the region they withdrew, leaving the country in disarray. It was not until some years later, when Bedouin Arabs led by Uqba Ibn Nafi captured Jerba and the southern province of Byzacena, that the Arabs made any territorial conquests. They founded a garrison at Kairouan (meaning 'arsenal'), which then served as the capital for Ifriqiya (the Arab name for Central North Africa), a dependency of Egypt. Berber attacks led by Kusaila and supported by the remnants of the Byzantines in 683, were fierce enough to defeat the Arabs, killing their leader Uqba and occupying Kairouan. The Arabs returned in 691 and retook Kairouan, fighting a series of battles against Berber forces led by the female warrior Kahina who was killed in 698. Carthage fell the same year; it was destroyed and abandoned in favour of Tunis, which was more easily defended against sea attack. With the destruction of Byzantine society, the country was plunged into lawlessness and disorder for several decades.

The Aghlabid dynasty: 800–909

In the late 8C the Abbasids called upon their governor in Algeria, Ibrahim Ibn Aghlab, to quell the disorder in Ifriqiya. He subdued the country and by the mid 9C the **Aghlabid** dynasty was powerful enough to mount a 25 year campaign which led to the conquest of Sicily. By conquering Sicily the dynasty gained control of the Mediterranean trade routes. An age of prosperity began; Kairouan, the capital city and the focus of the Saharan trade in gold, ivory, slaves and ebony, became the centre of both wealth and learning.

Trouble began when the heavy taxes imposed to finance the construction of the Aghlabid's royal city at Raqqada coincided with poor harvests and incursions from Shi'ite Muslims, who were intent on sowing dissatisfaction with the Abbasid Caliphate and its adherents. Their debauched lifestyles did nothing to improve matters and after a series of short-lived rulers the dynasty was overthrown by **Abu Abd Allah al Shi'i** in 909.

The Fatimid dynasty: 909–973

When Abu Abd Allah al Shi'i entered Ifriqiya in 910 he took the title 'Mahdi' (the 'expected one'). The Mahdi's ultimate goal was the creation of a Muslim state with himself at its head, and accordingly he took the title of caliph. Ifriqiya was governed much as it had been before but Abu Abd Allah's rule was deeply unpopular as he enforced the Shi'ite faith on the people. The majority of Muslims were Sunnites who followed orthodox beliefs and considered themselves the mainstream of Islam. The Shi'ites first grew up as a political faction, supporting Ali, son-in-law of Mohammed, as caliph. From then on, descent from Ali became central to Shi'ite beliefs, whereas Sunnites were content to follow leading Meccan families who had no connection with Ali. The Berbers revolted and Kairouan was sacked, forcing the Fatimids to flee to Mahdia. However, after military success in the Nile valley in the 960s and the founding of Cairo in 969, the Fatimids transferred their capital to Cairo; in 973 they left the Sanhaja Berber, Buluggin Ibn Ziri, the son of one of the Fatimid generals, as Governor of Ifriqiya.

The Zirids: 973–1160

Buluggin tested the Fatimids by expanding his territories to see if he could achieve independence, and to put him in his place they encouraged a Berber revolt. Destabilised, the country plunged into a 30-year power struggle after Buluggin's death in 984, during which 20,000 Shi'ites were killed. Al Muiz, Emir between 1016 and 1051, finally broke with the Fatimids by pledging his allegiance to the Abbasid Caliphate in 1049, making Ifriqiya Sunni Muslim once again. The stability he created allowed grain and olive production to flourish in the country and metalwork, pottery and weaving in the cities. With this new prosperity sprang up an exciting intellectual life, with the work of scholars such as Ishad Ibn Soulayman and his student Ibn Al Jazar in Kairouan. However, a decline in Saharan trade, the result of the **Zirid** lack of interest in ambitious building projects, namely communication links and fortifications, caused unrest to develop. The Fatimids sent in the Banu Hilal from the banks of the Nile in Upper Egypt. These Bedouin Arabs, almost a quarter of a million of them, descended on the country like a plague of locusts, destroying the agriculture and reducing cities to mere villages. The Zirids did their best to contain them, but were beaten in battle at Haidaran, just north-west of Kairouan in 1052. The city was sacked in 1057 and the Zirids fled to Mahdia. In 1078 a European coalition captured Mahdia and ransomed it back to the Zirids, who were so weak that they had to rely on the Normans for protection. Taking advantage of this situation, the Normans led by Roger II (1102–54) held brief sway over Sfax, Gabès, Jerba and the Kerkennah Islands, as well as the Zirid capital Mahdia, though they never managed to take Tunis.

Al-Muwahhid province: 1160–1227

In 1147 the Muwahhid Caliph in Marrakesh, Abd al Mumin, sent a military expedition to Tunisia to spread their Islamic faith and to gain more territory, and for the first and last time in history there was a unified North African Empire. However, it was not long before revolts in Ifriqiya demonstrated the fragility of the empire, and after the caliph's death in 1184, Marabit loyalists from the Balearic Islands led by Ali Ibn Ghaniya, captured northern Tunisia. Under pressure they retreated to the Jerid area in the south, and were eventually defeated in 1188. However, Ali's brother retook Tunis in 1203 and held it until 1205 when it was taken by General Abd-al-Wahid-Ibn Abi Hafs, the founder of the **Hafsid** dynasty.

The Hafsid dynasty: 1227–1574

The Hafsids played the interior tribes off against each other, establishing a reputation for strength, which led to their being asked by Spanish Muslims for help in their struggle against the Christian *reconqista*. Although they did not send help, Muslim refugees from Spain were welcomed to Tunisia and did much to revitalise the country. In the 1270s, the country was invaded by Europeans. The European powers were seeking to expand its territory, and an army was sent in the guise of a Crusade under the leadership of Louis IX of France who was fired by his religious beliefs. The force landed near Tunis where the invaders were struck down with dysentery and many, including the king, died.

After this debâcle, the Europeans contented themselves by employing corsairs to attack Muslim shipping in the Mediterranean. The Muslims responded in kind and during the 15C, both Christian and Muslim corsair activity increased dramatically. At the same time, the Hafsids found themselves squashed between two expanding powers, the Spanish to the west and the Ottomans to the east, and launched an attack against the Ottomans in Algiers. The Ottomans, led by **Barbarossa** (Khair-ed-din, died 1518), the most famous corsair of all, seized Tunis in 1534, deposing the Hafsids. In desperation, the Hafsids, turned to Charles I of Spain, who restored Sultan Moulay Hassen in 1535. The Hafsids retreated to the Spanish fortress at La Goulette when another corsair, Ilj-Ali, took Tunis in 1569. Tunis remained in Ottoman hands until 1573 when the Spanish again restored the Hafsids to power, but the Hafsid Dynasty fell to the Ottomans a year later, after which time the Spanish gave up the struggle.

Andalusian immigration

Although Muslim expulsions from Spain began around the 10C with the Christian reconquest, the repercussions were not felt in Tunisia until the 13C when Muslim Spain suffered considerable territorial losses. The first major territorial loss was in 1238 when Valencia was taken by Jaime I of Aragon. Spanish Christians, under Fernando III, then took Seville and in 1492, Granada. This created a huge refugee problem, which was increased by the failure of the Christians to respect the religious freedom of the Muslims in the lands they conquered. This led eventually to the mass expulsion of 'Moriscos' at the start of the 17C. Ifriqiya was a favoured destination as the country had political ties with Muslim Spain. Many refugees settled in the capital, Tunis, and significant numbers also found their way to other cities, as well as to rural locations. Kairouan, for example, had an Andalucian corner in the 13C, and in the 15C emigrants from Granada settled in Gabès, Sousse and Sfax. In the 17C refugees were housed in the Zuqaq al Andalus, in the medina in Tunis, from where they dispersed throughout northern Tunisia, namely to Cap Bon, the Mejerda valley and Bizerte. One colony established itself in Testour, and is known to have thrived after planting vines which produced an excellent wine.

The Andalucian population in Tunisia shrank in the 19C due to high taxation, but the Andalucian physical type persisted, as did their Spanish names, albeit in corrupted Arabic versions, and their domestic architectural style. These Hispanic-style villages with their monopitch pantile roofs can still be seen, as can the Renaissance style, Spanish-influenced mihrabs, with their columns and pediments. Minarets that are composed of a cone-shaped cylindrical lantern on a square tower are Andalucian in origin and copy models in Toledo, while octagonal towers on square bases are based on Aragonese models.

While there is little doubt that the Andalucian Muslims made a major contribution to Tunisia through the skills and ideas they brought with them, reaction from the local population was not always one of gratitude. People thought of the Andalucians as arrogant, as this story illustrates: Hammuda Pasha (1631–63) asked an Andalucian how he reaped wheat in his country, to which the Andalucian replied: 'with scissors'. The Pasha informed him that people reap with sickles not scissors, but the Andalucian maintained they used scissors in his country. The Pasha gave him 400 lashes for his stubbornness and then put the question to him again. The Andalucian again insisted that they used scissors in Andalucia. The Pasha then put lead weights on the Andalucian's legs and threw him into the Mejerda river, but as he was sinking under the water the Pasha saw the Andalucian thrust his hand up, out of the water, and defiantly open and close his fingers in a scissors motion.

The Ottomans: 1574–1705

Ottoman rule was welcomed by urban, but not by rural, peoples; therefore, initially the state derived more revenue from its corsairs than from its agriculture. This balance gradually changed, however, as the continuing influx of Andalucian refugees, who were provided with land and favourable tax status, helped to revitalise the economy. The Turkish military regime was initially ruled by a pasha, whose thousands of Janissaries were commanded by an agha, but a military coup by Janissary officers in 1591 robbed the pasha of power and placed it in the hands of a series of military commanders, called deys, who ruled until 1640. After this, power passed to Murad, a civil administrator, or bey, of Corsican origin, who was succeeded by members of his family. In 1705, after a conflict with Algeria, the title passed into the hands of Husain Ibn Ali Turki.

The Husainid dynasty: 1705–1881

Husain was a cavalry officer of Greek extraction who, after three years in power, was recognised by the sultan in Istanbul and granted the title of pasha. Despite this, he was challenged by his nephew Ali who, aided by Algeria, overthrew him in 1740. Ali was immediately challenged by Husain's sons, who declared war on him. In 1756 Ali II, Husain's younger son, came to power and the **Husainids** set about reforming the country by building schools and modernising the army; most importantly, they introduced the Ottoman style '*mamluk*' system, whereby non-Muslim slaves were specially educated for posts in the government and the bureaucracy.

Tunisia was still a very rural society: only 15 per cent of the population lived in urban settlements; half a million nomads, almost 50 per cent of the population, lived with their flocks in the arid inland regions. The Husainids stimulated urbanisation by granting special tax status and exemption from military service to city dwellers, and as a result commerce grew, especially the production of textiles, perfume and *chechias*.

When in 1814 a power struggle took place within the Husainid family, the European powers, who were all vying for this strategically positioned country, seized their opportunity. First, they demanded an end to corsair activity, and enforced their demand with a bombardment of Tunis in 1816 by the British fleet, and by an Anglo-French fleet in 1819. Then, following poor harvests in

Tunisia, which saw state revenue drop dramatically, the European powers lent Tunisia money, thus establishing a commercial foothold in the country. European pressure on Tunisia increased when France occupied Algiers in 1830, and European consuls competed fiercely for Tunisian government contracts and commercial privileges.

The European consuls also extended their judicial rights over their nationals in Tunisia, thus encouraging the number of Europeans in Tunisia to swell dramatically. Italian migrants came across the Mediterranean in large numbers, escaping from harsh economic conditions at home. Most settled on the land and formed the largest European national group in the country.

Ahmed Bey (1837–55) attempted to defend Tunisia against European imperialism by strengthening the army, introducing conscription and establishing the Bardo military school for the training of officers. His successor, **Mohammed Bey** (1855–59), however, played into European hands by executing Batto Sfez, a Jew, for blasphemy. Europe clamoured for reform, the French sending their fleet to force the Bey to guarantee civil and religious equality, introduce new legal codes and a constitution. Promulgated in 1861, the constitution allowed for a constitutional monarch and a Grand Council, to which the Bey's ministers were responsible. Many reforms, however, were blocked by the Prime Minister, Mustafa Khaznadar, who did further damage to the economy by awarding absurd contracts to the Europeans while creaming off a percentage for himself. With the country in debt again, the French supplied a high interest loan, the repayments of which absorbed half the total state revenue and necessitated increased taxes. This, coupled with further trading concessions for the Europeans, led to a revolt in Kairouan, El Kef and Sahel villages in 1864; in response, France and Britain sent in their fleets to 'protect their citizens', and France, in a change of policy, demanded that the constitution be rescinded. Finally under European pressure, the army was sent in and the revolt brutally suppressed. In 1866, the Prime Minister obtained another French loan to prop up the economy, but the situation became so bad that repayments had to be suspended, and an international debt commission under Khair-al-Din took control of the country's finances. Khair-al-Din ousted Prime Minister Khaznadar and pursued a policy of tax reform and economic growth. He was opposed by those who had grown fat on the old corrupt way of government, and he lost his position in 1877, after the French Consul demanded that he be removed from office. This cleared the way for the French to claim Tunisia, at the Congress of Berlin in 1878, when European powers agreed how they would divide up the Ottoman Empire. All France had to do was wait for some excuse to intervene in Tunisia.

The French Protectorate: 1881–1957

Although the Algerian border was little more than a line on a map, across which tribes wandered freely, the Khroumir tribes' 'raids' into Algeria in 1881 provided France with the excuse she needed to send 30,000 troops into Tunisia to 'stabilise the borderlands'. Within three weeks the French had reached Tunis, sparking off a revolt in central and southern Tunisia; the revolt was brutally put down, with 120,000 people fleeing into Tripolitania.

The following year the La Marsa convention was signed, which gave the French internal as well as external control of Tunisia. French settlers were given concessions on the purchase or rent of rural property, with the result that by 1900, 1.25 million Tunisian acres were in French hands, four times more than they had held at the start of the Protectorate. However, French rule, despite colonial exploitation, did bring very real benefits to the Tunisian people; there were great improvements in health, administration and infrastructure, as well as substantial investment in agriculture and industry.

There were some groups. such as the Salafiyya and the Young Tunisians, who were opposed to French rule, but it was not until 1912, when the Young Tunisians organised a boycott of the trams, that firm political action was taken. The government reacted by arresting and exiling the leaders and introducing a state of emergency.

In the First World War, 100,000 Tunisian troops served in France. Casualties were high: 40,000 were either killed or wounded. Afterwards, the veterans felt that for their loyalty and sacrifice to the French war effort, France should make concessions to their aspirations for autonomy. However, the Young Tunisians failed to win any concessions at the peace conference in Versailles in 1919; their failure led to the founding of the Destour (constitution) Party, which as the only opposition party in the 1920s, gained wide support. The Destour Party called for an elected assembly and government, with local councils, equal pay and compulsory education. In 1922 the Party even obtained the backing of Nasir Bey who ruled Tunisia from 1906–1922, and threatened the French with abdication if they made no concessions. France introduced a rather ineffective Grand Council, which was partly composed of Tunisians, but when Nasir Bey died in 1923, his successor Ahmed Bey failed to support the Tunisian people, and Destour Party members, such as the leader, Abd al Aziz Thaalbi, had to flee the country.

The Destour Party was effectively quashed by the restrictions on press freedom introduced by the French in 1926 and the opposition was taken over by a lawyer named **Habib Bourguiba**. Impatient with the failure of the conservative Destour Party, Bourguiba wrote articles for *L'Action Tunisien*, the newspaper he founded with his brother in 1931. Bourguiba propounded a radical view held by the young French-educated section of the Destour Party, opposing the economic policy of the Protectorate and arguing for full independence.

Bourguiba's newspaper was suspended and the Destour Party suppressed in spring 1933. Bourguiba then formed the Neo-Destour Party in Ksar Hellal, but within a year he was arrested and sent into exile in Bordj le Boeuf in the Sahara. He was released from exile in 1936 after the arrival of a new Resident General and immediately began his campaign for 'independence with a level of co-operation' between the two states. In 1938, after violent demonstrations organised by the Neo-Destour Party in which hundreds died, Bourguiba was again arrested and held in France. In prison at the start of the Second World War, he warned the Tunisian people not to collaborate with the Axis powers, but despite this he was released by the Germans in 1942. Bourguiba refused to join the fascists and returned to Tunis in 1943; after the Axis defeat in North Africa, he lobbied for political rewards in return for Tunisia's loyalty to France.

As France granted only limited concessions, Bourguiba went abroad in 1945 to gather international support. In 1949 he returned and began negotiating with France for Tunisian autonomy. As little progress was made, protest strikes were organised by the Union Générale Des Travailleurs Tunisiens (UGTT) in 1951. But the union's leader, **Farhat Hached**, was assassinated by a French-backed, right-wing terrrorist group, and in 1952 Bourguiba was again arrested.

The final struggle for independence was conducted by terrorist gangs in the cities and the 'Fallaqa', an armed peasant resistance movement, which attacked French rural property. With trouble also brewing in Algeria, the French acceded to demands for Tunisian autonomy and in 1954 began negotiations. Finally, in 1955, an agreement for internal autonomy was reached, and Bourguiba became Prime Minister of Tunisia in 1956.

The battle for Tunisia during the Second World War: 1942–43

Allied troops landed in French-controlled Casablanca, Oran and Algiers in November 1942. Their aim was to secure the North African coast in preparation for an assault on the Italian peninsula. In response, German parachute troops were dropped outside Tunis and heavy weapons and reinforcements poured into Bizerte and Tunis by sea. Within a week 5000 Axis troops, with tank and air support, had arrived in Tunisia.

The first battles

The British First Army advanced rapidly from Annaba (Bone) in Algeria into Tunisia, passing through Tabarka on 15 November and continuing to Bizerte, meeting Axis armoured forces at Nefza (Jebel Abiod) on 17 November. The First Army advance continued past Sejenane and for a further 25km, before being halted by Axis defences on 30 November. Meanwhile, Allied parachute troops had dropped at Jendouba (Souk el Arba) on 16 November, taking the airfield unopposed. They joined up with infantry, which had advanced overland from Algeria, in Beja on 19 November and launched a two-pronged assault on Tunis. One prong advanced to Mejez el Bab, from where it headed to meet the other prong, which had taken a more northerly route, at Tebourba. After a month's bitter fighting, the Allied advance on Tunis ground to a halt in heavy rain and mud at Jebel el Ahmera (Longstop Hill).

The Allied cemeteries of this phase of the Tunisian campaign are at Beja, where there are 396 graves; Mejez el Bab, where there are 2898 dead; Oued Zarga (between Mejez el Bab and Beja) where there are 247 graves; and at the Tabarka Rass Rajel Cemetery, where there are 500 dead. In the Thibar Seminary War Cemetery, west of Tunis, which is set in an agricultural college founded in 1895 by the White Fathers, 94 more soldiers lie buried.

Axis counter-attacks

The stalemate came to an end with an unsuccessful Axis counter-attack in the Tunis area on 18 January 1943, and a month later with a successful offensive through the Kasserine Pass in central Tunisia. Here the Africa Corps advanced through Gafsa, pushing the US First Armoured Division back to Thelepte and then to the Algerian border, while panzer divisions moved up through Sbeitla, from where one division pushed the US 34th Division back up to Sbiba, and another forced the 26th Armoured Brigade to retreat as far as Thala. The US troops suffered terrible losses, but the attack, which threatened Allied communications, was finally halted. Axis troops in the north then went on the offensive again with attacks on El Aroussa, Beja and Sejenane on 26 February.

In the meantime the British Eighth Army had advanced through Libya and arrived in southern Tunisia, occupying Ben Gardane on 15 February, Tataouine on 18 February and Medenine on 20 February; here they took up positions to the west of the town. To counter this advance, three panzer divisions in the south led a concerted attack down from the hills west of Medenine on 6 March, but they were met by the massed anti-tank artillery of the Allied forces and suffered heavy losses.

Assault on the Mareth Line
The Mareth Line blocked further Eighth Army advances into Tunisia. It had been built by the French to protect the country against Italian attacks from Tripoli and fulfilled a similar function to the Maginot line. It ran from the sea in the east near Zarat, up Oued Zigzaou, past Mareth on the Medenine–Gabès road, to the Matmata Hills near Toujane in the west. The Allied attack at outposts on the line began near the sea on 16 and 17 March, but these were unsuccessful and the Allies endured heavy casualties. On 18 March, the Allies gained control of a ridge overlooking the northern sector of the line, and on 19 March the assault began. After being repulsed by Axis forces the Allies mounted a fierce, 300 gun-barrage on the defences and briefly established a bridgehead over Oued Zigzaou.

Not having been able to break through the line, the Allies followed a route by the Long Range Desert Group, west of the Matmata Hills, advancing with New Zealand troops and the First Armoured Division to the Tabaga Gap, north-west of Matmata. They rushed the heavily defended Tabaga Gap, assisted by heavy air support, and broke through the Axis defences. The Allied troops advanced to El Hamma, 34km west of Gabès, and by so doing effectively outflanked the Mareth Line, which was taken on 28 March. Gabès itself fell on 29 March. Meanwhile, US forces had advanced from the north-west and taken Gafsa on 17 March and El Guettar the next day, thus forcing the axis troops to retreat towards the sea, east of a line running south-west from Meknassy.

The retreat north
With US forces threatening from the north-west, and the Allies in control of Gabès, the Axis forces drew up a defensive line along Oued Akarit, which crosses the narrow gap between the sea and the salt marshes of Chott el Fejaj, about 30km north of Gabès. At night on 6 April, the Allied forces attacked this line, and after severe fighting the Axis troops were forced to withdraw. They retreated northwards past Kairouan to Enfidaville, some 250km to the north, under constant Allied attack, the

Allies taking Sfax on 10 April and Sousse on the 12th. This left the Axis forces in control of Tunis, but hemmed in behind a line drawn from Enfidaville in the south, through El Fahs (Pont du Fahs) and Mejez el Bab, to near Sejenane in the north. 19 April saw an Allied attack on Enfidaville and the town was taken the following morning, although New Zealand troops met with strong resistance at Takrouna, a few kilometres to the west. The next attack was directed at the axis line to the east of Mejez el Bab, and Longstop Hill, on the north bank of the Mejerda river near Borj Toum, was taken on 26 April.

The last battles

In order to split the Axis forces, the attack on Tunis on 6 May was made through Massicault. By the evening the Allies were half-way to Tunis and on 7 May they entered the city; at the same time US troops, who had launched a simultaneous assault on Bizerte, entered Bizerte. After securing Tunis, the Cap Bon peninsula was cut off by the First and Sixth Armoured Divisions to prevent Axis forces from escaping, and the Allies moved south towards Enfidaville where Axis troops were holding out north-west of the town. Mopping up operations here were concluded at 11.45 on 13 May, when the last Axis troops surrendered. In all, 250,000 Axis troops were captured; under 700 managed to escape. At 14.15 on 13 May 1943 General Alexander sent the following message to the British Prime Minister, Winston Churchill: 'Sir, it is my duty to report that the Tunisian campaign is over. All enemy resistance has ceased. We are masters of the North African shore.'

At Massicault war cemetery lie 1578 Allied soldiers who died in the battles to take Tunis; 1500 German soldiers lie in a nearby plot. At Enfidaville there are 1551 more graves, and at the Sfax cemetery another 1254 soldiers lie buried.

The Tunisian Republic

The republic was created in 1957 with Bourguiba as its first president. After eliminating his rivals and securing power firmly in his hands, Bourguiba set about reforming the country, especially the Islamic institutions and practices. In 1960 he publicly broke the Ramadan fast and when the Kairouan religious authorities protested he moved against them and within five years had them within his control.

Responsibility for economic development was given to Ahmad Ben Salah, the Minister of Planning, but his land reforms proved unpopular and Bourguiba had him arrested and tried for treason. Following this, Bourguiba took personal control of more and more portfolios, surrounding himself with a small coterie of advisers. After a period of illness in the early 1970s when his hold on power appeared to be diminishing, Bourguiba had himself made 'president for life'. He introduced a free-market policy and encouraged foreign investment, but unemployment and poverty persisted and inflation was high. Tension exploded on 28 January, 1978, 'Black Thursday', when a general strike was organised by the UGTT. The protest was stimulated by the economic conditions and by frustration at the 'dictatorship' which governed the country.

Bourguiba had the unrest put down, disciplined the protesters, but offered them minimal concessions. On the second anniversary of Black Thursday there was another violent disturbance, this time in Gafsa when Libyan-backed guerrillas made an attempted coup. Bourguiba now installed Muhammad Mzali as prime minister, instructing him to liberalise political life and follow a moderate economic path. In 1984, under international pressure, Mzali removed subsidies from basic commodities, provoking violent riots. Bourguiba overruled Mzali and reinstated the subsidies, and following his recovery from a heart attack, dismissed him.

Bourguiba's fall came after the trials of members of the fundamentalist Muslim party, the 'Mouvement de la Tendence Islamique' (MTI) in September 1987. Several members were sentenced to death; however, the death sentence imposed on MTI leader Rashid Ghabbushi was commuted to life imprisonment on the advice of the interior minister, Ben Ali, who wanted to avoid creating martyrs. When on 7 November, Bourguiba appeared to have changed his mind about the commuted sentence, Ben Ali, who had in the meantime been appointed prime minister, removed Bourguiba from office on medical grounds.

President Ben Ali

Zine el Ben Ali was sworn in as president on 7 November 1987, according to the constitution, and introduced a more liberal flavour to Tunisian politics. Thousands of political prisoners were released from jails, and the State Security court, which had been responsible for the detention of political prisoners during the Bourguiba era, was abolished. Opposition parties were given back their rights, and newspaper censorship relaxed. Despite this apparent political liberalism, at the election in 1989 the governing party achieved 99 per cent of the vote, very similar to the 100 per cent vote achieved by Bourguiba. This is not to say that opposition parties have no support. What appears to be the strongest opposition party, the Hizb el Nahda (Renewal Party), which resembles the outlawed fundamentalist Islamic Salvation Front in Algeria, has not been able to stand in elections because it has not been able to register as an official political party.

BACKGROUND INFORMATION

A land between sea and desert

Tunisia, just 140km south of Sicily, at the northernmost tip of Africa, stretches back from the blue waters of the Mediterranean Sea into the arid depths of the great Saharan sand sea; the country, just 897km from north to south and 330km from west to east, is caught in a struggle between these two dramatically different environments.

The influence of the Mediterranean, vital for the agricultural coastal strip, is strongest in the north, but extends only a short distance inland and only 20 per cent of Tunisia receives enough rainfall to support Mediterranean type crops. The winds across the Mediterranean lose much of their moisture as they pass over the tail-end of the Atlas Mountains in the north of the country. The Khroumerie range, which, just inland from Tabarka is 700–800m high, is the wettest area in Tunisia and receives 1500mm of rainfall a year. It is also the most verdant area of the country and the hills are covered in dense forests of cork oak. Further to the east the hills of the Atlas range are lower, the Mogod range behind Bizerte being just 300–400m high. Composed of soft tertiary limestone overlaid with beds of sandstone that are deeply folded and eroded, the hills receive 600mm of rainfall and are covered with the maquis vegetation typical of the Mediterranean.

The real climatic divide between the Mediterranean and the central steppe, however, occurs further south, where the Dorsale Mountains stop the rain-bearing winds from reaching the steppe, and the hot dry desert winds from parching the north. The Dorsale Mountains enter Tunisia from Algeria, just north of Kasserine, and run eastwards for 220km to Zaghouan and the Cap Bon peninsula. They are the highest mountains in the country, standing between 1600m and 1300m high, and are covered in parts with Aleppo pines and holm oaks. To their east is the olive-growing region of the Sahel, which means 'coast' or 'border', and to their south is the semi-arid steppe, which is 600–800m above sea level and extends southwards as far as the great salt lakes, known as the chotts.

South of the chotts is the Grand Erg Oriental, which is the beginning of the Sahara, and the Dahar uplands, the homeland of the Berbers. This range of hills, some 600m high, runs south from Gabès and separates the Sahara from the coast.

The name Sahara derives from the Arabic 'Sahra', which means 'empty area', an apt description for a place where it is possible to drive for 500km and not see any vegetation. The desert, 5000km wide, is the largest in the world and surely ranks as one of its most inhospitable environments. The Grand Erg Oriental, south of the Chott el Jerid, is, as the name 'erg' suggests, an area of dunes and sand seas. Dunes are wind-formed features and as such are constantly shifting and changing, making navigation very difficult. They vary enormously in size but are often over 30m tall and many kilometres long.

In the Saharan part of Tunisia, the sky is deep blue during the day and at night the stars are very bright and clear, as the atmosphere is so dry. However, when there is a wind, which is quite often, fine particles of sand are picked up and the air becomes hazy and yellow, so much so that shadows become indistinct. When the strong winds blow in October and November, at the beginning of the winter rains, there are sand-storms. Huge quantities of sand are picked up and swept to a height of 1km, and the sand-laden wind sandblasts everything it comes in contact with, until the rain comes and turns the landscape to mud. Dry, hot air from the Sahara occasionally blows north, raising temperatures there by 10°C. This sirocco, known locally as the 'Chehili', blows in Kairouan for 31 days a year, in Sousse for three or four days, and in Tunis for one or two days a year. Its Mediterranean adversary, the 'Chergui' wind, carries sultry sea air from the west, and is most prevalent at Gabès, where it blows for 125 days a year.

Flora

Before the Saharan region dried up about 4000 years ago, and before the Romans deforested the region in their efforts to increase the area of agricultural land in Africa Proconsularis, much of Tunisia was covered by evergreen forest. The little evergreen forest that remains today is restricted to the Atlas and Dorsale mountain ranges in the north and is composed of holm oak, kermes oak, cork oak, Aleppo pine, maritime pine, carob, umbrella pine and laurel. The rest of the country, not under cultivation, is covered in vegetation of three levels of degradation:

Maquis. This typically Mediterranean vegetation is seen on the lower hills of the north, especially around Bizerte, and grows up to 2m high. It is dense, thorny, dark green and resinous and is composed of sclerophyllous-leaved shrubs and trees such as olive, tree heather, myrtle, judas tree, wig tree, broom and terebinth.

Garigue. This type of plant cover grows on poorer and drier soils than those that can sustain maquis, and is formed of spiny and woody, aromatic plants with grey-green leathery leaves, which are covered in fine hairs that trap moisture. It grows to under 1.5m in height and contains many of the culinary herbs that have found their way into European gardens, such as thyme, sage, lavender and rosemary.

Steppe. Where the soil has been destroyed, either by erosion or by heat and loss of moisture, and the rock is partially exposed, the vegetation tends to be very deeply rooted or highly seasonal. In the steppe, with up to ten hours a day of sunlight between June and September, the flowering season is early. Perennials flower brilliantly in early spring, and annuals in late April, before the summer drought sets in. By June the seeds have been shed and the plants may have dried out and withered, apart from thistles and mints. Plant cover here is composed predominantly of asphodel, thistles and esparto grass, the latter being cropped and exported for the manufacture of paper.

As well as deforesting and cultivating the land, man has made his mark on the landscape in another way. Over the centuries many plants foreign to the region have been introduced and have become so widespread that they appear to be part of the natural vegetation. The Phoenicians were the first to import plants, bringing such species as the olive, of which there are now some 30 million trees, the pomegranate, and the fig from the east. Later the Arabs introduced citrus fruit, most notably the orange from China, and the palm from Arabia. In the last 300 years the invasion has continued unabated with eucalyptus and acacias arriving from Australia, the boulevard palm from the Canary Islands, bougainvillea from South America, and the prickly pear from Central America (originally brought to Spain by Christopher Columbus).

Travelling around Tunisia, one of the commonest plants to be seen is the globe thistle, which flowers between May and August and has a beautiful pale-blue flower-head. Also very much in evidence, especially in the drier south, is the prickly pear or Barbary fig, as it is also known. This grows 2–5m high and is used to fence in land, to keep animals both in and out. It has bright yellow flowers which form ovoid fruit between April and July. The fruit can be eaten but care should be taken as the plant and fruit is covered with fierce and irritating spines. Another common cactus is the century plant, which has enormous rosettes of pointed, fleshy leaves and great candelabra-like flower-heads. The leaves grow up to 2m and have tough spines, while the flower-stems grow up to 10m, shooting up within a month when the plant is 10–15 years old. Each plant flowers once in its lifetime, dying afterwards, although side-shoots may continue to grow.

Fauna

BIRDS
There are a wide variety of habitats in Tunisia, supporting a wide range of birds, and although more than half of the land is arid desert or semi-desert and supports little vegetation, a surprising number of bird species manage to find a niche. Although a number of the birds are also common to Europe, there are many that are peculiar to the region, and these have been listed below, grouped according to habitat. Tunisia is visited by many species of migratory bird, a number of which stay only for short periods; these have not been included in the list.

Forest or Woodland
Red Kite
Moussier's Redstart

Oases or Palmeries
Common Bulbul
Palm Dove (easily recognisable song:
  'oh-cook-cook-oo-oo')

Cliffs or Mountains
Griffon Vulture
Barbary Falcon
Black Wheatear

Marsh or Shallow Water
Great Flamingo (the only flamingo in
  the region, it has pink plumage,
  red and black wings and a hooked
  bill that it uses to sieve the water
  for food. It likes shallow water and
  can be seen in large numbers
  around Menzel Temine on the Cap
  Bon peninsula. The black stripes
  on its wings are only seen in
  flight, when it is also possible to
  hear its goose-like honking. It
  nests on piles of mud heaped up
  out of the water)

Purple Gallinule
Black-Winged Stilt
Lesser Shore Toed Lark

Shingle
Little-Ringed Plover

Steppe or Grassland
Bittern
Little Egret
Cattle Egret
Black-Shouldered Kite
Long-Legged Buzzard
Bonelli's Eagle
Steppe Eagle
Egyptian Vulture (breeding only)
Little Bustard
Dupont's Lark
Black-Headed Bush Shrike
Fan-Tailed Warbler
Spotless Starling
Brown-Necked Raven

Semi-Desert
Stone Curlew
Scrub Warbler
Red-Rumped Wheatear (on edge of desert)

Desert
Cream-Coloured Courser
Crowned Sandgrouse
Pin-Tailed Sandgrouse (not in open desert)
Black-Bellied Sandgrouse (not in open desert)
Hoopoe Lark
Temminck's Horned Lark
Desert Lark
Bar-Tailed Desert Lark
Thick-Billed Lark (stony desert)
Thekla Lark (not near villages)
Trumpeter Finch (stony deserts)
Desert Sparrow

ANIMALS

A range of animals also manages to survive under the extreme conditions of the desert. Many of the animals are nocturnal and exhibit special characteristics which are adapted to desert conditions. Camels are one of the best examples, for they have flat feet that expand with pressure and help to keep the animal 'afloat' in the sand, and blood vessels which are adapted to keep the head temperature low, even though the rest of the body may be very hot. Camels carry fat reserves which can keep the animal fed for up to six months, as long as it does not have to work; their bodies can tolerate saline water and are able to form water directly from the air by combining free hydrogen and oxygen. They can live for two weeks without water, but when they do find it they can consume as much as 150 litres at a time.

Other desert animals are equally resourceful. Lizards, known as sand-fish, literally swim in the sand and live at some depth below the surface where the environment is cooler; while the addax and the gazelle can survive without drinking as they obtain their water from the vegetation.

Visitors to the Sahara are very lucky if they catch a glimpse of the rarer desert species, which include the desert cat, addax, oryx, mountain goat or moufflon, desert fox, hedgehog, gazelle, fennec and jackal. More common and easier to spot, especially at dusk, are the desert hare, sand rat, gerbil and jerboa.

Care should be taken to avoid the desert's two poisonous inhabitants: the scorpion and the horned viper. There are ten different types of scorpion of varying size and colour, and all of them give a persistent and painful sting; these include two deadly species, which are found in the regions south of Kairouan and Sousse. The horned viper, a real danger to walkers, hides under the surface of the sand with only its horns protruding, waiting for its prey to pass. Its sting is similar to a cobra's and can kill in four hours. This is the snake used by the local snake charmers, who before a performance take the precaution of extracting the poison from the gland in the snake's neck.

The horned viper is one of 22 species of snake that live in the country, only five of which are poisonous, including the Levant viper which lives in northern regions. Also in the north, Atlas deer and wild boar inhabit the thickly wooded mountains behind Tabarka. Just to the south, around the Mejerda valley, there are otters and porcupines. In the centre of the country, the striped hyena patrols the steppes. Off the coast, seals can be seen at various remote islands; the best-known are the communities of Monk seal which can be found off the Gallite Isles north of Tabarka, and at the Zembra and Zembretta Isles off Cap Bon.

Ancient gods

In museums and at archaeological sites around the country, visitors will come across depictions of the Carthaginian and Roman gods and the symbols which represent them. It is useful, therefore, to have some idea of the character of the principal divinities of both religions and the symbols which were used to represent them.

Baal Hammon, the principal Carthaginian divinity, was god of the sky and fertility. The god is depicted as a dignified old man with a beard, his head surmounted by rams' horns. He sits on a throne with a high back and rams' heads as armrests. He is linked with the Egyptian deity, Seth, and the Greek divinity, Kronos, who ate his own children. He was associated with Saturn in Roman times and many temples of Saturn in Tunisia look out over fields, which befits the god of fertility. Baal's symbols are the twin rams' horn, grapes, pillars, a spear and an axe.

Tanit, the principal Carthaginian goddess associated with Baal Hammon, was known as 'the face of Baal'. She was originally an ancient 'Libyan' goddess who gradually assumed some of Baal's roles. Her symbol, found frequently on stele, was a cone or triangular shape truncated at the top by a disk. This symbol with its stylised upraised arms may represent a blessing from the goddess. Other symbols associated with the goddess are grapes, doves and the crescent moon.

El was head of the Carthaginian pantheon and the 'father of years' who made the world run. He was omnipresent and preceded the birth of the gods. With **Asherat**, goddess of the sea and 'mother of the gods', he produced 70 children, including Baal. El's favourite son, however, was **Mot**, god of the harvest, who ruled the dry land. Mot was sacrificed at harvest time by the goddess **Anat** but was soon reborn, only to be beaten in combat by Baal's son and abandoned by his father when the rains came.

Ashtart was the consort of Baal, who with him produced **Aleyin**, the god of water and spirit of springs. Aleyin was honoured in temples called 'memnonia' which were situated at the mouths of rivers. Anat, the virgin daughter of Baal and sister of Aleyin, was involved in the ritual sacrifice of Mot, her function being to preserve the gods' lives through frequent sacrifices.

The daughter of the rain god, Anat was connected with water, her speciality being dew, 'the fat of the earth'.

The **Roman pantheon** in Africa Proconsularis was dominated by the trinity of Jupiter, Juno and Minerva and it was to them that the main temple in every town, the capitol, was dedicated. **Jupiter** was the god of light, the sun and the moon as well as the elements. He later became the protector of the city, justice and the state, and his symbol was the thunderbolt. **Juno**, goddess of light, marriage and childbirth, was the female equivalent of Jupiter, and his sister and consort. She is shown with a sceptre, veil and peacock, but may also have a shield and spear or be carrying a child. **Minerva** was the goddess of trade, commerce and schools, but she also became a warrior and her symbols include a helmet and a coat of mail. She was widely venerated and is also often shown with wings and holding an owl.

The other frequently represented Roman god is **Saturn**, god of the fertile land and tender of vines. He was celebrated in rural festivals, the 'Saturnalia', which were held on 17 December and the following seven days. These celebrations ended with a massive feast which lasted all day and brought everything else to a halt. Saturn is represented carrying a sickle or some ears of corn.

Along with the gods, a number of natural deities were popular, especially the **nymphs**, who were the spirits of the springs and rivers. **Diana**, goddess of light and mountains and woods, and **Venus**, goddess of spring, fruitfulness and love, are also depicted in mosaics and statues.

Mosaics in Tunisia

The discovery of the earliest true mosaic in the world in Carthage, supports the idea that it was the Carthaginians who invented the technique and not the Romans. This mosaic dates back to the 5C or 4C BC and is a simple chequerboard pattern. Nearly all the remaining mosaics in Tunisia today, however, are from 1–7C AD.

The earliest Roman mosaics produced in the 1C were of relatively simple design but by the end of the century, mosaics had become considerably more sophisticated and influenced by Italian geometric designs in black and white. Some of these early African mosaics (examples have been found at Oudna) included polychrome panels in the borders, which were imported ready-made from Italy. In fact it appears that Italian workmen were also brought over during this period, specifically to train local pupils, who then established mosaic workshops around the country.

Of the early workshops, those at El Jem and Sousse were particularly successful, and their work spread far from the original workshops, for example, the mosaics decorating two baths in Acholla, on the coast south of Ksour Essaf, came from the El Jem workshops. The Trajan Baths of 115–120 have a mosaic of Dionysus with satyrs, nymphs and centaurs, while the later, more conservative Thiasos Baths, have a marine scene set in a larger decorative composition. (Both of these are now in the Bardo museum.) However, mosaics became so popular that very soon nearly every city had its own atelier with a 'pictor' who drew the cartoon to which the '*tessellare*' (the craftsman who laid the stones on the mortar) worked. Individual ateliers often had distinct styles, such as that at Thuburbo Maius which specialised in mosaics with large floral garlands and wreaths.

By the 2C, the simple, flat, decorative forms of earlier mosaics had developed into richly coloured and modelled figurative forms, where volume was conveyed through subtle gradation of colour, and compositions were more complex and cluttered. From the mid 3C, production declined due to a general slump, and the depiction of form became more impressionistic, with suggestion and economical description in place of detailed representation. Single viewpoint compositions were abandoned in favour of friezes, registers and free compositions, and instead of the figures being placed against flat abstract backgrounds, they were now placed in landscape settings.

The 4C and 5C, the golden age of mosaic production in terms of the quantity laid, saw a more abstract style evolve, with what were formerly subtle gradations of colour becoming vivid stripes running down the form. Far greater emphasis was placed on the linear qualities of the composition and the background, with scrolls of vines once again assuming a rather rigid, abstract form.

The subject-matter used in mosaics is fairly conventional and there are a number of popular themes: the hunting scene depicting wild animals, and perhaps including the patron and his estates, is one of the commonest subjects, even outliving Roman rule to be adopted by the Vandals. Allied to this theme are scenes from the amphitheatre, where whole zoos of fabulous animals are depicted—a veritable catalogue of slain animals. In one such mosaic, from Thuburbo Maius, Diana is shown surrounded by a gladiator, an antelope, a bear, boar, bull, deer, goat, ram, horse, and even an ostrich. There are also scenes from the circus, where charioteers are often shown at full tilt. In a third-century mosaic from Dougga, a charioteer holds a palm, whip and crown while being pulled by four horses; in another mosaic, from the Trifolium house in the same city, a celebrated circus horse is depicted.

During the 3C rural scenes became popular, especially those depicting the seasons. Ploughmen are shown at work with their oxen, and shepherds with their flocks; no doubt in many cases these were representations of real estates, as in the 'Sorothus' mosaic in Sousse, where Sorothus' stud farm is shown with all its fine horses. Banqueting scenes, depicting patrons with tables piled high with food, are also common; and there are drinking scenes, whose function seems to be have been to welcome guests to the house. Marine scenes were common in private houses; these mosaics show fishing boats at sea with their nets out, and marvellously accurate fish pictures, but they also give a picture of the local coastline as it was 1500 years ago. Mythological subjects, with Venus being one of the most popular, were also common in private houses. On a mosaic in Bulla Regia, Venus is borne by tritons in a cockleshell and flanked by two erontes mounted on dolphins, who are carrying her mirror and jewel-box. Dionysus was also very popular and 14 depictions of him have been found in El Jem. These Dionysian mosaics usually show the god being carried on a leopard, or as a child on a tiger, or in triumph driving a chariot, but are often also mildly erotic.

In the Christian era of the late 4C, mosaics were laid in many churches, though these were of an inferior quality which by the 6C had almost become pastiche. They were often large and floral, the composition being basically geometric; established by vine scrolls and interspersed with Christian symbols. At the same time, tomb mosaics, which are unique to Africa, started to appear. They were laid on the church floor and had inscriptions and in some cases half- or full-length portraits of the deceased, such as those found at Sfax and Tabarka. Many were also non-figurative, for example the fifty tomb mosaics found in the church of the priest Felix in Kelibia; these have ornamental borders and an epitaph in a crown flanked by a pair of palm trees.

Glossary

Abu	see Bou
Acanthus	prickly plant used in the design of ancient capitals
Aid	festival
Ain	spring
Atrium	central courtyard in Roman house
Baal	principal Phoenician god. The term is also used in general to mean lord or master
Baal Hammon	protecting god of Carthage
Bab	gate
Berber	indigenous tribespeople
Bey	ruler of Tunis
Bordj	fortress
Bou	father or owner
Caldarium	hot room in Roman baths
Calèche	horse and trap
Capitol	principal temple in Roman city
Cardo	road following north–south axis through Roman city
Chechia	red felt hat worn by Tunisian men
Cella	inner sanctuary of Roman temple
Chott	salt lake
Columbaria	niches inside Roman tomb for cinerary urns
Curia	town hall in Roman city
Dar	Arabic house designed around central courtyard
Decumanus	road following west–east axis through Roman city
Destrictarium	room in Roman baths where bodily hair was removed
Dey	governor of Tunis
Doliman	large terracotta storage jar
Dolmen	megalithic tomb made of stone slabs
Esparto grass	steppeland grass used to weave baskets
Exedra	semi-circular recess in Roman building
Faience	painted ceramic ware
Fondouk	inn for travellers and caravans
Forum	central square of Roman city
Frigidarium	cold room in Roman baths

Ghorfa	Berber store room or granary with barrel-vaulted roof
Haik	wrapper for body and head
Hammam	Turkish bath
Hanefites	Islamic school founded by Abu Hanifa in the 9C
Hypocaust	underground heating system used in Roman baths
Hypogeum	underground burial place
Ifriqiya	Arabic name for central North Africa, comprisingTunisia, part of Algeria and Libya
Impasse	no-through road
Impluvium	basin in central courtyard of Roman house for collecting rainwater
Insula	housing block in Roman city
Jebel	hill or mountain
Kalaa	fortress
Kasbah	citadel
Koubba	domed mausoleum
Ksar/Ksour	fortified granary/ies or village/s
Maghreb	name given to north-west Africa, comprising Tunisia, Algeria and Morocco
Malikites	Islamic school founded by Melik Ibn Anas in the 8C
Marabout	holy man of Islam; his mausoleum
Medersa/medrese	koranic school
Medina	old town centre
Mihrab	prayer niche in mosque
Muezzin	person who calls faithful to prayer, usually from minaret
Narthex	church porch or entrance hall
Necropolis	burial ground
Nymphaeum	fountain dedicated to water nymphs
Opus Sectile	mosaic of marble paving
Oued	river bed that only flows with water after rainfall
Palaestra	place for physical exercise in Roman cities
Peristyle	courtyard surrounded by columns
Proscenium	front part of stage in ancient theatre
Rass	cape or headland
Ribat	fortified monastery
Sahel	area between desert and coast
Sidi	lord or master
Skifa	dog-leg entrance hall
Souk	market
Stelae	upright tomb stones
Sudarium	sweat room in Roman baths
Tanit	Phoenician goddess
Tepidarium	warm room in Roman baths
Tesserae	small square block used to make mosaic
Tophet	place of sacrifice and burial
Triclinium	dining room in Roman house
Unctuarium	room in Roman baths where dead skin was removed
Zaouia	centre of a religious brotherhood

I TUNIS AND ANCIENT CARTHAGE

1 · Tunis

TUNIS, the capital of Tunisia, sprawls over low hills north-west of two lakes, the Lac de Tunis and the Sabkhit as Sijoumi, the suburbs extending for more than 10km from the city centre. Reflecting its turbulent history, the city is one of contrasts, with modern development competing with architecture of the past, and colonial styles with the labyrinthine structures of the Arabic souks. It is unlike any other city in Tunisia, having a much more western feel and a sense of space in which, as a tourist, you can feel relatively anonymous. Coming back to Tunis, having travelled around the rest of the country, is something like returning home.

The city has two distinctive areas: the French colonial part and the medina. The colonial city, built on reclaimed land in the 19C, lies west of the port of Tunis and extends inland to the walls of the medina. It was laid out by the French planners on a regular grid plan of wide, tree-lined boulevards, and forms the administrative and financial heart of the city as well as being the hub of accommodation and transport. The medina, the historical and old commercial centre of the city, is immediately to the west of the colonial city. Its maze of narrow streets and alleys covers an area approximately 1.5km by 1km. The bustling streets along the tourist routes and around the major historic monuments are lined by shops stocked with souvenirs. However, much of the medina remains as it always has, the preserve of small shops and one- or two-room manufacturing workshops. Off the main routes it can be quiet and appear almost deserted, and in contrast to the French colonial city, is pleasantly traffic-free.

Tunis' growing population lives in the residential suburbs that spread further out each year into the surrounding countryside. These vary in character from the exclusive villas around Carthage to the north, to the grim cement apartment blocks that extend along the coast as far as Hammam Lif in the south.

The French colonial city and the medina form a compact city centre, best explored on foot or by public transport. Having a car is both unnecessary and a nuisance. If you have arrived in Tunis by car, the best idea is to park it in a custodian car park such as that near Place 3 Août on Rue Yougoslavie, although care should be taken to ensure that nothing is left visible inside. Should you be staying in the *Hotel Afrique* you can make use of their private car park.

- **Airport**. Tunis–Carthage Airport, 9km north east of Tunis, tel. (01) 236000. Shuttle service No. 35 from TGM or *Hotel Afrique* every 20 minutes from 06.00 to 21.00 (takes 20 minutes).

- **Airline companies**. Tunis Air, 48 Ave Habib Bourguiba, tel. (01) 785100. Tunisavia, 19 Ave Habib Bouguiba, tel. (01) 254239.

- **Arrival by sea**. La Goulette, tel. (01) 730300. This dock is 10km from Tunis, but is connected by the regular TGM train to Tunis Nord which is within walking or bus-ing distance of the city centre. Bus No. 3, 11, 12 and 38 go from Tunis Nord up Ave Habib Bourguiba, the main artery of the city.

- **Maritime companies**. Navitour, 8 Rue d'Alger, tel. (01) 249500. Tirrenia– Compagnie Tunisienne de Navigation, 122 Rue de Yougoslavie, tel. (01) 242801. Tour Afrique, 52 Ave Habib Bourguiba, tel. (01) 341488.

- **Railway stations**. TGM, Tunis Nord, Place du 7 Novembre. A small electric train runs from here along the coast west of Tunis to La Marsa. Gare SNCFT, Place Barcelone. Trains run from here to Bizerte, Beja, Jendouba, Tabarka, El Kef, Sousse, Monastir, Mahdia, Sfax and Gabès.

- **Bus stations**. SNTRI, Gare Routière Nord de Bab Saadoun, tel. (01) 562299/562532. Services to: Ain Draham, Beja, Bizerte, Jendouba, El Kef, Tabarka, Teboursouk and Testour. SNTRI, Gare Routière Sud de Bab Alleoua, tel. (01) 495255/490358. Services to: Ben Gardane, Douz, Gabès, Gafsa, Kairouan, Kasserine, Kebili, Mahdia, Matmata, Medenine, Nefta, Sfax, Sousse, Tataouine, Tozeur and Zarzis.

- **Metro**. Gare Centrale, Place Barcelone. The metro comprises a simple network of green trams. Nos 2 and 3 run in a north–south direction, No. 4 branches west from Place Palestine in the direction of Bardo Museum, although it is only built as far as Rue 20 Mars.

- **Louage stations**. Bab Saadoun for northern destinations. Bab Alleoua for southern destinations. Garage du Bois, 37 Rue el Jazira, for Sousse and Sahel destinations.

- **Taxis**. Place du 7 Novembre and throughout the city, although it is often hard to get a taxi on Ave Habib Bourguiba.

- **Hotels**. Most hotels are to be found on and around Ave Habib Bourguiba. *Hotel Afrique*, tel. (01) 347477, the tall blue block at No. 50 is not only a city landmark but one of the top hotels. More moderately priced accommodation can be found in side streets, such as the *Hotel Atlantique*, tel. (01) 240860, at 106 Rue de Yougoslavie. For budget accommodation look around the medina walls, but be prepared for basic and often none too clean facilities; women travelling alone should be very wary. Under 25s can use the youth hostel, *Maison des Jeunes de Medina*, 23 Rue Saida Ajoula. Accommodation is quickly filled and it is recommended to book in advance where possible, or at least check in before lunchtime. The tourist office holds listings of classified hotels. Bookings can be made from the airport.

- **Restaurants**. There are a great many restaurants in Tunis, particularly at the cheap end of the market where the standard fare is spit roast chicken and couscous. For something a little different and more upmarket, try the *M'rabet* in the Souk et Trouk in the medina. *Le Malouf* at 108 Rue de Yougoslavie is less pricey and popular with tourists as wine is available; the food is bland but safe. For cleanliness you cannot beat *Prince*, the self-service restaurant on Place Barcelone (81 Rue Ave Farhat Hached), which is air-conditioned and has a colourful selection of foods. Alcohol is not available: if you need to slake your thirst with a beer, head for one of the pavement cafés on Ave Habib Bouguiba where you can sit outside and watch passers-by, or one of the less prestigious beer houses on Rue de Yougoslavie.

- **Post office**. PTT, Rue Charles de Gaulle (open Mon–Thurs, 07.30–12.30, 17.00–19.00; Fri–Sat, 07.30–13.30; Sun 09.00–11.00). Place Pasteur. Ave Habib Thameur.

- **Tourist information**. ONTT, Place du 7 Novembre, tel. (01) 341077, (open summer Mon–Sat, 08.00–13.30, winter Mon–Sat, 08.00–12.00, 15.00–18.00). Regional Tourist Office for Tunis, 29 Rue de Palestine, tel. (01) 289403.

- **British Embassy**. 5 Place de la Victoire, tel. (01) 245100.
  USA Embassy. 144 Ave de la Liberté, tel. (01) 282566.
  Canadian Embassy. 3 Rue Didon, tel. (01) 286577.

- **Medical care**. Hôpital Charles Nicolle, tel. (01) 663000. Ambulance, tel. (01) 341250.

- **Festivals**. Music festival, February; theatrical festival, March–April; festival of youth music, November; festival of the Medina; Ramadan.

- **Entertainment**. The Parc du Belvedere, Belvedere Park, (No. 28 bus from Ave Habib Bourguiba to Place Pasteur) makes a pleasant break from the city. Covering an acre, it has a zoo, cafés, a 17C pavilion and a modern art museum. Parc Thameur, Thameur Park, is another pleasant green area, a formal gardens with wide walkways and palms (open daily 09.00–17.00), originally the site of a Jewish cemetery. If you have children there is a fairground on Ave Mohammed V (metro tram No. 2 from Place Barcelone to Ave Mohammed V).

- **Shopping.** The Medina is where most tourists go shopping. Many of the Medina shops are given over to tourist souvenirs, but genuine articles, such as chechias (red felt hats) and textiles are also to be found. The largest supermarket is the monoprix on Rue Charles de Gaulle. There is a good covered food market on the same street.

History

Tunis, an early Numidian settlement, was one of the first to fall into Carthaginian control. The rise of nearby Carthage and the expansion of its power in the surrounding region after the 7C BC, cast Tunis into relative insignificance. It was, however, to suffer the same fate as Carthage and was destroyed with it in 146 BC by the Roman Scipio Aemilianus. Rebuilt as a colony by Caesar and Augustus in the 1C AD: Tunis remained in the shadow of Carthage, which had also been rebuilt, until the destruction of that city by the Arab invaders acting on behalf of the Umayyad Caliph, in Damascus. After destroying Carthage in AD 698, the Umayyad leader, Hassan Ibn al-Numan, abandoned the site in favour of Tunis which was more easily defended against sea attack. Throughout the subsequent centuries, though Tunis was an important city, the Arab capital was at Kairouan and then Mahdia, and it was not until the establishment of the Hafsid dynasty in 1228 that Tunis was to become the leading city in the region. Under Hafsid rule the city flourished, the population grew rapidly and business prospered. Tunis became the centre of religious, cultural and intellectual life, and was soon the most important commercial port in the Maghreb, attracting traders throughout the Mediterranean.

During the 16C, the city was caught in the struggle between the Ottoman Empire and the Spanish for control of the North African shore and the western Mediterranean. Control of the city changed hands several times between 1534 and 1574 before falling eventually to the Ottomans who remained its distant rulers until the French Protectorate was declared in 1881. The French remained the colonial masters during the Second World War, witnessing the occupation of Tunis by the Axis powers in November 1942 and its liberation by the Allies in May 1943. In 1956 Tunisia achieved independence and Tunis, the capital of the new republic, began its rapid expansion from a population of around 500,000 to its present figure of nearly two million.

The following itineraries have been divided into seven sections (A–G); the first deals with the colonial city, which can be seen in an hour or two, the next five concentrate on the medina. Walking quickly, the medina could be covered within a morning, but this is not the best way to see it. The last section is dedicated to the Bardo Museum which easily fills a half day.

A. Nineteenth-century Tunis

Avenue Habib Bourguiba, built by the French in the 19C, connects the port and the medina and forms the centre of the city. With its cinemas, theatres, restaurants, hotels and cafés, it is Tunisia at its most western. A wide, pedestrian boulevard of neatly clipped trees shading benches, with newspaper kiosks and flower shops, runs down the centre between the three lanes of traffic on either side.

The western end of Avenue Habib Bourguiba meets **Place de l'Indépendance**, a noisy and busy junction for both cars and trams. On the south side of the square is the **French Embassy**, a grand colonial villa built in 1861, which is set back from the road in a spacious garden, behind high railings. It is a stone's throw from the newly cleaned façade of the French Catholic church, **St Vincent de Paul**, 1882, which stands on the north side of the square. From the façade, a statue of St Vincent, protector of European slaves, looks down into the square from the top of a central lunette which is decorated with a golden mosaic. Above, at the top of the façade, stands a bust of God the Father, and on either side rise twin towers; a direct import from French Gothic architecture. The large interior, dimly lit by stained-glass windows and somehow suffering from a gloomy dampness even in the height of summer, is divided into three aisles. Its high dome is decorated with blind-arcading, a feature that is echoed in the upper walls of the apse, around the lower walls of which is an ambulatory. The focus of worship, which takes place in French with occasional sermons in English, is a statue of the Madonna.

Outside the church, at the centre of Place de l'Indépendance, four palm trees mark out a small garden around the turbanned **statue** of the great Islamic philosopher and historian, **Ibn Khaldun**.

Ibn Khaldun was born in Tunis in 1332 and died in Cairo in 1406. He worked as a diplomat for the Hafsid dynasty and the Marinids of Morocco, and took part in the Syrian campaign against Tamerlane. In his retirement he wrote a history of North Africa which unusually for its time included a sociological study of the conflicts in Maghreb society between urban and nomadic people.

Walk along **Avenue de France**, a modern commercial street which is the continuation of Avenue Habib Bourguiba west of Place de l'Indépendance. After crossing over Avenue de Rome, a wide street lined with imposing colonial architecture, the next left is **Rue Charles de Gaulle**. This is a bustling market street with stalls selling cheap clothing and cosmetics, and has a large Monoprix supermarket on the left and, further down, on the right, there is a good covered market, selling fresh fruit, vegetables, meat and fish.

Continue west along Avenue de France, beneath the arcades that shelter shops on either side, to **Place de la Victoire**. This is a large square on the fringes of the medina, which was created by the flattening of the Hafsid medina walls in the 19C. It was named after Bourguiba's return from exile in 1955. In it stands the solitary but monumental arch, **Porte de France**, which was built in 1848 on the foundations of the old city gate, Bab el Bahr. It is constructed of soft yellow sandstone, which is widely used throughout the old city, with a harder white limestone for the horseshoe-shaped arch and the decorative crenellations on top. On the far side of Place de la Victoire, the **British Embassy** presides over the medina entrance, occupying a turquoise-shuttered building with balconies and a studded door. On the ground floor is the **British Council Library** (open Tues–Fri, 10.00–17.00, Sat, 09.00–12.00; July and August Tues–Fri, 08.30–13.00; closed mid-July to mid-August).

B. Place de la Victoire to Zitouna Mosque and the Three Medersas

THE MEDINA

The following five walking itineraries cover the medina which is the largest in Tunisia. There is much more to the medina than a string of monuments, so allow time to have a good browse and do some shopping. Regarding shopping in the medina, there is probably a lesson to be learned from Paul Klee's diary; after visiting the medina in April 1914 with his old friend Louis Moillet, Klee wrote: 'We strolled through the souks. He [Louis] bargained hard over an amber necklace. When it was all done, a nearby connoisseur declared: "Ce n'est pas de l'ambre."'

From Place de la Victoire, with your back to the Porte de France, take **Rue Djamaa ez Zitouna**, the left hand of the two main arteries that lead through the medina. Although the street is not covered, the sky is barely visible

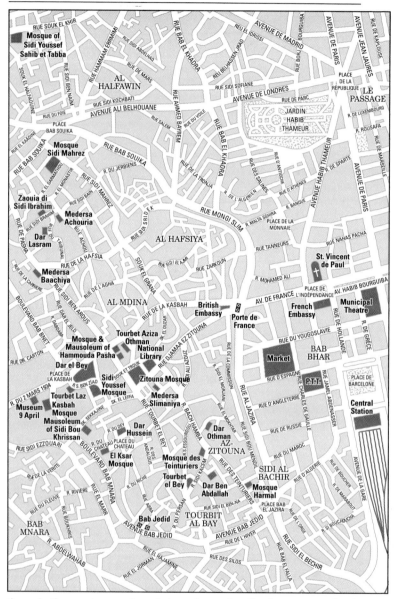

through the awnings and profusion of merchandise hanging overhead. Likewise the flagstone pavements, which are piled with souvenirs, such as the engraved brass which craftsmen tap out in the entrances to their shops. More genuine workshops can be found along Rue Sidi Sabeur, off right, approximately 200m from the medina entrance.

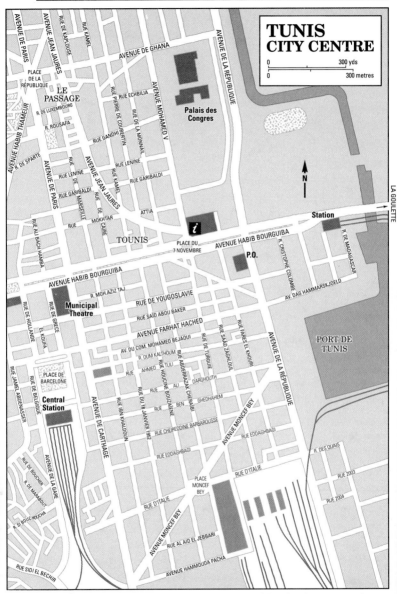

Before Rue Sidi Sabeur, on the left, is the arched façade of St Croix, a former church which is now converted to government offices.

Zitouna Mosque

Rue Djamaa ez Zitouna emerges from a dark vaulted passage at the foot of the ****ZITOUNA MOSQUE** walls. The mosque, the spiritual heart of the city, is hemmed in by souks on three of its sides, while the fourth side, which rises from the square in front, has steps leading up to a portal with an architrave made of a 2C chunk of Roman masonry. The mosque itself stands on a terrace, screened from view by an elegant **loggia** that was added in the 15C by the Hafsids. The **courtyard** of the mosque (open daily except Fri, 08.30–12.00) is based on the design of the Great Mosque at Kairouan with well-heads for drawing water from a cistern below. The mosque was first built in 732 by the Umayyads on the site of a great olive tree (which is supposedly how it got its name), then reconstructed in 864 under the Aghlabid Emir, Ibrahim bin Ahmed, whose court was at Kairouan. It was partly built with stones plundered from ancient Carthage, and there are no fewer than 184 Roman columns, arranged in 15 rows in the prayer hall. It was at the foot of these columns that religious instruction took place until the university was founded, earning the mosque its reputation as one of the foremost centres of theological learning along the North African coast. The most recent addition to the mosque is the **minaret** (1834), an imposing square tower some 13.5m high, decorated with Moorish tracery work after the minaret of the Kasbah Mosque.

Leave the Zitouna Mosque by heading south along the covered **Rue des Libraires** towards the **Three Medersas complex**. The first of these medersas, all of which were built in the 18C as religious schools under the Husainids, is on the right at No. 11. Built in 1714 under the founder of the Husainid dynasty, Husain ben Ali, **Medersa en Nakhla** still serves as a Koranic school. Its studded door, set in a stone-carved portal, leads into a small courtyard which is surrounded by the students' cells and has a palm tree at its centre, so giving the building its name.

The entrance to the second medersa, **Bachiya Medersa**, built in 1752 by Husain's nephew, Ali Pasha I, is on the right, under the Rue des Libraires's vaults, beyond the red and green pillars. It now houses a women's crafts institute, so it is necessary to ask for permission before entering. The door, set in a black and white striped portal, gives way to a small tiled hall lined with benches and niches. This leads through to an enclosed courtyard surrounded by slim columns and decorated with delicate stucco designs. Off one side of the courtyard is a large domed room, also decorated with plaster tracery work, which would once have been a lecture and prayer hall.

Back in the Rue des Libraires, opposite the Bachiya Medersa, is **Hammam Kachachine**, a Turkish bath. The entrance is through a barber's shop which has a colourful red, yellow and green front, with black and white stripes outlining the arched doorway.

The third medersa, **Medersa Slimania**, is further along on the right, its columned portal forming the corner of Rue des Libraires and Souk el Kachachine. It was built in 1754, also by Ali Pasha I, for his son, Sliman, who was said to have been poisoned by his brother. A horseshoe arch decorated with black and white bands leads from the portal into a domed entrance hall which is lined with panels of Andalucian-style tiles. The spacious courtyard beyond the entrance hall is surrounded by brick arches resting on tapered limestone columns; the upper walls are decorated with intricate plaster designs. The rooms surrounding the courtyard, originally students' cells, now house the offices of the Medical Association.

C. Southern medina

From the Three Medersas complex, a circular walk can be made of the southern medina, much of which is marked by 'tourist route' signposts provided by the Tourist Board. Start by heading south beneath the high arches and vaults of **Rue el Khomsa** which is lined with elegant arched portals and decoratively studded doors. Take the first alleyway on the right, Rue du Trésor, and turn left onto **Rue Tourbet el Bey**, another fine vaulted street with studded doors and carved portals. Down an impasse on the right is a domed building, **M'sed el Kobba**, believed to be the entrance to a mosque where Ibn Khaldoun taught during his early career in Tunis in the 14C. It is built of yellow sandstone with horseshoe arches resting on sections of antique columns and a mixed selection of eroded capitals.

Continuing along Rue Tourbet el Bey, the next right turn, **Rue du Riche** is noted for its prestigious houses. As its name suggests, this was a wealthy quarter: the stone doorways are markedly larger and façades are more decorative, both in stone carved detail and in the use of faience tiles.

Return to Rue Tourbet el Bey and keep walking to the tiled domes of the Husainid mausoleum, **Tourbet el Bey** (open daily 09.00–16.00), which are sadly shedding their green enamel surface. Built by Ali Pasha II (1758–82), the mausoleum is made up of a series of domed rooms containing the tombs of the entire Husainid sovereign family as well as favoured courtiers and ministers. The monument is centred on a courtyard, off which are three large chambers filled with sarcophagi. Those of women have plain headstones at the head and foot, while the men's have a single headstone composed of an Arabic inscription stone topped by a turban or fez, according to rank. The chambers themselves are decorated in the Italianate style, then in vogue, with marble facings and pilasters cladding the walls of the main room, and faience and stucco throughout.

From Tourbet el Bey you may wish to explore the southern quarter of Bab el Djemilla. Head south-west of the mausoleum for 300m along Rue des Juges and Rue de Forgerons to the gate Bab Jédid which was built by the Hafsids in 1276. The quarter outside this gate, on the other side of the main road that encircles the medina, is known as Bab el Djemilla. The main street through the quarter, Souk des Armées, has a lively street market. The El H'Laq Mosque at the end of this street dates from 1375 and can be recognised by its squat square minaret. Place aux Chevaux, a short distance further, is a dusty square alongside the Marché du Blé, which is now a flea market.

Back at Tourbet el Bey, continue by heading east around the mausoleum walls. Take the first left along Rue Sidi Kassem passing under a series of arches before turning right onto **Rue ben Abdallah**. This impasse leads through an opening with blue doors into a small courtyard enclosed by buildings with arched doorways. The blue studded door in the corner on the right leads into the **Musée des Arts et Traditions Populaire de Tunisia** (open Tues–Sun 09.30–16.30) which is housed in the 18C palace, Dar ben Abdallah. The palace was acquired in 1801 by an Ottoman official who had it refurbished in the Italian style. A tiled hall leads into a marble-paved courtyard, surrounded by columns and decorated with faience tiles and stucco work, with an Italianate marble fountain at the centre. There are four rooms leading off the courtyard containing exhibits illustrating the daily life of the wealthy classes in 19C and early 20C Tunis, such as cribs, circumcision clothes, cooking utensils and jewellery. There is also a small hammam with all the items used in it.

Retrace the route back to Rue Sidi Kassem and turn right, following the street to the end. Turn left onto Rue des Teinturiers which is presided over by the colourful minaret and large green dome of the **Mosque des Teinturiers**. The mosque was built in 1716 by the founder of the Husainid dynasty, Husain ben Ali, of simply but deftly carved local sandstone. Under the vaults on Rue des Teinturiers, adjoining the mosque, is the blue studded door of a Koranic school that was built at the same time.

Take the first right turn under the vaults of Rue des Teinturiers down an alleyway, signposted to Dar Othman. The alley, covered by high arches, opens out into a small square, at the right side of which is the palace of **Dar Othman**. It houses the Consérvation de la Medina offices and is not open to the public, although a museum is planned for the future. The façade is strikingly decorated, with black geometric designs set around the marble portal and in the black and white lunette above. Othman Dey, who had the palace built, was a 16C corsair who retreated to this protected corner of the medina with his booty until his death in 1610.

Return to Rue des Teinturiers, once a street of dyers but now dominated by second-hand clothing shops, and take the first left turn, Rue el Ariane. Follow this road until it meets Rue Tourbet el Bey, from where you can either retrace your steps to the Zitouna Mosque or continue with the next itinerary.

D. Rue Tourbet el Bey to Souk el Lefta

From the junction of Rue el Ariane and Rue Tourbet el Bey, head northwards along Tourbet el Bey, turning left just before the vaults into Souk el Kachachine. This open-air souk leads into Rue du Dey where there is an Institute of Music. Turn left after the institute onto Rue Mohsen which opens out into the **Place du Château**. Along the east side of this small square is the white façade of **Dar Hussein** which now houses the Institut Nationale di Patrimoine but was originally built as a minister's palace in the 18C. Although the interior of the building is closed to the public, it is possible to look inside the inner courtyard. On the ground floor, which is where the reception rooms would once have been, generous arches rest on slender marble columns with neo-Corinthian capitals. The walls are lined with variously designed tiled panels, vividly coloured in yellow, green and blue, with stucco work decorating the upper walls and a black and white prayer niche on the east wall. The first floor, surrounded by wide walkways with wooden balconies and double columns, has a series of doors leading off, formerly the palace bedrooms. Should you be fortunate enough to be shown inside you will see the Louis XV-style décor, dating from the 19C renovation, with splendid stucco ceilings

Back on the Place du Château, on the other side of the square, stands the striking minaret of the **El Ksar Mosque**. The mosque was built in 1106 from giant blocks of sandstone, the original stonework being visible on the side wall. The square minaret, Hispano-Mauresque in style, was a later addition, and dates from 1647. It is made up of three distinct layers each with designs picked out in contrasting dark and light sandstone. The lower level is decorated with blind arches with inscriptions inserted in a plait motif; the middle section has square panels holding geometric designs; the upper part has horseshoe arches and is topped by a small square lantern.

From the Place du Château, head north along Rue ben Mahmoud, which twists and turns before finally reaching the **Mausoleum of Sidi Bou Khrissan** (open daily except holidays, 09.00–12.00, 14.00–17.00) at No. 12. The entrance, an unassuming blue door set in a horseshoe portal, is normally closed, so knock and wait for someone to appear, and be prepared to give a donation. The door leads into a small courtyard, surrounded by living quarters, which was built on the site of one of the earliest cemeteries in Tunis. Numerous tombstones are dotted about the place, most dating from the 11C, and there are Arabic inscriptions set into the walls. The mausoleum itself occupies a corner beneath some shady trees at the far side. According to the worn inscription, it was erected in 1093. Founded by his two sons, it contains the body of the Khorassan sovereign who hopefully is not really interred in the decrepit wooden coffin that is sheltered beneath the high brick dome. The dome rests on a deep sandstone drum decorated with half-columns, arches and scallop motifs, and the walls have attractive designs created by the use of contrasting coloured sandstones.

Continue by heading north along Rue ben Mahmoud and turn right into **Souk Sekajine**, a covered street that was built under Husain ben Ali at the start of the 18C as a saddler's workshop. It runs straight into **Souk el Leffa**, which has a motley selection of shops ranging from groceries to pottery and textiles. From here, either head eastwards back to the Zitouna walls or continue with the next itinerary on Souk el Berka which leads north off Souk el Leffa.

E. Western medina

This itinerary starts at **Souk el Berka**, built by Youssef Dey (1610–37), which is a covered street of jewellers, leading north off Souk el Leffa. Midway along the street, lined with brightly lit windows crammed with gold, there is a small square, the Berka, surrounded by ornate fretted wood façades. Six red and green spiral-striped columns support a white vaulted ceiling, an attractive setting for what used to be a slave market. Chained and fettered Europeans kidnapped by pirates at sea, and black Africans brought from the Sudan, were sold here until 1841 when Ahmed Bey, who sought European favour, closed the market down.

In 1605 **St Vincent de Paul**, then 23, was obliged to make a journey to Marseilles. When returning by sea he was captured by some Tunisian corsairs. His account is as follows: 'The procedure of our sale was that we were gagged, stripped quite naked, and only allowed to wear a cap and a couple of strands of wool. We were marched through the town with chains at the neck, and having made five or six promenades we were taken at last to the slave-market. Here the merchants came to inspect us in the same way as they would a horse or a bullock, making us open our mouths to see our teeth, fingering our ribs, probing our wounds, making us walk, trot and run, testing our strength with heavy weights, and subjecting us to 1000 other brutalities. I was bought by a fisherman, who, finding that I was but an extra vexation added to those of the sea sold me almost immediately to a quack doctor.' St Vincent was later freed by a Christian convert.

Continuing along Souk el Berka, the vaults open out at the corner of the **Sidi Youssef Mosque**, which is on the left. It was built by Youssef Dey in 1616 as a Hanifite mosque to serve the local Turkish community. The sandstone minaret, with its wide overhanging balcony painted yellow and blue, towers over the street. To one side of the minaret is the monumental tomb of its founder and his family, which has a distinctive conical roof with green enamel tiles, and arches decorated with bands of black and white stone. On the other side of the minaret, a doorway leads through the walls and up into a courtyard that surrounds the mosque.

Keep following the walls of the Sidi Youssef Mosque along **Rue Sidi ben Ziad**. On the left are the extensive hospital buildings of Aziza Othman, named after the daughter of Bey Othman, which are partly housed in barracks built by Hammouda Pasha II. Rue Sidi ben Ziad eventually emerges at the wide open expanse of **Place de la Kasbah**. On the left, nestled against the hospital walls, is **Tourbet Laz**. This was the last monumental tomb to be built under the Turkish regime in the 18C and contains the body of the last Turkish ruler. It has a domed roof covered with green enamel tiles and sandstone walls decorated with blind arches.

The adjacent Place de la Kasbah is the site of the ancient citadel of which only a few vestiges of walls remain. The now devastated mound was a naturally well-defended spot, strategically positioned between the Lac de Tunis and the lagoon, Sabkhit as Sijoumi. From the 12C onwards it was the political heart of the city and the seat of the Hafsid caliphs amongst others until the 18C when the Husainids moved out to the Bardo leaving the citadel largely abandoned. Today, although the old buildings no longer exist, the government offices are once again centred here. On the hill summit a modern building houses the Maison du Parti, the headquarters of the ruling political party. There is also a UN building here and the Sadiki College, a private school run on European principles which was founded in 1875. At the foot of the hill, to the left, is the **Kasbah Mosque**, the only substantial remnant of the Hafsid citadel. It was built between 1231 and 1235 by the founder of the Hafsid dynasty, Abu Zakariyya. Its most outstanding feature is the fat, square minaret, which is decorated with a distinctive relief design, woven like a lattice. The design, which originates from Morocco, is seen throughout Tunisia but is generally poorly reproduced.

Behind the Kasbah Mosque there is a small museum, the **Museum 9 April**, the entrance to which is on Rue du 2 Mars 1934. Housed in an ex-prison, where Bourguiba was once held, the museum exhibits include photographs and documents recording the Tunisian campaign for independence.

Head back into the medina, passing through the **Place du Gouvernement**, on the right side of which is the **Dar el Bey** palace, the Prime Minister's residence and seat of the Foreign Office. The heavily guarded façade dates from the late 18C and early 19C, although the building actually stands on a 17C groundplan. The later structure was built under Hammouda Pasha II who also commissioned work on Souk el Bey, a wide arcade at the end of the palace on the right. **Souk el Bey**, which was built over an already existing arcade in 1782, has textile shops, selling furnishings and curtains, recessed in the arcaded façades at either side.

At the bottom of Souk el Bey stands the minaret of the Sidi Youssef Mosque (see above). Take the first left after the minaret into the covered ****Souk et Trouk**. This is one of the most elegant streets in the medina, wide and spacious, with high airy vaulting. It was built in 1630 during the reign of Youssef Dey, by Ali Tabet, one of the Dey's favourites. It is lined with smart carpet and kilim shops, several of which advertise panoramic roof terraces, the views from which are exceptional. One of the best-known of the medina restaurants is also to be found in this souk, the *M'rabet*. Even if you are not going to eat there, it is worth taking a look. A passage leads through to a small courtyard with red and green columns with, curiously enough, a tomb to match. The restaurant is arranged around a series of small courtyards beyond, overshadowed by the Zitouna minaret. From here, either return to the Zitouna Mosque by continuing straight ahead and turning right, or continue with the fifth walking itinerary.

F. Northern medina and souks around the Zitouna

From Souk et Trouk head north, leaving the vaults, following Rue Sidi ben Arous. A brief diversion off left takes you into the **Souk des Chechias** which has two parts: a Petit Souk des Chechias and a Grande Souk des Chechias. It was constructed during the reign of Bey Mohammed el Hafsi (1675–84) as a centre of production for chechias, the red fez-style hats worn by Tunisian men.

> **Chechias** were first made in Tunis by Andalucian immigrants in the 17C. The technique today follows the old traditional methods. The hat is first knitted twice the size it needs to be from natural hand-spun wool. It is then washed, carded, soaked in oil and compressed, so shrinking it. Next it has to be dyed crimson, after which it is carded once again and stretched on to a form with the help of a press. Chechia makers sit in their small workshops carding the hats over and over until a smooth felt-like surface is achieved.

Returning to Rue Sidi ben Arous, the **Mausoleum of Hammouda Pasha** lies directly opposite. Built in 1655 on a square groundplan, it is constructed of attractive stone and coloured marbles. Decorative arches are flanked at either side by pretty red marble columns, with a striking black stone inlaid in the white marble.

Adjoining the mausoleum is the **Mosque of Hammouda Pasha**, its sandstone walls decorated with blind arcading. It has an octagonal sandstone minaret with attractive black and white arches and a zig-zag design, incorporating the black star motif used in the mausoleum, running below its wide overhanging balcony. The balcony, originally used by a muezzin to call the faithful to prayer, but who has now been replaced by loudspeakers, has a brightly painted red, blue and gold roof.

From the mosque, turn right along Rue de la Kasbah for less than 70m, before turning right again onto Rue el Jelloud. At the end of this street, along the impasse Echemmakhia at No. 9, is the **Tourbet Aziza Othman**. The koubba holding the tomb is in the courtyard of someone's house, but visitors can get in by ringing the bell and making a donation. Daughter of Othman Bey, Princess Aziza died in 1646 leaving behind a reputation for piety and kindness. Her tomb is in the first room on the right near a false door created from ceramic tiles. Other tombs in this room, and also a second koubba, belong to the Othman family. The second koubba is more richly decorated than the first, with fine plaster carved ceilings and ceramic tiles.

An optional diversion, involving a walk of over 500m north, would be to the dilapidated palace of **Dar Lasram**. Its restoration is planned but in the meantime you must content yourself with its extensive façade, dating from the 19C, which is pierced by horseshoe-arch windows. 330m further north of Dar Lasram is the **Sidi Mahrez Mosque**. Built around 1675, it is modelled on the Ottoman mosques of Istanbul, having a large central dome and four smaller domes at each corner. The prayer hall, preceded by a stairway, is surrounded on three sides by porticoes and courtyards. Inside, there are four massive, ceramic clad piers that support the central dome, and attractively tiled walls. The Zaouia of Sidi Mahrez is on the opposite side of the road and holds the tomb of Sidi Mahrez. 100m due north of the mosque is Place Bab Souika, to the north of which stretches the quarter of Bab el Souika. The main street through the quarter, Rue Souk el Halfaouine, leads to Place el Halfaouine which is overlooked by the **Mosque of Youssef Sahib et Tabaa**. Built in 1812, the mosque is modelled on that of Sidi Youssef, but richly ornamented with Italian marbles and stone.

The final stretch of the itinerary takes in the souks around the Zitouna Mosque. Retracing your steps along Rue Sidi ben Arous to Souk et Trouk, turn left onto **Souk el Attarine**, the souk of the perfumers. Built by the founder of the Hafsid dynasty, Abou Zakkariya (1225–49), it is still filled with perfume shops and boutiques selling the paraphernalia that accompanies circumcision and wedding ceremonies. At the far end of the souk there is an entrance into the Zitouna Mosque, known as the **Bab el Bouhour**. It has an inscription stone dated 1081 resting on columns that flank the doorway. It leads into the mosque courtyard which in the summer is covered with rush mats used for prayer. Opposite Bab el Bouhour there is an ablutions room, the **Midhat as-Soltan**, which was added in the 13C.

Head back through Souk el Attarine, turning left into the **Souk des Etoffes** which dates from the 15C and was commissioned by Abu Amr Othman. Red and green columns run through the souk and as its name suggests it sells textiles, both traditional and modern. At the end of the souk at No. 37, a beige door with black studs leads into the **Medersa Mouradia** (open daily 09.00–14.00) which was built in the 17C. It was set up as a Hanefite religious school by the Muradite princes (1684–1702) at a time when most of Tunis' population belonged to the Malekite sect. Today it houses a craft school, but during visiting hours you can go into the colonnaded courtyard which is encircled by its original wooden balcony on the first floor. The students' cells punctuate the walls on three sides, while on the fourth a marble horseshoe arch leads into the prayer room.

The Souk des Etoffes leads into the **Souk des Femmes**. The theme is still textiles, although here you will see the traditional white haik, loincloths for the baths and headscarfs for women. Midway along the Souk des Femmes, it is crossed by the **Souk du Coton**. Following the right-hand branch of this souk you will wend your way through the labyrinth into the **Souk des Orfevres**, the jeweller's market.

Head back along the Souk des Femmes and turn right just before the Souk des Etoffes down **Souk de la Laine**. This narrow covered street follows the south wall of the Zitouna Mosque. Midway along the street there is a gateway through the mosque wall known as **Porte Imam**. It is particularly interesting as it is built of finely-carved ancient Roman masonry, thought to date from the Severan period (193–235).

Keep on down Souk de la Laine until meeting the Rue des Librairies which leads left into the small courtyard in front of the Zitouna Mosque. You can leave the medina by retracing your steps along Rue Damaa ez Zitouna to Place de la Victoire.

G. Bardo Museum

The ****BARDO MUSEUM** (open summer daily except Mon, 09.00–18.00, winter daily except Mon, 09.30–16.30), Tunisia's national museum, is over 5km from the city centre but can be easily reached by public transport. Take either a No. 4 metro from Place Barcelone to Rue 20 Mars (which is 500m before the museum, the line is due to be extended to the Bardo stop), or a No. 3 bus from Avenue Habib Bourguiba. The entrance to the museum is on Rue Monji Slim, where there is a large car park on the left inside the museum gates. The ticket office and a refreshments' kiosk are on the right beneath a colonnade.

The Bardo is made up of various palaces, built over a succession of eras dating from the 13C Hafsids to the 19C Husainid Beys who based their government here. The museum is housed in the Little Palace, built in 1831, and some of the state rooms of the Great Palace. The other palace buildings, which face onto Rue 20 Mars, are the seat of the National Assembly. The museum collection is made up of some of the finest mosaics in the world from ancient sites across the country, ranging from fine mosaics used to pave the floors of Roman villas, to coarser mosaics that covered tombs in Byzantine North Africa. Other archaeological artefacts include a fine collection of Punic stelae and other funerary objects, and Roman statues. The museum also has an Islamic department which contains ethnic objects and a good collection of pottery. The Bardo is currently under a long-term project of rearrangement which means that you may find a number of rooms temporarily closed.

From the entrance hall, **Salle I** on the right contains a ticket desk, publications for sale, and a scale model of Gigthis. **Salle II** is dedicated to the Carthaginian god, Baal Hammon, to whom children were sacrificed at the Salambo Tophet in Carthage, which is the provenance of most of the exhibits in this room. The **votive statues** and **terracotta masks** date from the 6C BC. The two basic types of mask seen here are smiling ones, to bring good luck, and grimacing ones, to ward off evil. The ceramics collection, also in this room, is most notable for the **black and red ware** that was imported into Tunisia from Greece in the 7–5C BC, and the **Punic ceramics** from the 4–2C BC. In addition there are **terracotta statues** that have been laboriously pieced back together. Many of these statues are copies of Greek originals thought to have been imported from Sicily. They include **Demeter** seated on a throne (goddess of agriculture and fertility), **Kore** (Persephone) and **Ade** (Pluton).

Salle III is closed. **Salle IV** contains a chronologically arranged collection of Punic funerary objects.

Corridor B is the hall of the **stelae of the Ghorfa** which holds a collection of carved stelae from central Tunisia, dating from the 2C BC to the 1C AD, showing how Punic beliefs survived into Roman times. The stelae are carved typically with three representational parts: the lowest section depicts a Herculean figure slaying a bull or a hydra; the middle section shows the entombed person, set within a classical temple façade, the pediment of which is decorated with the Punic symbol of Tanit; the upper section has three gods, a female and male deity flanking a central god with a vase in each hand, one containing pomegranates (a symbol of Tanit) and the other grapes (a symbol of fecundity). At the very top is the crescent symbol of Tanit, surmounted by a woman's head.

Salle V is a room of mosaics taken from early Christian and Byzantine churches, dating from the 4–7C. In the centre of the room stands a marble **cruciform baptismal font**, used as a model by the millionaire George Sebastian for his four-people bath. It comes from a church in El Kantara on the Isle of Jerba and dates from the 6C. Amongst the most impressive mosaics mounted on the walls are those designed to cover tombs, a technique that was peculiar to churches in North Africa. To the right of the entrance, there is a charming group of **three panels**, dating from the 4–5C, from the Chapel of Martyrs in Tabarka.

Salle VI, dedicated to Bulla Regia, contains mosaics and statues from the city at its heyday in the 2C and 3C. The mosaic of **Perseus and Andromeda**, dating from the 3–4C, comes from the dining room of a wealthy villa. The statues come from the 2C Apollo temple of Bulla Regia and are of Apollo, Ceres and Aesculapius.

Salle VII contains various **busts of Roman emperors** dating from 1–3C.

In the **Salles Paleo-Chretiennes** there is a collection of mosaics, fonts and architectural fragments from churches throughout Tunisia dating from the

4–7C. Most notable is the 6C cross-shaped **immersion font** found on Cap Bon.

Return to Salle V and leave through the door on the left, where you will pass a fine mosaic of **Daniel in the Lion's Den** (A253) which decorated the tomb of Blossius Honratus of Furnos Minus.

Corridor D, a brick-vaulted hallway, contains **sarcophagi and stelae** dating from the 2–5C. Amongst the numerous finely carved tombs is one of the early 4C from Carthage (Inv 3158) which is carved with symbols of the sciences representing the deceased. There is also a particularly expressive **Herculean funerary statue** (Inv 3047) dating from the 3C.

On the left of Corridor D there is an entrance to the Islamic Museum which is listed here as a separate entry after the main Bardo collection.

Salle VIII, the Thuburbo Maius Room, contains 3–4C mosaics and sculptures from wealthy villas, public monuments and temples in the ancient city. Against the end wall is a fine marble **statue of Hercules** (C1352), which according to the inscription was commissioned by a guild of cloak-makers.

Return to Salle V again and take the main staircase up to the first floor. The walls either side of the stairs are clad with early Christian mosaics from Tabarka. A **statue of Apollo** stands at the top of the stairs and the door on the left leads into the **Carthage Room** (IX). This spacious colonnaded hall with its Italian style ceiling is lined with **Roman busts and statues** excavated from the odeon and theatre in Carthage. At the centre of the room there is an **altar stone** (Inv 2125) dating from the end of the 1C BC and early AD 1C with fine relief carvings on each of its four sides: a) Aeneas fleeing from Troy with his father and son; b) Rome in Amazonian costume; c) sacrifice of a calf; d) Apollo, protector of Augustus. Overlooking the altar is a large **statue of a Roman empress** (C933), most probably Faustina II, the wife of Marcus Aurelius. On the floor in front of the altar there is a **dining room mosaic** (A103) taken from a house at Oudna, dated 2–3C. It shows Dionysus presenting a vine to the Attic king Ikarios, surrounded by the four seasons and cupids harvesting grapes.

The statue collection, which dates on the whole from the 2–3C and mostly comes from Carthage, includes **Crepereia Innula** (C39); **Bacchus** (C979); **Empress Giulia Domna** (C22), the wife of Septimius Severus; **Hercules** (C943); **Emperor Hadrian** (C932), resembling the god Mars; **Emperor** (C1212); unidentified, **woman** (C945) holding ears of corn and poppies, the symbols of the goddess Ceres.

Salle X is a former banqueting hall and has a high-domed ceiling decorated in gold. The room is dedicated to Hadrumetum, modern-day Sousse, which is the place of origin of the centrepiece on the floor, a mosaic of the **triumph of Neptune** (A1). It was found in a massive dining room and comprises 56 medallions and hexagons, which hold sirens, tritons and nereids, arranged around Neptune riding his chariot. On the far wall are three **semicircular mosaics** (A25, A26, A27) which are of interest for their representation of everyday Roman life and architecture. On the left wall there is a Byzantine mosaic of **chariot racing** (A19) found at Gafsa. Below it is a 3C mosaic of the head of **Oceanus**. The mosaic on the remaining wall of **Seigneur Julius** (Inv 1) gives a unique insight into aristocratic life in Roman North Africa during the 4C. The central panel depicts the noble villa. Above to the right is summer, to the left winter and in the middle Julius' wife sits in the shade of cypress trees. Below on the left is spring and next to it Julius collecting donations; on the right is autumn and Julius holding a parchment that has his name inscribed on it.

Salle XI, the Dougga Room, has a scale model of the city and exhibits, mainly dating from the 3–4C, from the city's excavation. Clockwise, there is a 2C **triumph of Neptune** (A292), from Chebba, which depicts Neptune with the four seasons, here represented by women. The 4C **Eros and the circus games** (A262), from Dougga, shows two horses named as Amandus and Frunitus, and is the central panel of a larger mosaic. **Fishermen at sea** (A179), from Carthage, was found in a 2C apse. The 3C **Cyclops forging thunderbolts** (A261) is from the frigidarium of the baths at Dougga. The last **mosaic** (A188) comes from a 3C villa at Carthage and is made up of fruit, flowers, peacocks and gazelles.

Salle XII is dedicated to El Jem, the site of ancient Thysdrus, which was at its pinnacle under the Severan emperors during the 3C, the date of most of the exhibits in this room. In the mosaic of the **triumph of Bacchus** (A287), Bacchus rides his chariot drawn by a pair of tigers. Other mosaics include a **hunting scene** (A288) represented in three layers, and a mosaic of the **nine muses** (A289) who are depicted in circular medallions. A huge dining room mosaic (A268–284) is decorated with animals, birds and still-lifes.

Return to the Carthage Room and turn left into **Salle XIII**, the Althiburos Room, formerly the palace concert hall with wide balconies at either end and a wooden painted ceiling. The most interesting mosaic in this room, all of which come from the ancient city of Althiburos, is the one in the centre (A166). It provides a remarkable document of fishing vessels in the 3–4C showing some 26 different types of boats, each with its name in Latin and Greek. Above the door there are two mosaic fragments: the **head of Oceanus** and a **triton** (A239). There are several mosaics based on hunting themes: a **grand hunt** (A117) from the 4C; a **hunting scene** (A171) from the same era which has a sacrifice to Apollo and Artemis at the centre; and the **centaur Chiron teaching Achilles the art of hunting** (Inv 3618). Also of interest is the **banqueting scene in an arena** (Inv 3361) which comes from El Jem and dates from the 3–4C. It depicts five hunters, two of whom on the left are drunk, seated at a triclinium.

Salle XIV, the Oudna Room, houses finds from ancient Uthina. Formerly the palace dining room, the mosaics here are made from small tesserae which produce particularly fine detail. Moving clockwise, there are panels of detached mosaic fragments of the **four emblems** (A150–152) dating from the 2C. **Orpheus singing to the wild beasts** (A148), which shows Orpheus semi-nude, includes the name of the craftsman who made the mosaic: Masurus; and the people who commissioned it: Laberianus and Paulina Laberianus. Also of note are **Europa raped by Jove** (A125), **Venus at her toilet** (A123), and the **goddess Selene** (A128) watching over a sleeping shepherd. **Hercules seducing Auge** (A267) shows the semi-nude Auge resisting Hercules. **Neptune on a sea horse** (A111) is one of the rare depictions of Neptune astride a horse rather than riding a chariot.

Salle XV, reached by a short flight of steps up from the Carthage Room, is the Virgil Room. It has a cruciform plan centred on an ornate plaster dome and faience tiles decorate the walls. Fomerly the centre of the harem, the doors off it lead into the palace private apartments, now administration offices. At the centre of the domed room on the floor is a **hexagonal mosaic** dating from the 3C, depicting the seven days of the week and the 12 signs of the zodiac. The left arm from the central dome holds the masterpiece **Virgil with the muses** (A226). The mosaic is so fine that its depiction of Virgil holding a parchment, listening to Clio on the right and the masked Melpomene to the left, has a painterly quality.

Salle XVI (closed for rearrangement) is devoted to prehistoric finds in Tunisia, mainly tools and implements dating from before the arrival of the Phoenicians in the 12C BC, and Punic jewellery and ornaments.

Salle XVII–XXII have been closed for almost a decade awaiting rearrangement. They contain finds from a sunken ship, found 5km offshore from Mahdia, dated 81 BC. Archaeologists discovered it was a cargo vessel, still loaded with ancient Greek bronze statues in excellent condition and marbles bound for import into Tunisia. Marble statues include **Hermaphrodite** (F109), **Eros androgeny** (F216) running with a flame, **Eros** (F210) bejewelled and dancing, **Mercury** (F208) posed as an orator, and **young satyr** (F209). Amongst the bronze statues are **Agone** (F106), an allegorical figure holding two palms in the left hand and probably part of the group **Mercury and Dionysus** (F107). Other exhibits include a pair of **marble vessels** (C1204–1205) used to mix wine and water and decorated with reliefs of Bacchus; two beds with their original bronze decoration; and parts of the wreck itself including naval instruments.

Salle XXIII (closed for rearrangement) is the room of **marine mosaics**. The vast mosaic, now in fragments at the entrance to the room (Inv 2722), dates from the 5C and decorated a vast exedra. It depicts urban life by the sea. Another large mosaic of marine life (Inv 2807), covering the wall facing the entrance, was found at Carthage and dates from the 4C. **Neptune** (Inv 2787) is shown being pulled along by horses and surrounded by nereids riding sea creatures. On the floor is a mosaic of the **hippodrome races** (Inv 3632) with an inscription dedicated to the 'blues', one of the competing teams. A mosaic from a **fountain** (C58) features a cupid on a dolphin.

Salle XXIV (closed for rearrangement) is called the Mausoleum Room after the 2C **tomb** (Inv 2993) from Carthage, which is carved with reliefs on all four sides. The room also contains mosaics from Thuburbo Maius and Carthage. Starting from the left is the **hunt** (Inv 2706), showing hunting dogs and hunters on horseback, **Venus at her toilet** (Inv 2997), **fishermen, cupids and dancers** (Inv 2804) from the 4C, the 3C **Hercules at the feet of Onfale** (Inv 2788), which shows Onfale seated with a leopard skin and Hercules on the floor below. **Fishermen with trident** (Inv 124) dates from the 3C and comes from an atrium at Oudna. The intricate mosaic of a **still life** (Inv 1394) dates from the 5C.

Salle XXV called Mosaique, as if everything else was not, is reached by retracing your steps to the Carthage Room and taking **Corridor F** (with its mosaics from Carthage, Thuburbo Maius and El Jem); or you can return via

Salle XII. The mosaics displayed here include a **Bacchus and Ariadne** (Inv 1394) seated on the back of a panther enveloped by a vine. There are statues of **Mercury** (Inv 3641) and a **Venus Pudica** (C981), which is a Roman copy of the Cnidos Venus of Praxiteles. There is also a mosaic of a **peacock fanning its tail** (A11), the peacock's tail being a symbol of eternity and immortality.

Salle XXVI is a small hallway containing a mosaic from the frigidarium of the baths at Thuburbo Maius, featuring Dionysus and cupids harvesting grapes.

Salle XXVII, the Ulysses Room, is named after a fragment of a mosaic (Inv 2884A) taken from an impluvium at Dougga, dating from the 4C. The hero is tied to the mast of a ship while the sirens tempt him with their melodious voices, singing from a rock to the right. Another fragment of the same mosaic (Inv 2884B) shows Bacchus punishing the pirates of the Tyrrenhian Sea by transforming them into dolphins. At the top of the wall is the **triumph of Neptune and Amphitrite** (Inv 2980); the two are shown riding a chariot drawn by four sea horses across the sea where there are three boats, which contain Venus and Bacchus amongst others, driven by cupids. The **myth of Apollo** (Inv 529) is the theme of a large mosaic which depicts a musical contest between Apollo and the satyr Marsyas, arbitrated by Athena. Above is a mosaic of the **seasons** (Inv 399) where, in a medallion on the right, there is a portrait of a bearded man, Xenophontes, thought to be a Greek writer. The mosaic of **Dionysus** (Inv 2808) shows the god at the centre surrounded by eight rectangles that hold satyrs and bacchants. The **triumph of Venus** (Inv 3126) is taken from a 3C house in Kasserine and shows the bejewelled goddess astride a sea monster.

Salle XXVIII has a mosaic of **Venus crowned by two female centaurs** (Inv 3650) to the right of the door. A 4C **dining room mosaic** (Inv 2403) from Carthage patterned with geometric designs shows the T-shape of the table layout. The position of the table is marked by a peacock fanning its tail, in front of which are four horses. At the centre of the room is the **torso of Victoria** (C1026), a Roman copy of a Hellenistic statue, executed in black marble.

Return to the main staircase and continue up to the second floor where there is a statue of **Concorde Ponthee** from Gigthis. Turn left into **Salle XXIX**, the Gallerie des Terres Cuites, Verres et Bronze, which looks down onto the Carthage Room. The numerous bronze and terracotta figurines, dating from the 2–3C, were found in necropoli at Sousse and El Jem.

Salle XXX (closed for rearrangement) has further mosaics including the 3C **Theseus killing the Minotaur** (A372) from Thuburbo Maius. The 4C mosaic of the **cupids harvesting grapes** (Inv 3331) is from Dougga. The 3C **tragic poet** (Inv 1396) from Thuburbo Maius shows two tragic masks behind the poet. The 3C **deer hunt** shows the animals in cages possibly to be taken to the circus, or used for hunting game.

Salle XXXI (closed for rearrangement) has amongst its most interesting mosaics a **Diana the Huntress** (Inv 2983) which dates from the 2C. A tree grows out from the centre, its branches covering the entire mosaic, with the goddess on the left.

Salle XXXII (closed for rearrangement) has a 3C pavement on the wall to the right of the entrance taken from the caldarium of the baths at Thaene. Two of the medallions show Diana taken by surprise by Atteone and Ila while she is bathing.

Salle XXXIII is dedicated to Acholla which is where most of the mosaics, mainly dating from the 2C, are from. To the left of the entrance is a **centaur raping a nymph** (Inv 3586) and next to it is **Dionysus riding a tiger** (Inv 3600). The masterpiece of the room is the **triumph of Dionysus** (Inv 3602). The god is standing in a chariot drawn by two centaurs, surrounded by medallions decorated with allegorical symbols, including spring on the left and winter on the right. Another good piece is the **tasks of Hercules** (Inv 3588), dated c 184, showing the T-shape of a dining table with thirteen panels below depicting Hercules' feats. There are also some bronze, marble and terracotta figurines. The bronze figurine of **Bacchus** (Inv 3039) is a Roman copy of a Greek original in the style of Praxiteles.

Salle XXXIV and XXXV are stairwell rooms off the galleries that surround the Carthage Room. They hold various mosaics of marine subjects, circus games and hunting scenes, mainly from Dougga and El Jem.

The **Islamic Museum** is housed in the Husainid Palace (1824–35), which is connected by a hall on the first floor, but is best entered from the main entrance on the ground floor off corridor D. Steps lead up from the corridor into a richly tiled chamber, once a room of the harem, with a scale model of the ribat at Sousse at its centre. A door on the right leads into the ground floor of the museum (closed for rearrangement) which surrounds a central courtyard and holds a collection of **Islamic ceramics**, including Berber pottery, Tunisian majolica, 16C ceramics from Tunis, and tiles from Turkey, Morocco and Italy.

Central courtyard, Islamic Arts Section, Bardo Museum

Returning to the entrance room a door on the left leads up to the first floor of a courtyard around which the palace is arranged. Walking around the courtyard in an anticlockwise direction, the first room off the courtyard holds old **maps**. The second room is arranged as a traditional **19C reception room** with an ornate plaster ceiling and decorative faience tiles on the walls. The third room contains a collection of **Jewish cult objects**. The fourth room has **prints** dating from the 16–17C of views of Tunis. The fifth room is a hallway, off which, in a large room with a fine wood-panelled ceiling, is a further collection of Islamic artefacts including **copper**, which dates from the 17–20C, **jewellery** from Morocco and Algeria, **objects in silver** such as a tea set, perfume bottles, trinkets, scissors and embroidered cloths.

2 · Tunis to Carthage

Tunis to Carthage is 17km via La Goulette. Although it is an advantage to have a car to get around Carthage, the sites being fair distances apart, it is equally possible to use the TGM train which leaves from Tunis Nord at the port end of Avenue Habib Bourguiba and stops at five locations in Carthage itself. The TGM train runs to its destination, La Marsa, every 15 minutes during the day and hourly at night, stopping at the following stations: Tunis Nord—Le Bac—Goulette Vieille—Goulette Neuve—Goulette Casino—Kheredoine—Aéroport—Le Kram—Salambo—Carthage Byrsa—Carthage Demech—Carthage Hannibal—Carthage President—Carthage Amilcar.

The railtrack runs alongside the road from Tunis Nord on a spit that traverses the Lac de Tunis, where in November flamingoes touch down on their migration route from Europe to Kenya. It reaches the coast at Le Bac, an industrial zone, before arriving at the walls of (10km) **La Goulette**. If you have a long day ahead of you in Carthage, save your energy and press onwards. The old walled town and its **kasbah** are run-down and semi-abandoned, only coming to life when theatrical performances are staged here during the summer. During the 16C, La Goulette was one of the most feared ports in the Mediterranean; it was from here that the corsair Barbarossa terrorised Christian shipping off the African coast. Not only did he plunder their goods, he also took slaves.

Khair Al Din Barbarossa (1466–1546), named Barbarossa because of his red beard, was born in Lesbos. His father, Jacob, was a retired Janissary turned potter, and his mother was the widow of a Greek Christian priest. He had several brothers, but it was Aruj, an older brother, who led Barbarossa into piracy. The two began their pirate careers when they arrived on the African shores in 1504. They first tried their hand off the coast of Jerba, but were unsuccessful, and turned instead to La Goulette, the port of Tunis. La Goulette offered a good sheltered harbour for their two boats, which were open, and had 17 oars on either side, each manned by two sailors. The two pirates traded mainly in slaves, creating a flow of slaves for the Sultan's harem. An account of the period describes how 'a great procession was formed of Christian captives marching two and two, four young Christian girls were mounted on mules and two ladies of noble birth followed on Arab horses'.

By 1510 Aruj and Barbarossa were the richest men on the Mediterranean and operated from both La Goulette and Jerba. From their base in Jerba, they led an expedition to Bouggie in Algeria where, losing his arm, Aruj called off the attack and returned to Tunis. En route the pirates captured a Genoese boat belonging to the Lomellini family. In revenge the Genoese sent a fleet in 1512, under Andrea Doria, to destroy the pirates' ships, which they did after finding them at anchor at La Goulette. The Barbarossa brothers escaped to Jerba to rebuild their boats; then they set out again to attack Bouggie, only to be met by Spanish ships which forced them once more to retire. By 1516, however, they had established a pirate city state in Algiers; here, after Aruj's death in 1518,

Barbarossa was obliged to ask the Ottomans for help in order to keep the Spanish from grabbing parts of the coast. Barbarossa was appointed admiral of the Ottoman fleet in 1534 and with the Ottoman navy at his disposal attacked the Hafsids in Tunis. He held his command until his death in 1546.

In 1535, the Hapsburg Emperor Charles V (1500–58; Charles I of Spain), built the kasbah at La Goulette in response to requests from the Hafsids who had been ousted from their capital. Spanish troops were successful in regaining Tunis and reinstalled the Hafsids. Piracy reared its head again, however, after the Ottoman conquest in 1574. The state encouraged piracy and the kasbah was rebuilt with extensive dungeons to hold slaves who were later sold in the local market, Souk el Berka, in the medina.

A few hundred metres beyond the kasbah walls the train stops at **Goulette Neuve**, a modern, whitewashed suburb. After the next stop, **Goulette Casino**, the track joins the mainland, passing through the modern suburb of **Kheredoine**. There are two more stops, Aéroport and Le Kram, before the train reaches **Salambo**, the first of five stops that punctuate the site of ancient Carthage.

3 · Carthage

Ancient Carthage mingles with the modern suburb, the building of which has been responsible for a good deal of damage to the ancient remains. As a result of the modern developments, the ruins present a series of isolated sites, spread some distance apart, making it difficult to envisage the ancient city as a whole. Tourists often use the horse-drawn calèches to travel from one site to another. The train can also be used, although the stations are rather distant from some parts of the sites. Covering the site on foot is also possible although it makes for a long and tiring day.

All the sites are covered separately in geographical sequence from south to north. However, you may well want to be more select and concentrate on the more important sites: the Salambo Tophet, the Punic harbours, the Paleo-Christian Museum, the Byrsa hill museum and ruins, and the Antonine Baths. One ticket serves for all the sites but must be shown at each entry. For some of the sites a torch would come in handy to explore underground vaults and for peering into cisterns.

■ **Hotels**. Accommodation in the suburb of Carthage tends to be expensive but is convenient for visiting the ruins. The *Amilcar* near the Basilica of St Cipriano, tel. (01) 740788, is at the top of the range and has air-conditioning. *Reine Elyssa Didon*, on Byrsa Hill, tel. (01) 275447, is also air-conditioned but less prestigious. *Residence Carthage* tel. (01) 731072 on Rue Hannibal, near the Salambo Tophet is next down in the range. There is also a youth hostel at Dermech, tel. (01) 275762.

■ **Festivals.** International Cultural Festival of Carthage, July and August.

History

Carthage originated as one of a number of Phoenician settlements along the coast of North Africa and became the capital of a federation along the Tunisian coast. Legend has the founding of the city as 814 BC when Dido, daughter of the King of Tyre, is said to have asked the chief Iarbus for as much land as she could cover with a bull's hide (*byrsa* in Greek). She cunningly cut the hide into strips and encircled the hill of Byrsa, the earliest site of Carthage. By the 6C BC, Carthage had become the leading power in the western Mediterranean, with colonies in Sardinia, Corsica, the Balearics and Sicily. It was in Sicily that Carthage came into conflict with the Greek city states, one of which, Syracuse, defeated Carthage in 480 BC at the Battle of Himera. Sicily was again the territory which brought Carthage and Rome into conflict leading to the three Punic Wars between the two cities. The third and final war brought about the total destruction of Carthage; the city's defences were breached by Scipio Aemilianus in 159 BC.

In AD 44 Julius Caesar founded a new Carthage, that was to be completed by Augustus and called Colonia Julia Carthago. It expanded rapidly, soon becoming the third largest city in the Roman Empire, and the capital of the Roman African Proconsularis. In 439 Carthage fell into the hands of the Vandal Genseric who retained control until 533 when Belisarius took the city in his campaign to win the African province for the Byzantines. It remained in Byzantine control until 692, when it fell into Arab hands and was destroyed and finally abandoned.

Archaeological work began on the site in 1857. In 1973 the excavation of the city was put under the direction of UNESCO and continues to this day with at least 14 countries participating in the work.

A. Salambo Tophet

The **SALAMBO TOPHET** (open winter daily, 09.00–17.00, summer daily, 07.00–19.00), the remnants of an overgrown Carthaginian burial ground, is almost a kilometre from the Salambo railway station. Take Avenue Farhat Hached off Avenue Habib Bourguiba, and the third left, Rue Hannibal, which is signposted 'Sanctuaire Punique'. The site entrance is on the right, after the hotel *Residence Carthage* and the *Restaurant Baal*.

The sanctuary, which is said to be the spot where Dido first landed, was discovered in the 1920s. It once contained a temple and a sacred stone where sacrifices were offered, and gradually assumed the nature of a massive burial ground, covering an area of some 2 hectares, most of which is now covered with housing.

The tophet, a word that is derived from the Hebrew for a similar sanctuary outside Jerusalem, is a burial ground for children. The earliest burials contain a proportion of animal bones, but the sacrificial victims increasingly became human over time so that by the 4C BC, 68 per cent of bones belonged to children aged between one and three and 30 per cent to newborn children. Most of the burials were of children from wealthy families.

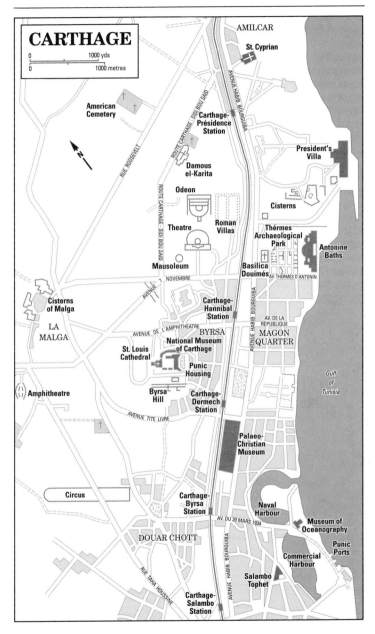

CARTHAGE

| 0 | 1000 yds |
| 0 | 1000 metres |

AMILCAR

St. Cyprian

American Cemetery

Carthage-Présidence Station

ROUTE CARTHAGE, SIDI BOU SAID

AVENUE HABIB BOURGUIBA

President's Villa

RUE ROOSEVELT

Damous el-Karita

Odeon

Cisterns

ROUTE CARTHAGE, SIDI BOU SAID

Theatre

Roman Villas

Thérmes

Archaeological Park

Antonine Baths

Mausoleum

Basilica Douimés

AV. THERMES D'ANTONIN

NOVEMBRE

AVENUE

Cisterns of Malga

Carthage-Hannibal Station

AV. DE LA RÉPUBLIQUE

AVENUE DE L'AMPHITHEATRE

LA MALGA

BYRSA

MAGON QUARTER

St. Louis Cathedral

National Museum of Carthage

AVENUE HABIB BOURGUIBA

Amphitheatre

Punic Housing

Byrsa Hill

Carthage-Dermech Station

Gulf of Tunisia

AVENUE TITE LIVRE

Palaeo-Christian Museum

Circus

Carthage-Byrsa Station

AV. DU 20 MARS 1934

Naval Harbour

Museum of Oceanography

Punic Ports

DOUAR CHOTT

Commercial Harbour

AVENUE HABIB BOURGUIBA

RUE TAHA HOUSSINE

Salambo Tophet

Carthage-Salambo Station

The sacrifices may have been a type of high class birth control: the inheritance laws stipulated that property be divided between all heirs and a family's power would be weakened if its property was divided too often.

The Romans frowned upon human sacrifice and used its practice as propaganda against the Carthaginians. The ancient Greek writer Diodorus Siculus stated that the Carthaginians 'were filled with superstitious dread, for they believed that they had neglected the honours of the gods that had been established by their fathers. In their zeal to make amends for their omission, they selected 200 of the noblest children and sacrificed them publicly; and others who were under suspicion sacrificed themselves voluntarily, in number not less than 300. There was in their city a bronze image of Cronus, extending its hands, palms up and sloping towards the ground, so that each of the children when placed thereon rolled down and fell into a sort of gaping pit filled with fire'. The guilt Diodorus mentions comes from the families having substituted slave children for noble children in former sacrifices. It was this evocative image of human sacrifice that inspired the final scenes of Flaubert's 'Salammbo'.

From the ticket office, which is on the right of the gate, follow the narrow footpath between the shady palms and bushes. Look for the remnants of an **oven** on your right, identified by four steps that lead up to it. It dates from the 9C BC and is said to have served as a crematorium. The path heads down to a hut on the right. To the right of the door there is a **funerary urn**, originally plugged with clay and capped with an inverted bowl, then set into a stone block which would have been buried underground.

Inside the **hut**, should you find someone with the key, there is a large collection of stelae, dating from the 6C BC which was when they first came into use. Prior to this, urns were simply protected by stone slabs rather like a dolmen. The stelae, which are small and pointed in the Egyptian style, have inscriptions. The inscription sometimes indicates the type of sacrifice: the child of a wealthy family is *mulk ba'al*; and child of a commoner, *mulk adam*. Sacrifices were made to Baal Hammon, and from the 5C BC also to Tanit, the goddess of Carthage. Once a burial patch was full, more earth was piled on top and the process began again, a fact that accounts for the different levels of the land.

The path continues down, and on the left there is a **single stelae** with the well-preserved symbol of Tanit, a triangular shape, truncated at the top by a disk, with an inverted crescent above. A little further on, the path is lined with some of the oldest stelae on the site, so old that they are almost worn completely away. The path next climbs up onto a newer layer where there is a clearing filled with stelae just like a modern graveyard. There is another graveyard, somewhat overgrown, further along the path on the left, set below a group of palm trees.

From here the path leads down to an **underground vault**, which was built in the 4C by the Romans as a granary store. If you have a torch, you may be able to make out the large stone slab at one end which the Romans used, said to be a stone sacred to Baal Hammon.

Heading back towards the entrance gate the path is lined with stelae, one of which has a carving of a woman holding a child.

B. Punic Harbours

The **PUNIC HARBOURS** are 500m from Carthage Byrsa railway station, and about 800m from the Salambo Tophet. From the railway station head down Avenue du 20 Mars 1934 until meeting Rue Hannibal on the right. Rue Hannibal runs from the tophet to the first of the two Punic harbours, the **commercial harbour**, from where grain and olive oil were shipped. There is nothing very remarkable to see; once polygonal in shape, dug out by mammoth human effort from the clay and sand to a capacity of 125,000 cubic metres, nature has reclaimed it and reduced it to a marshy wasteland. Originally it was connected to the sea by a channel 21m wide which could be closed off by a chain; it was from here, in the 5C BC, that the Phoenician admiral Hanno sailed off on his voyage down the west coast of Africa.

Rue Hannibal continues to the edge of the second Punic harbour, the naval harbour. Turn right onto Rue du 20 Mars 1934 and cross over the bridge that spans the channel connecting the two harbours. Straight ahead is the gateway into the Institut National Scientifique et Technique d'Oceanographie et de Pêche, which houses the **Museum of Oceanography** (open summer, Tues–Sat, 14.00–17.00, Sun, 10.00–12.00, 14.00–17.00; winter, Tues–Sat, 14.00–16.00, Sun, 10.00–12.00, 14.00–17.00). The collection—nautical objects, catalogues of freshwater and Mediterranean fish and explanations on fishing techniques in Tunisia—is arranged on the first floor of this spacious villa, from where there are fine views over both the Punic harbours and the Gulf of Tunis beyond.

At the museum turn left to the **naval harbour**, the entrance to which is on the left. Just inside the entrance on the right there is a small museum (open daily, 08.00–18.30). It houses models and drawings of the two ports, giving a very good idea of how they once were. The model of the commercial harbour shows it as it would have been in Roman times around AD 200. The model of the naval harbour shows the Punic version dating from 150 BC, before the Romans added a circular colonnade, a small temple and an octagonal building. It has 30 ship sheds around the admiralty island, Ilot de l'Amirauté, each with a covered slipway leading into the water.

> The dimensions of the ramps indicate that the boats, numbering some 220 in all, would have been 5.5m wide and 37m long. They were made of prefabricated parts, designed for maximum assembly speed and had a battering ram on the keel which was capable of breaking off under great stress, thus preventing damage to the vessel. In 1969 a dredging vessel struck a Punic warship which was found to be 35m long and had 17 oars on each side. Each oar would have been worked by two rowers so that the boat had a total capacity of about 100 men. In addition the boat carried food supplies in the form of oxen, sheep, goats and pigs as well as marijuana tea.

In the courtyard outside the museum there are pieces of masonry dating from Punic and Roman times that were found in the port area. Amongst the fragments are some pieces of Carrara marble imported from Italy, indicating the extent of Mediterranean trading and the wealth of Carthage.

From the museum courtyard follow the footpath across the island, which has a diameter of 325m. You will pass the fallen chunks of giant columns, strewn near the foundations of the **Roman temple** which is divided into three chambers. Close by, the circular foundations can be made out of another Roman building, an **octagonal structure** of unknown origin. Follow the path to the edge of the island where pillars can be seen flanking what would have been a **ramp** for boats to enter the water, but which was blocked off in Roman times. If you continue around the island to the north side, where an arched gate stood in Roman times with a causeway connecting it to the mainland, you can see where the boats entered the sea.

C. Paleo-Christian Museum

From the port area head back inland along Avenue du 20 Mars 1934 to rejoin Avenue Habib Bourguiba. Turn right and after about 300m cross over to the gates of the **PALEO-CHRISTIAN MUSEUM** (open summer, daily, 07.00–19.00, winter, daily, 08.00–17.00). Set back from the road, this small purpose-built museum stands on the site of a Byzantine basilica and ecclesiastical complex. The exhibits were found in local excavations undertaken by an American UNESCO team and cover the period from the 4C to the 7C. The display in the entrance hall reveals some alarming statistics concerning the 20C destruction of ancient Carthage. There are photos of building sites where ancient remains are being bulldozed to make way for swimming pools, cellars and garages. The entrance hall also has a collection of Paleo-Christian **masonry** mounted on the wall.

The first part of the museum is dedicated to the construction of the basilica complex, with good explanations in French and English. It was built after the Byzantine reconquest in 534 on the site of an earlier basilica that dated from 400. There are various finds, constituting the fabric of the basilica, including **terracotta tiles** of local production decorated with palmettes and crosses, **hollow terracotta pipes** used to construct vaults and domes, a technique that Byzantines borrowed from North African architecture, pieces of plaster walling with **frescoes imitating Chemtou marble**, and a 6C **mosaic of a peacock**, the symbol of immortality.

The second part of the museum, which follows on from the first, has finds from the House of the Mosaic of the Greek Charioteers including the mosaic itself. It dates from 400 and shows **four Greek charioteers**, with the names of each competing faction above them.

Outside the museum are further masonry fragments and detached panels of mosaics. To the left, beneath a corrugated roof, are the scant remains of the **Basilica of Agileus**.

D. Magon Quarter

From the Paleo-Christian Museum continue along Avenue Habib Bourguiba, where there are pizzerias, cafés and a supermarket, for about 500m. Then turn right and proceed for another 200m down Avenue de la République, a wide street lined with palms which leads to the sea.

Alternatively take the train to the Carthage Hannibal station which is on the corner of Avenue de la République, 300m from the site.

The ruins of the **MAGON QUARTER** (open summer, daily, 07.00–19.00, winter, daily, 08.00–17.30), a housing district, originally Phoenician, but later built on by the Romans, lie at the southern end of Avenue de la République along the sea-shore. The entrance is just before the sea-wall on the right. Inside the entrance on the right is the **first antiquarium** which holds various small objects that were found during the excavation of the site by a German team. There are also maps and photographs with explanations (in French and German) as to the origins of the quarter, and a maquette of El Haouaria, the underground limestone quarry on Cap Bon. On the wall, a section of **plaster frieze** has been preserved complete with its painted egg and dart decoration. It would once have decorated the walls of a Punic house and dates from the 4–3C BC. The two benches at the back of the room are covered with **mosaics**, that on the right being Punic, and that on the left Roman. The **second antiquarium** has models and diagrams showing how the Punic quarter was reshaped in Roman times. One of the most notable changes was the straightening of the sea-wall, which allowed more housing to be constructed. The remnants of part of the Punic sea-wall and great blocks of sandstones that were placed as breakwaters from 5–3C BC can be seen just outside the second antiquarium, 25m towards the coast.

> The Punic city wall was 13m high and 9m thick. On the landward side it comprised a triple wall with a four-storey tower every 59m and stalls for 4000 horses and 300 elephants in casemates. The length of the walls is not known, but a 2C commentator cited them as 34km long, which if accurate this would make it the longest wall in ancient history.

Follow the footpath which leads beyond the two antiquariums to an extensive area of **Punic housing** dating from the 5–2C BC, which was discovered during deep excavation of the ground. In places the Punic houses, many of which bear traces of monochrome mosaics, have been used as cisterns and cellars for Roman houses that were built on top. It is also possible to walk along **Cardo XIX**, the road the Romans built parallel with the coast, and which dates from the 2C. For a complete view of the site go to the entrance on Rue Septime Sévère where there is a viewing terrace.

E. Antonine Baths

From the Magon Quarter it is no more than 300m to the Antonine Baths, which are set in a shady archaeological park, below the stark white walls of the Tunisian President's villa. To get there head back up Avenue de la République and take the first right, Rue Septime Sévère, until meeting Avenue des Thermes d'Antonin, on the far side of which is the entrance to the **PARC ARCHEOLOGIQUE DES THERMES** (open summer, daily, 08.00–19.00, winter, daily, 09.00–17.00), the site of the Antonine Baths. Inside the main gates, the ticket office is on the left. From the entrance, follow the wide leafy avenue, **Cardo XVI**, which is lined with ancient tombs and masonry, to **Decumanus IV** and turn right. Follow Decumanus IV until reaching a viewing terrace from where you can look down on the **Antonine Baths**, spectacularly located on the coast. The plan on the terrace shows the principal rooms and the symmetrical layout of the baths, of which one wing was used by men and the other by women. At the centre of the baths you can identify the frigidarium, which was almost the size of an Olympic swimming pool, measuring 22m by 47m, by the vast granite column.

Construction began on the baths, which are the fourth largest baths in the Roman Empire, under the Emperor Hadrian (118–138); the work was completed under Antoninus Pius (145–162). Water was carried from the Zaghouan aqueduct into the Borj Jedid cistern which had a capacity of 30,000 cubic metres, for the baths alone consumed 32 million litres of water a day. The baths were destroyed during the Vandal period and plundered for stone thereafter so that only the basement and ground floor are seen today.

> A Roman bath session started by undressing in the vestibularium from where one proceeded to the unctuarium to be oiled down. Next came a gym session in the palaestra. After building up a sweat, one went to the destrictarium to be scraped down. To recover from all this one sat in the dry heat of the sudarium before proceeding to the tepidarium for a warm bath. Next came a cold bath in the frigidarium, then finally another warm dip in the tepidarium.

Take the steps down from the viewing terrace to the ruins themselves, a giant maze of towering piers and vaults. Directly opposite the steps are a series of **octagonal chambers**, many complete with their vaulting. At the centre is the **caldarium** which has a series of arches meeting in the middle. A vaulted gallery leading off the south end of this complex of rooms shelters a collection of masonry fragments with acanthus carvings and a fragmented inscription.

The gallery emerges into the vast sandy expanse of the **palaestra** which is strewn with chunks of tumbled masonry as well as some finely carved sections of architrave and part of an inscription. There are also numerous segments of fine marble columns lying around. From the palaestra, a ramp leads up to the **gymnasium**, where an elegant **fluted column** has been restored and several crisply carved Corinthian capitals lie around.

Head back to the viewing terrace, passing through the largest room in the baths, the **frigidarium,** marked by a **giant granite column** complete with its Corinthian capital, one of eight that once stood here. Each of these columns weighed about 50 tonnes, had a diameter of 1.6m and stood at a height of at least 20m. The one that stands here is raised on a concrete plinth to compensate for the present lower level of the floor, and gives some idea of the original height at which the baths once stood, with the vaults of the ceiling some 30m high. Running from one side of the room to the other is a deep channel that would have carried water from the cistern.

From the viewing terrace, return along Decumanus IV, part of the Roman grid network of roads. Built into the slope on the right of the road are a series of barrel-roofed **cisterns** which today house fragments of mosaics and fragments of carvings. On the left are the remains of a **Roman house** built around a central courtyard. Further along the road, steps lead up on the right to a **burial area**, with Punic stelae dating from the 6–5C BC. At the crossroads with Cardo XVI, the main avenue from the entrance, steps lead up on the right into the ruins of another **Roman villa**. In places parts of mosaic and broken columns are still intact, and in one underground barrel-vaulted room there is a mosaic of a fish.

Continue along Decumanus IV until meeting **Cardo XV**, along the right side of which are the extensive remains of a Roman building called the **Schola**. The house has a central courtyard, off the north side of which is an apsidal room which contains a **mosaic** of children entwined with garlands and vines, dancing beneath a tholos draped with canopies. It is believed that the building was used as a meeting place for the associates of an imperial cult.

South of the Schola, concrete steps lead down to the **Chapel of Saiida**, a 7C funerary chapel. The tiny entrance hall has a mosaic of fish; in the chapel itself there are further mosaics of birds set in circles and Solomon's knots.

Heading uphill from the Schola along **Cardo XIV**, take the steps up from the west side to the ruins of two basilicas, the best preserved of which is the Byzantine **Basilica Douimes**. An inscription was found here from the Epistle to the Romans: 'If the Lord be with us who can be against us?' The nave, which was originally divided into five aisles, still has some of its slender columns although most of them stand no higher than half their original height. The floor is covered in geometric design mosaics which are currently under restoration.

Beyond the basilica ruins, at the highest part of the park, there is a Punic necropolis with graves dedicated to Baal Haamon and Tanit.

F. Roman villas and theatre

From the Antonine Baths follow Avenue des Thermes d'Antonin back to Avenue Habib Bourguiba. Cross over and continue straight ahead along Rue Mohammed Ali Novembre. After passing under the railway bridge take the first turning on the right, following the signs to Villas Romaines. You pass a private health clinic, Clinique Carthage, on the left before reaching the gates into the site of the **ROMAN VILLAS** (open summer, daily 08.00–19.00, winter daily, 09.00–17.00). This residential quarter of the city was built by the Romans on the site of a Punic necropolis that dates from the 3–2C BC. From the ticket office, which is on the left, a path leads uphill past two barrel-roofed water cisterns. Steps climb up into the housing remains which were excavated in the early 20C. There is little left standing, apart from low walls and door jambs, but these make it possible to follow the grid system upon which the houses were built. On the right there is a pair of wells indicating the existence of an underground cistern. To the left is the long wall of the **Maison Cryptoportique**. The wall, or portico after which the house is named, shelters a collection of mosaic panels that have been lifted from the site. The ruins of the villa, which is a peristyle, run alongside it. In the central courtyard, with its neat rosemary hedges, patches of the original mosaic clad the surrounding walkways. An oecus (a reception room) leads off one side and is preserved with parts of its marble paved floor.

The real show-piece of the site is the villa on the hill-top above. Follow the paved road off left after the Maison Cryptoportique, passing an overgrown section of housing to the right where there is little to be seen but low walls and the occasional well. At the first junction along this road turn right and continue to the top of the hill before turning right again into the **Maison de la Voliere**, sometimes alluded to as Hannibal's Palace. This 3C Roman peri-style villa has had its courtyard rebuilt around an octagonal flowerbed, using the original marble columns. The courtyard also contains sections of mosaics of pheasants, peacocks and other birds, statues, and pillars carved with diagonal lines. Beyond the courtyard there is a ****panoramic terrace** with broken marble columns and larger granite ones complete with their Corinthian capitals. The view is exceptional, taking in the ruins of Carthage, the coastline as far as Sidi Bou Said and the presidential palace below, near which are the Roman cisterns of Borj Jedid.

Returning to the paved road, it is possible to continue uphill to the **odeon**. However, the paving soon peters out and the terrain beyond is overgrown, dangerously concealing the occasional well. When the odeon was built in 205–210 it was the largest in the Roman world. However, it was plundered for stone by the Vandals and all that remains is the floor with a low wall along the back which would have held niches for statues, and a vague outline in the hill-side where the seating would have been.

Head back to the main road, Rue Mohammed Ali Novembre. Turn right and continue until you see a pair of mock columns marking the turning on the right to the **THEATRE** (open summer, daily, 08.00–19.00, winter, daily, 09.00–17.00). It is approached by a road lined with carved stone fragments and column capitals, off the right side of which is a car park. Inside the gates there are reproduction Roman busts, and paths leading both left and right into the theatre. Erected at the start of the 2C, it was described by the Roman writer Apuleius, who was born in 123 and educated at Carthage, as having a multi-storeyed stage building and a golden coffered ceiling over the stage. It was restored many times before being destroyed by the Vandals in 439. Little of the present-day structure is original with the exception of some of the lower rows of seating. The once grand stage building has been replaced by a bland white stone edifice with a central niche and most of the seating, as well as the colon-nade around the top, is modern. It does, however, at least function as a theatre, and is the venue for many of the spectacles held during the International Cultural Festival of Carthage in July and August; it was from here also that Winston Churchill addressed the Allied troops in June 1943.

G. Byrsa Hill

To get to the top of the Byrsa Hill on foot is a stiff walk in the heat of the day. From the theatre, wind up **Rue Florus**, a wide avenue lined with prestigious villas, until meeting **Avenue de l'Amphithéatre**. Turn right onto this boule-vard, which carves a wide channel right through the centre of ancient Carthage, and either scramble up one of the footpaths to the hill summit or continue up to Rue Pasteur on the left. Alternatively take a taxi or a *calèche* from Carthage Hannibal railway station.

At the top of the hill is the massive salmon-tinged façade of the French cathedral, the **ST LOUIS CATHEDRAL** (open summer, daily 08.00–19.00; winter, daily, 09.00–17.00).

History

King Louis IX, to whom the cathedral is dedicated, was the founder of the French monastic order of the Pères Blancs. He led the Eighth Crusade, which arrived in Tunisia in 1270, but failed in his attempt to convert El Mustansire, the Hafsid ruler. The crusade was abandoned when the king and many of his troops died of the plague. However, the Pères Blancs order lived on and in 1881 Cardinal Lavigerie set out to convert North Africa to Christianity. In the same year he founded this awe inspiring cathedral which was finished nine years later in 1890. It was the seat of the Archbishop of Carthage up until 1965, but is now deconsecrated.

The cathedral has a distinctly Moorish style with its horseshoe arches and Arabic twin windows. Yet the twin towers that flank the façade and the decorative crenellations are decidedly Gothic, while the high dome with its tight band of decoration around the drum is Byzantine in inspiration. The interior, which has recently been restored, is also a blend of styles. Grand horseshoe arches supported on fine marble columns line the central aisle at either side, and form a rood screen across the apse. The ceiling, clad in wood coffering, is decoratively painted, while Arab style windows are filled with Gothic stained glass. The upper walls are decorated with coats of arms, above which there is a balcony running right the way round the central aisle.

Facing the cathedral façade, head along the right side, where drink and snack stalls line the way to the entrance of the ****NATIONAL MUSEUM OF CARTHAGE** (open summer, daily, 08.00–19.00, winter, daily, 09.00–17.00). From the ticket office on the left, which also sells publications and postcards, head up a ramp to the vast terrace, overlooking Carthage and the bay beyond, which marks the summit of Byrsa Hill. The museum entrance is on the left.

This newly arranged museum, housed in the spacious ex-convent of the cathedral, is one of the best in Tunisia. It has a very well displayed and informatively labelled (in English and French) collection, which is organised chronologically. Inside the large entrance hall, on the right are three Roman statues dating from the 2C: **Aesculapius**, the Greek god of medicine, with his serpent; **Ceres**, the goddess of fertility, with her ears of corn and bunches of grapes; and **Prospera**, now headless.

To visit the museum in chronological order start from the first floor. The stairs are along a hallway, in which there are details of the excavations of the Punic and Roman remains on Byrsa Hill. At the top of the stairs there is a large gallery of mosaics, at the far end of which is the **Punic Hall** which holds the oldest exhibits in the museum, coming mainly from the Salambo Tophet, which was in use from the 9C BC to the fall of Carthage in 146 BC. At the entrance to the room there is a large heap of catapult shot which would have been used during the last defence of Carthage in 146 BC when women are thought to have cut off their hair to make the catapults. The collection starts with imported ceramics, including **terracotta masks**, some of which still bear traces of their painted decoration; one dating from the 6C BC has a bronze earring, another from the same era has a silver ring through the nose. Other masks dating from the 6–5C BC are painted on **ostrich egg shells**.

Next is the main hall which is arranged according to colour code: beige for Punic; blue for Roman; pink for Christian and green for Islamic. Oil lamps span the ages from Punic to Islamic, showing the course of their development in design. The **Punic collection** includes some fine pieces of jewellery, small burial objects to ward off evil spirits, and imported ceramics including Corinthian ware from Campania in Italy and Attic-ware from Greece which were found buried in graves.

In the **Roman collection** is a prize sculpture of **Silenus carried by four satyrs**, pieced together from 45 fragments. There are also the white marble fragments of two colossal statues of **Victory** which decorated a 2C monument on Byrsa Hill. Also of interest is the **hemi-spherical funerary urn** which is decorated with fluting.

The **Christian section** has a fine collection of **terracotta tiles**, which are decorated with scenes from the Old Testament and symbolic animals, as well as original moulds from which the tiles were made.

The **Islamic section** is fairly small and comprises mainly glazed ceramics and a collection of weights. The **Amphora Hall** has a comprehensive collection of amphorae with explanations on how to identify the period and provenance of amphorae by examining any marks, the rims and the handles.

Return to the **Mosaic Hall** which has a mosaic collection mostly from a wealthy Roman villa near the amphitheatre. A pair of 3C **semicircular mosaics** from basins depict fishing scenes, showing different fishing techniques. A very large **geometric mosaic** decorated with animal and fruit motifs bears an inscription to Scorpianus, the owner of the villa from which the mosaic was removed. There is also a mosaic of **Venus** dating from the 4C with a palm branch, a mirror and an apple representing love, vanity and beauty respectively. The finest mosaics are above the stairs and are fragments taken from a large pavement depicting **animals**.

On the ground floor of the museum there is a **Salle Chretienne** off the main entrance hall. There are several fine carved sarcophagi here including the **Sarcophagus of the Good Shepherd** which dates from the 4–6C. There are also mosaics from tombs, some of which have inscriptions. One such tomb has a photograph next to it of the two children that were found interred in it.

Outside the museum, along its north side, there is a small **garden** which contains antique mill-stones and a collection of ancient column fragments and carved capitals.

Return to the **large courtyard** in front of the museum entrance and make your way to the marble plinth at its centre where there is a map of Byrsa Hill in Roman times. In Punic times the summit of Byrsa Hill was the acropolis, the site of a temple to Euchmon. When the Romans founded their city here, they not only levelled the temple, but sliced a herculean 7m off the top of the hill to make a larger area, big enough to hold the capitol. A vast retaining wall was built traversing the Punic housing that once clad the hillside, using the fallen stone to build supporting vaults. From the map you can see that the capitol once comprised a (2C) library, in which you are now standing, two temples (the main one of which, built in 40 AD, had porticoes down two sides) and a terrace looking out over the sea. It also held a large forum and a basilica, built in the late 2C, both of which were connected to the temple precinct by a portico.

A dusty path leads down from the terrace of the capitol, past two cisterns which now house a collection of column fragments, and down some steps to an area of **Punic housing**, dating from the 3–2C BC, which covers the south-east side of the hill. Laid out on a regular grid plan, even though there are no roads, only steps, the houses originally stood on two storeys and each surrounded a courtyard, beneath which was a water cistern. Wandering through the ruins you will see the vast piers were built right though the Punic city to support the Roman capitol.

Within the housing block, named **insula C**, the houses were found to be of very precise measurements. Each house was 15.65m by 31m, which in the Punic measuring system was 30 by 60 cubits (1 cubit=52cm). It is also interesting to note the paving visible in some places, known as '*pavimentum punicum*', which is made up of a grey cement-type substance impressed with chips of terracotta and grey marble. Another typical feature is the pink plaster used to cover the walls.

The next housing block, **insula E**, has all but disappeared beneath a mountain of earth, piled on by the Romans to make up the terrace. However, one Punic house has been excavated and has a circular impluvium to collect rainwater in its central courtyard.

The last housing block, **insula D**, is believed to have been an area of 4–3C BC metal workshops, as traces of metals have been found in the ground.

On the north-west side of Byrsa Hill are the remains of a **Punic necropolis**. Dating from 7–6C BC, the tombs mainly take the form of underground chambers. It was at the doorways to chambers such as these that the terracotta funerary masks in the Carthage museum were found.

H. Carthage suburbs

The sites on the fringe of Carthage are poorly preserved and are best visited by private transport.

The **amphitheatre**, set in a pine forest to the west of Byrsa Hill, is now razed to the ground but at one time was the largest edifice of its kind in North Africa. It measured 156m by 128m, and had an arena of 65m by 70m, which is equal to that in Verona. Built in the 1C, it was expanded in the 2C to seat 36,000 spectators. A hundred or so metres to the south is the site of a stadium, now no more than depressions in the ground.

The **circus**, further south of the amphitheatre, was a Roman hippodrome, 516m long, capable of holding 200,000 spectators, but very little remains to be seen today.

The **Roman cisterns of Malga**, north of the amphitheatre, are enormous chambers covered by vaults, dating from the late 2C. Now used as depots, they were once filled with water carried by the Zaghouan aqueduct. There were originally 24 of these cisterns, each one measuring an impressive 95m by 12.5m.

The remaining monuments on the outskirts of Carthage constitute two Christian basilicas both of which are in a ruinous state. The first is **Damous el Karita**, a vast basilica complex, which lies to the north of the Roman theatre, alongside the cemetery of the Pères Blancs. The core of the complex is a large nave, 65m long, which at one time was divided into nine aisles, terminating in a rounded apse. Today there are a number of broken columns on plinths which were erected during restorations in the early 20C. Amongst the surrounding debris, along the north-east side of the nave stood a chapel and a cloister. To the south-west are the remains of what are thought to be monastic cells, and beyond these are the foundations and underground chamber of a circular edifice, possibly a grandiose baptismal font or a storage place for reliquaries.

The second basilica, **St Ciprian** (open summer, daily, 08.00–19.00, winter, daily, 09.00–17.00), which is on the road to Sidi Bou Said, was excavated at the end of the 19C. It is still possible to follow the outline of the walls, and broken columns mark the position of the nave which was divided into seven aisles. To the south-east of the basilica is a colonnade built over a cistern from where there are fine views of the coast.

4 · Carthage to Sidi Bou Said and La Marsa

Carthage to Sidi Bou Said is 3km, with La Marsa a further 2km beyond. The drive north of Carthage along the rocky coastline is scenic, but there is little to stop for, and the excursion is more easily made by the TGM train, particularly as both the resorts, Sidi Bou Said and La Marsa, have parking problems in the summer. The TGM train from Tunis departs every 15 minutes during the day, and hourly at night. It passes through the following stations from Carthage to its destination, La Marsa: Carthage Byrsa—Carthage Demech—Carthage Hannibal—Carthage President—Carthage Amilcar—Sidi Bou Said—Sidi Dhrif—La Corniche—La Marsa.

It is no more than 15 minutes from Carthage to La Marsa, and the railway stations at both resorts are within easy walking distance of the town centres. Sidi Bou Said is the more select of the two resorts but less convenient as its beach is reached by steps down a cliff. La Marsa is the better resort for children, and although it is less picturesque, it has a happy seaside atmosphere. Both resorts have a selection of accommodation and restaurants, although prices tend to be higher than in Tunis, and rooms are quickly filled during the holiday season.

SIDI BOU SAID

Sidi Bou Said, just one stop from the last of the Carthage stations, is amongst the most picturesque resorts in Tunisia thanks to a preservation order that was clamped onto it in 1915. The painter Paul Klee, who came here on 13 April 1914 with his artist friend August Macke, wrote in his diary: 'The town lies so beautifully up there and looks far out to sea, which accompanies us with its deep breathing as we climb.' The town is set high on the promontory of Gebel Manar, the site of a lighthouse, and is indeed something of a climb from the railway station.

Coming out of the station, turn right onto **Place Novembre**, which is overlooked by a modern white mosque surrounded by cactus bushes. From the left side of the square, the main drag through the village, a charming flagstoned street, starts its ascent. Whitewashed houses with blue painted grilles over the windows and blue painted doors line the way, interspersed with simple drinking fountains built of sandstone. Midway up there is a car park, on Place Sidi Aziz off on the right, after which point the street is pedestrianised. Towards the top, the souvenir shops start to thicken and, playing on the resort's associations, there are reams of prints and watercolours for sale. On the right, look out for the **covered souk**, where there are yet more tourist shops and jewellers. At the top of the hill there is a clutch of cafés and restaurants, including the famous **Café des Nattes**. Preceded by a flight of stone steps, the café owes its fame to August Macke who made it the subject of one of his paintings. The village is named after the 13C marabout, Abu Said, who is buried in the **Sidi Bou Said Mosque**, at the top of the hill.

> Abu Said was born c 1207 and settled in Sidi Bou Said as a teacher of Sufism. He attracted a large following, particularly amongst Andalucian immigrants. In 1574 at the end of Spanish rule, Andalucian pirates settled here, adopting Abu Said as their protector and 'lord of the sea'.

Today, it is a highly revered spot, well-attended by pilgrims, and tourists are not encouraged. Should you wish to take a discreet peek (definitely not during prayer time), the door is on the left, before Café des Nattes. A flight of steps leads up to the terrace on which the mosque stands. The mosque was built in the 13C after the marabout's death and was restored under the Husainid Beys who also added the square minaret. A vaulted walkway leads through to the tomb, which is on the right. It is attended mainly by women and is housed in a tiny room with a very low ceiling behind a blue fretted screen. The mosque, which is on the left of the walkway, is preceded by red and green striped columns. The courtyard in front of the mosque is used for outdoor prayer during the summer, and has a fine mihrab decorated with faience tiles and stucco.

From the top of the hill, to the right of *Café des Nattes*, take **Rue el Hadi Zabrouk**. This elegant flagstoned street, lined with fine stone portals framing decoratively studded doors at either side, is known as the Passeo, a popular promenading spot. But for the occasional glimpse of the sea far below between the houses you do not realise that you are walking along the top of the Gebel Manar promontory. The street ends at a panoramic viewing spot where dark rock thrusts vertically down into the sea below. A steep cobbled road leads down to some sheltered coves which hold the marina and a beach. The beach, which is sandy, can also be reached by steps.

Leave Sidi Bou Said either by the coastal road, or by train for two stops, to La Marsa. Both road and rail pass through Sidi Dhriff where the coast starts to get less rocky and eucalyptus forests begin. **LA MARSA** sits on a flat and sandy stretch of the coast which extends for 5km to Gamart, another coastal resort.

The railway station at La Marsa is at one end of the main street, which leads to a palm lined promenade and a wide sandy beach, lapped by shallow water. A holiday atmosphere pervades the town, as balloon and ice cream sellers wander up and down, and the shops are piled high with good things to eat, particularly cakes and pastries.

A wide pedestrian arcade, **Avenue 20 Mars 1956**, leads off from the main street to the central square, **Place du Saf Saf**, which is filled with café tables. Rising above the square is the gaunt minaret of the main mosque which was first built during the Hafsid period. On the other side of the square, opposite the mosque, is the **Café Saf Saf**. The café, a series of bright blue wooden kiosks that offer shade in the summer and have shutters that can be closed to keep in the warmth in winter, is run by a French family who make doughnuts on the premises and fresh fruit juices. In the courtyard is a Hafsid well which is attended during the tourist season by a white camel and a camel man.

II THE NORTHERN COAST

5 · Tunis to Bizerte

The direct route from Tunis to Bizerte, calling in at Utica, is 66km on highway GP8, which is a busy and reasonably surfaced road. The coastal route to Bizerte is 98.5km on steep, winding and often pot-holed roads from Utica via Aousja to Gar el Melh; then along the coast, taking in Raf Raf and Rass Jebel, with an excursion to Cap Zebib.

By public transport there are four trains a day from Tunis Station SNCFT (Place Barcelone), to Bizerte. SNTRI buses from Gare Routière Nord de Bab Saadoun run every hour or so to Bizerte, with 11 buses a day to Ras Jebel and one a day to Gar el Melh.

Leave Tunis from the north of the city, following signs to the airport. The road weaves through wealthy suburbs before reaching a large junction. Continue to follow the signs to the airport and then to Bizerte on the GP8 which is signed off left, just before the airport itself. The GP8 continues through a further 8km of suburbs known as Ariana. A gentle range of hills finally carries the GP8 out of Tunis and into rolling countryside which is neatly culti-vated with olive groves and vineyards. At (5.5km) **Cebalat**, also known as Sabalet ben Ammar, is passed on the left. It stands on the edge of the vast allu-vial plain created by the Mejerda, the longest river in Tunisia. The plain sweeps up to (10.5km) **Pont de Bizerte**, a small town named after the bridge to the right of the GP8, just beyond it. Now disused, the bridge was built in 1858 during the French colonial era and has seven wide stone arches.

Another 4km beyond the river there is a right turn signposted to the peace-fully located Utique Ruines on RN337. This narrow and poorly surfaced road winds between olive groves and vineyards for 2km to the site museum which is on the left.

UTICA

History
Utica is almost three centuries older than Carthage. According to tradi-tion it was founded in 1100 BC by Phoenician traders, although no archaeological evidence exists earlier than the 8C BC. The city, once situ-ated on the coast, was a half-way point between Tyre and Cadiz, where the Phoenicians traded in metals. Along with Motya, another Phoenician colony off the west coast of Sicily, it had strategic importance as it guarded the Sicilian Straits.

In 310 BC the Greek tyrant Agathocles, ruler of Syracuse, under siege from the Carthaginians, decided to take the battle to Africa and landed at Cap Bon with 14,000 men. Having literally burned his boats, he pillaged the countryside and took control of Utica, where he based his army for

three years while he built a new fleet. Utica once again suffered occupation when in 204 BC, during the second Punic War, the city was taken by
Publius Cornelius Africanus Scipio. With an army of 30,000 men, Scipio
set up his headquarters just outside Utica, and coerced the city into
helping him launch a decisive attack on Carthage. In the third Punic War
Utica was allied to Rome and in 149 BC supported the siege of Carthage.
With the fall of Carthage in 146 BC, Utica was rewarded with the status
of a free city, and was nominated the capital of the Roman Proconsularis
of North Africa.

In 46 BC, Cato the Younger, who had sheltered and aided the Pompeian
rebels, committed suicide at Utica. After learning of Caesar's victory over
the Pompeians at the Battle of Thapsus, he threw himself onto his sword
and is said to have pulled out his own guts.

Caesar treated Utica mercifully, and the city prospered under Roman
rule, reaching its heyday under Septimius Severus (193–211) who
boosted the city's economy by granting it immunity from taxation.
However, towards the end of the 3C the Mejerda river silted up the port
and the maritime commerce upon which Utica's wealth depended dwindled. Although Utica remained the see of a bishop up until the 8C, it was
a shadow of its former self and was abandoned after a series of Arab raids.

The small **MUSEUM** (open summer, daily, 08.00–16.00, winter, daily,
08.30–17.30), composed of two rooms, houses archaeological finds from the
site. The **first room** contains a collection of **Punic amphorae**, distinct for
their tall, slender form, and items excavated from the Punic necropolis, dating
from the 4C BC to the 1C AD. Amongst the burial objects on display are
imported **Greek vases**, including Attic red-figure ware dating from the 4C BC
and black-figure ware dating from the 6C BC. Some of the Greek pottery
depicts scenes from the Trojan War. There are also **Punic and Roman oil
lamps**, and jewellery which includes beads made of bone.

The **second room** contains five of the seven **Roman mosaics** depicting
hunting scenes taken from the Maison de la Chasse. There are also a number
of statues. The lifesize statue of **Hercules**, in good condition apart from a
missing arm, dates from the city's heyday in the 3C. The 2C **sleeping
Ariadne** statue once decorated a fountain. Also from the 2C is the small
statue of **Aesculapius**, which depicts the god of medicine with his symbol,
the serpent, at his feet.

Outside the museum, mounted on the wall, are segments of **geometric
mosaics** and the other two **hunting mosaics** from Maison de la Chasse.
Dotted about the gardens are fragments of antique masonry and next to the
path a **sarcophagus**, which still bears faint traces of the red paint with which
it was painted.

The excavated ****RUINS OF UTICA** lie 800m north-east of the museum. To
get there continue on the road past the museum, taking the first right fork down
a rough track. There is a parking area on the left, and the gates to the site on the
right, which is open the same hours as the museum. The site is attended by a
custodian who will issue you with a ticket if you do not already have one from
the museum.

The excavations consist of a complete Roman housing block, an insula, and part of a Punic necropolis. From the gates, head down to **Decumanus A**, which is paved in parts. From here, enter the first house at the corner of the block, the **MAISON DE LA CHASSE**. Shaded by cypress trees, the walls of the house, which are built of large blocks of stone, stand little above knee height. The **central courtyard** contains a **well** and two fluted **Corinthian columns** and capitals. Paved with white monochrome mosaic, the courtyard is littered with the broken fragments of the other columns with which it was once surrounded. In the north corner of the courtyard is a small, marble paved room with a **mosaic of four wreaths** depicting the four seasons.

Return to Decumanus A and continue westwards to the back entrance, which is flanked by cypress trees, of ****MAISON DE LA CASCADE**. Built in AD 69–96, this is the best preserved of the houses here and also the largest, stretching from one side of the insula to the other. You enter a **peristyle garden**, once surrounded by columns, complete with its original **sun dial** and the marble basin of a **monumental fountain**. The basin is lined with a mosaic of the sea showing fishermen and fish. Off the left side of the courtyard is a large **dining room** with a marble paved floor. The marble, which is laid in a geometric design with circles, is of various colours, including green which comes from the Greek island of Euboea and yellow from the Chemtou quarry in Tunisia. Off the south side of the dining room is the **fountain,** with a mosaic of fish in the sea, after which the house is named. Returning to the garden, head north to the vestibule at the front of the house where there is another **fountain** with a green marble basin lined with a fish and sea mosaic. The **front door** to the house is very well preserved, complete with the holes into which the beams supporting the ceiling overhead would have been fitted. In a small room off the west side of the vestibule are the remnants of a **staircase** that originally led up to private apartments on the first floor.

Leave the Maison de la Cascade by the front door which gives onto a paved road, **Decumanus B**. Turn left, passing by the very scant remains of **Maison du Trésor**, named after a stash of coins that was found here during excavations. It was built between the end of the 1C BC and the start of the 1C AD, but was demolished in the 4C. It has a curious **rectangular basin** at its centre thought to have been a grain store.

Continue a little further along Decumanus B to the modern steps on the right that lead down to the **Punic necropolis**. Excavated from under the Roman city, at a depth of 6m, the Punic sarcophagi date from the 8C BC and have been left in their original positions. A footpath leads north from the necropolis to the **capitol**, a large paved area scattered with broken granite columns. Along the east side are four steps of a 1C **hexastyle temple**. The scant remains of the **Forum Novum**, with its white monochrome mosaic floor, lie to the east of the necropolis. The sea, now 10km away, once lapped the defensive walls of the city. One section, which was reinforced in 47 BC, can be seen to the west, next to the footpath.

Back on Decumanus B, on the east side of Maison de la Cascade, are the remains of **MAISON DES CHAPITEAUX HISTORIÉS**. It takes its name from **two columns**, that remain of an original 12, with historical and mythical scenes carved on the capitals. The carvings are very worn but the figure of

Masion des Chapiteaux Histories

Hercules with his club on his shoulder and the busts of Minerva and Apollo are just about discernible. The house, built of granite from Cap Bon, originally had two storeys and surrounded a central courtyard.

Other parts of the city remain unexcavated. The **Great West Baths**, built in the mid 2C, which once looked out over the sea, are west of the insula. The 1C **theatre** and **amphitheatre** are in the vicinity of the site museum. The **circus**, also dating from the 1C, lies to the east of the museum, but is now no more than a slight depression in the ground.

From Utica, the itinerary continues along the RN337, a narrow and potholed road, for 3km to the modern village of **Utique Nouvelle**. Continue for a further 3km to a left turn signposted to Aousja. After 3km on this poorly surfaced road, turn right onto the MC69. After 2km the road forks left into **Aousja**, 2km beyond which is a junction right to (8km) Ghar el Melh. The road winds towards the coast and then skirts the edge of **Lac de Ghar el Melh**, a shallow lagoon which is cut off from the sea by a spit. Just south of Lac de Ghar el Melh, the Mejerda river, which has its source in Algeria 365km away, empties into the sea.

> Lieutenant Colonel R.L. Playfair wrote in his *Handbook of Algeria and Tunis* (1878): 'The Mejerda is none other than the famed Bagradas, on the bank of which took place the combat between the army of Attilius Regulus and the monstrous serpent, 225 years before Christ. They besieged it with *ballista* and implements of war, as one would have done a city. It was 120ft long and its skin and jaws were preserved in a temple at Rome.'

GHAR EL MELH, a small fishing village with three fortresses, lies on the slopes of the Jebel Nadour hills, on the north side of the lagoon. From the 15C, up until silt deposits carried by the Mejerda river eventually filled the lagoon during the 18C, it was an important port and a notorious base for pirates. Nowadays the shore is some 50m from the village and the shallow water is choked with seaweed, although this has not stopped the development of holiday villas in the surrounding hills.

As the road comes down into the village, the first of the three fortresses is passed to the right. Now the seat of the National Guard, this well-preserved **Ottoman fortress** stands on a square ground plan with low towers at each corner and has an arched gateway. The main road, **Avenue Habib Bourguiba**, dips down to a small square where there is a café, before passing through a **vaulted tunnel**. On the left, as you come out of the tunnel, there is a small restaurant, serving very reasonable food.

A little further down Avenue Habib Bourguiba, the **second fortress** is on the right. Dating from the 17C, the orange stone of the fortress, with its four black-and-white painted arches, has been unsympathetically restored.

On the opposite side of the road, directly opposite the second fortress, stands a small 17C **mosque** with a green tiled dome and a square minaret. Next to it is a **tomb** set back from the road behind black railings and a row of **ablution fountains** beneath a colonnade.

Walk down **Rue des Martyrs**, which descends steeply from the left side of the second fortress, and enter the **port** through a vaulted passage on the left. The port, enclosed by a wall, has an impressive arcade of 17 wide arches, most of which have been converted into lock-up boat workshops. It was built as part of the arsenal complex initiated by Ahmet Bey in 1837, but never put to use due to the silting up of the harbour. A few small fishing boats now rest in the shallow water where corsair galleys once anchored. In 1654, the harbour was the scene of an attack led by the British Admiral Blake which destroyed nine corsair boats and most of the port.

Leaving the port by the arched gateway at the end of the colonnade, the **third fortress** is on the opposite side of the main road. Now whitewashed and partly inhabited, the fortress once served as a prison. It has a fine, stone horseshoe-arch portal with an **Arabic inscription** above, but the interior is dark and dingy, with living quarters surrounding the central courtyard.

Fishing, still one of the main forms of livelihood at Ghar el Melh, is centred around the modern harbour on a mole at the mouth of the Lac de Ghar el Melh, 3km from the harbour. Signposted to Port du Pêche, the road traces the northern shore of the lagoon. The **fishing port**, with its purpose-built fish market, looks out to a small island offshore called **Ile Plane**, and offers good views back to the mainland where rocky hills sweep up from the sea.

An excursion from the Port du Pêche road leads to the sandy beach of **Sidi Ali el Mekki**. The turning is on the left, 1km before reaching the port. It leads down a 4km dirt track which is only negotiable at speeds less than 30kph. The beach, which is 2km long, is named after the marabout, Sidi Ali el Mekki, whose whitewashed **tomb** sits on a shoulder of the hills above. The white walls are merely a façade for the chamber that is hewn from the rock behind. The beach is wide and the water is shallow, making it a suitable place for children, although it can be a windswept spot at times. A holiday complex has long been planned, but as yet there is no more than a handful of villas, a café and a few beach huts. The bay is enclosed by the headland of **Cap Farina**, on the skyline of which is the **tomb** of the marabout Sidi Haj Bareck.

Cap Farina, known in ancient times as Promontorium Pulchri, was an important boundary. In the pact of 507 BC between Carthage and Rome, Roman vessels were allowed no further south than here, except in the extreme circumstances of a storm. The pact was breached in 204 BC by Publius Cornelius Africanus Scipio who landed on Cap Farina with 30,000 men before making his headquarters outside Utica in preparation for an attack on Carthage.

There is another fine white sand beach on the other side of Cap Farina, known as Raf Raf. However, there is no road along the coast from Sidi Ali el Mekki and it is necessary to return to Ghar el Melh. From Ghar el Melh take the road back towards Aousja, forking right after 8km onto the PK3. After 1km the road crosses over the small river Oued Saadane, between gently rolling hills where some of the best table grapes in Tunisia are grown. Continue for 4km to the coast, from where the road forks right to Raf Raf (3km). At the town outskirts the road forks, the left fork leading to the town, and the right to the beach.

Raf Raf, a popular seaside town, is packed with Tunisian holidaymakers during the summer. The town lies on the slopes of Jebel Nadour looking down on a sandy, crescent-shaped beach below and the striking, wind-eroded **Island of Pilau**, which lies just offshore. The town is renowned for its embroidered bead-work, which is worn in the local traditional costume. The town's main livelihood is the tourist trade and every year new developments gradually spread further.

From Raf Raf, retrace the 3km back to the fork and keep straight on for 10km to **Rass Jebel**. This large agricultural town sits in the coastal plain 3km from the sea. It is the market-place for the surrounding farmers who produce a wide range of crops from potatoes to vines. Friday, market day, is when the town is at its most animated, with market stalls lining the narrow streets and causing mayhem with the traffic. Rass Jebel is also a centre for textiles and has a French-run Lee Cooper factory which is passed on the right at the town outskirts. The road passes through the centre of Rass Jebel and continues westwards along the coast.

At 8km from Rass Jebel the road divides into a three-way junction above which stands the hill village of **Metline**, thought to be the site of Roman Beneventum. The right fork leads to **Cap Zebib**. The road winds through ancient olive groves and terraced hills for 3km before ending at a small harbour. Tuna is fished here; in spring large nets are laid ready to catch the fish on their way to their spawning ground. The nets are usually drawn in during May and June, and the fish are slaughtered at the quayside.

Head back to the junction and take the MC70 left to Bizerte. The road crosses two small rivers before climbing up into pretty hills where fields of grain and vineyards are divided by hedges of prickly pear.

> The prickly pear, or Barbary fig as it is also known, is not an indigenous plant but was introduced by Christopher Columbus. It grows to a height of 2–5m and has bright yellow flowers which form ovoid fruit from April to July. It is easily propagated and roots quickly, making it a suitable hedging plant which has the added advantage of being prickly and so keeping out animals.

Elalia, which is 6km from the junction, lies to the left of the road on the slopes of Jebel Hakina. Occupying the Roman site of Uzalis, the village was built by Andalucians during the 17C, following the mass expulsion of 'Moriscos' from Christian Spain. The Muslim refugees were at first housed in Tunis, and then dispersed throughout north Tunisia. Although the number of Andalucian inhabitants shrank in the 19C due to high taxation, the physical type persists and you may notice in Elalia that some people have fairer complexions. The village's buildings have also retained some Hispanic character with their monopitch pantile roofs and decoratively studded doors. The Andalucians also introduced the cultivation of thistles in the area; these were used for the felting of chechias, the traditional red hats.

Continue on the MC70 for a further 8.5km, passing through El Azib, to the main highway GP8. Turn right onto the GP8 in the direction of Bizerte which is a further 9km. The GP8 follows the eastern edge of the vast lake, **Lac de**

Bizerte, which is lined with platforms and jetties for fishing. At the far side of the lake, on its western shore, smoke belches from the factories at Menzel Bourguiba. The arsenal for the French naval base of Bizerte was situated here; the buildings are now used as factories. At 6.5km from the junction with the MC70, there is a turning on the right to ****Remel Plage**. The road to Remel Plage heads through a wood, where there is a hotel and campsite, for 3km before arriving at a car park in front of a large dune, at the other side of which is a wide sandy beach.

6 · Bizerte and the Cap Blanc Promontory

BIZERTE

Bizerte is approached by a steel swing bridge, finished in 1980, the central section of which lifts up so that ships can pass through the 244m wide canal to the port. The main industrial port in the region, its chief exports are oil, iron ore, cereals, cork and cement. The town itself lies to the north of the canal and has two distinct parts: the French colonial town which is laid out on a grid plan, and the labyrinthine Arabic town which surrounds a picturesque harbour. Thomas Hammerton wrote of Bizerte in 1959 as 'profoundly depressing. The natives looked seedy and down at heel to a degree I saw nowhere else in Tunisia, and their portion of the town resembles them. I wandered through the town in search of any surviving relics of the fastidious Hafsid ruler El Mostaneer Bihillar, who, in the middle of the 13C, built a palace here amidst gorgeous gardens, but nothing is left'. Since then tourism has had limited impact on the town centre which remains in a rather decrepit but charming condition, concentrating more on the corniche north of the town.

- **Airline companies**. Tunis Air, 76 Ave Habib Bourguiba, tel. (02) 432201.

- **Maritime companies**. Navitour, 29 Rue de Algerie, tel. (02) 431440.

- **Railway station**. SNCFT, Rue de Russie, tel. (02) 431317. Lines for Menzel Bourguiba–Mateur–Tunis, Mateur–Beja–Jendouba, Sejenane–Nefta–Tabarka.

- **Bus station**. SRTB, Quai Tarak Ibn Ziad, tel. (02) 431317. Services to the Corniche, Menzel Jemil, Tunis. SNT, Rue d'Alger, tel. (02) 431222. Services to Mateur–Menzel Bourguiba–Tabarka, Ras Jebel–Raf Raf–Ghar el Melh.

- **Louage stations**. Rue d'Alger, and under swing bridge. Services to Ain Draham, Ghar el Melh, Raf Raf, Rass Jebel, Remel Plage, Menzel Bourguiba, Tabarka, Tunis.

- **Taxi**. *Taxi-bébé*, Ave Habib Bourguiba.

- **Hotels**. There are half a dozen hotels in Bizerte. Those in the town centre, near the medina, are cheap but not recommended. More upmarket, but at the cheap end of the middle range bracket, is the *Hotel Continental* on 29 Rue de 2 Mars 1934. There is also a newly opened hotel at the western end of Ave du President Habib Bourguiba. There are several larger hotels on Rue de la Corniche, 2–3km from the town, and a youth hostel, tel. (02) 431608.

- **Restaurants**. The best restaurants in Bizerte are outside the town with the smart hotels on Rue de la Corniche. They are mainly fish restaurants and so prices are quite steep. In Bizerte itself there is not much to choose from; the *Sport Nautique* on Quai Tarak Ibn Ziad in the French part of the town is amongst the best.

- **Shopping**. Along the west side of the port there is a branch of ONAT (Office National de l'Artisanat), which sells ceramics, textiles and furniture at rates fixed by the state. Monoprix is at the western end of Rue d'Espagne.

- **Post office**. 6 Avenue d'Algerie. Rue el Medina. Place Pasteur.

- **Tourist information**. Commissariat Régional, 1 Rue de Constantinople, tel. (02) 432703.

- **Medical care**. Hôpital Régionale Habib Bourguiba, Rue Saussier, tel. (02) 40231422.

- **Festivals**. Festival of Bizerte, July–August. Sidi el Bechir, first Thursday of September.

- **Entertainment**. Cafés around the old harbour. Promenade beneath palms along Quai Tarik Ibn Ziad. Discos and bars in hotels along Rue de la Corniche.

- **Children**. There are two children's playgrounds: one in the French town on Place du 7 Novembre; the other at the southern end of the old harbour, just south of ONAT.

- **Sports**. Watersport facilities at Club Nautique, Quai Tarak Ibn Ziad, tel. (02) 432262, and on the beach in front of Nador Hotel, Rue de la Corniche. Horse riding is organised on the beach between the Nador and El Kebir hotels on Rue de la Corniche.

History

Bizerte was first settled by the Phoenicians who dug a canal from the Lac du Bizerte to the sea, forming a sheltered port. In 310 BC the settlement was taken by Agathocles of Syracuse, and, along with Utica, served as a base for the rebuilding of his fleet. The Romans gave it the status of a colony and named it Hippo Diarrhytus. However, the mountains that had protected the Phoenicians from tribal invasions were a barricade to inland transport in Roman times and prevented the colony's expansion.

In 661 Bizerte was taken by Arabs and renamed Benzert. In the 9C the Aghlabids rebuilt the town and over the next few hundred years Bizerte was endowed with fine palaces and gardens. The 16C saw the start of the Turco–Spanish struggles with the corsair Barbarossa taking the town from the Spanish in 1534. The town changed hands many times, ending up an official corsair base under Youssef Dey in 1610.

The French ensconced themselves in Bizerte in 1882, establishing a naval base. The opening of the Suez Canal gave Bizerte a strategic importance for the French who were vying with the British for control of the trade route to India.

In November 1942 German troops were parachuted into Bizerte, to secure it as a base from which to forestall the Allied advance from Algeria. After the Allied success six months later Bizerte fell once more into the hands of the French who held onto it even after they had relinquished control of the rest of Tunisia. After the hijacking of a French plane in Tunisian airspace and the bombing of a village in the late 1950s, fighting broke out between French and Tunisian forces in Bizerte in 1961. The Tunisian militia shot at a French helicopter in the naval base, to which the French replied with a ferocious assault on the local Tunisian garrison, killing 1300 people. The eventual withdrawal of the French on the 15 October 1963 is still celebrated as a public holiday, the Fête de L'Évacuation. The dead are remembered by a monumental arch, Monument of the Martyrs, on a hill-top south-west of the town.

The most attractive part of Bizerte is the **old harbour**, filled with brightly painted fishing boats and surrounded by whitewashed houses and cafés. Until the French colonial period, the harbour was split into two parts with an island at the centre. The French filled in the northern part, forming what is now **Place Lahedine Bouchoucha**, which is lined with low houses backing onto the medina. At the south end of Place Lahedine Bouchoucha there is a big, covered fish-market, to one side of which is the **Rbaa Mosque**. The mosque has a severe, modern façade and a very large square minaret topped by a balcony.

At the north end of Place Lahedine Bouchoucha, on the corner of the road that leads between the medina and the crenellated kasbah, is the **fountain of Youssef Dey**. Built in 1642, it comprises a horseshoe arch, outlined in black and white, which is set in white marble. The fountain is now dry, but the Arabic inscription in the centre of the arch tells passers-by that the water is to make Bizerte more enjoyable before the time comes to drink the water of Paradise.

Turn left after the fountain, following the west wall of the **kasbah**, to a simple stone gateway on the right. A vaulted passage leads through the walls to a small square, at one side of which is the **Kasbah Mosque**. Built in the 17C as a Hanefite mosque, it has black and white bands decorating the central horseshoe arch, and a single window painted in brilliant turquoise. The squat minaret is square, topped by a conical green roof which rests on a decorative band of tiles. From here, a warren of squalid alleyways, some vaulted, others spanned by arches, weaves through the kasbah. To view the kasbah from less close quarters head for the artillery terrace on the north bastion.

Return to the kasbah gate and continue a little further along the west wall of the kasbah, before turning left onto **Rue des Armuriers**. This narrow cobbled street lined with tailors' and shoemakers' shops is the main artery through the medina. On the left is the **Zaouia Sidi el Mostari** with its simple whitewashed façade and horseshoe arch. It was built in 1672 as a college and has a pair of shallow domes over the lecture halls. Next to it is the **Great Mosque**, hidden behind a retaining wall. Tourists must be content with a view of the 17C octagonal minaret which is decorated with tiles and has an attractive overhanging balcony. Continuing along Rue des Armuriers, take the next right into the **Souk des Forgerons**, a narrow street of blacksmiths' workshops.

Return to the kasbah walls and continue to **Place du Marché** which is filled by a café. It lies at the north-west corner of the kasbah, from where the road heads to the foot of the hill upon which the **Spanish fort** is built. An impressive wall climbs almost vertically up the hill, as does the footpath, to the ruined fort, to the right of which is a large **cemetery** with cypress trees. The fort was built by a Turkish corsair named El Eulj Ali, between 1570 and 1573, to defend the city against the Spanish. It was restored in the 17C by Youssef Dey, but is now totally derelict and there is little to see except the ruined walls and a few cannons. It does, however, offer a commanding view over the town and lake, and in the summer it is the venue for theatrical performances.

From the north-west corner of the kasbah, follow the road below the cemetery before turning right to the **Mosque des Andalous** which stands in an Andalucian quarter that was settled in the 15–17C. Its light blue doors with their swirling designs in black studs are typically Andalucian, as is the mosque's minaret which is square and has a balcony topped by a green tiled roof.

Bizerte's museum is housed in the small fortress, **Sidi el Henni**, at the mouth of the harbour, opposite the south-east bastion of the kasbah. The entrance is on Boulevard Habib Bougatfa. The fortress was built in the 17C at the same time as the kasbah to guard the entrance to the harbour and has a small mosque with a square minaret. The museum, **Musée de la Mer**, has a dozen or so fish tanks with a wide variety of fish on display. On the first floor there is a pleasant terrace with a small café looking out to sea.

A scenic excursion can be made from Bizerte to the **Cap Blanc promontory**. Leave the town along Boulevard Habib Bougatfa and fork right to the bridge that crosses the mouth of the old harbour. Fork right again after the bridge, following signs along Rue de la Corniche to '*quai*'. After 2.5km fork right again and follow the promenade for a further 2.5km to where the road forks right at a coastguard's tower. After 1km fork right again to the headland, where the road ends after 2km in front of a National Guard building. The headland, with its sandy coves and white rocks, is the most northerly point of Africa. From Cap Blanc either retrace the road back to Bizerte, or make a circular route, heading back via the hamlet of Nadhour, through the pine-clad hills of Jebel Khara.

7 · Bizerte to Tabarka

Bizerte to Tabarka is 147km via Menzel Bourguiba, Parc National de l'Ichkeul, Mateur, Sejenane and Nefza. After Mateur the road is winding and the surface poor. An alternative route of 125km on minor roads via Teskraia travels closer to the coast before joining the main road at Sejenane. There are two buses a day from Bizerte to Tabarka, calling at Menzel Bourguiba and Mateur. Louages depart more regularly, up to five times a day. The railway line to Tabarka is closed at present.

Leave Bizerte by the RN11 in the direction of Menzel Bourguiba. At 3km from the centre, the modern arch of the **Monument of Martyrs**, which commemorates the Tunisians killed in Bizerte by the French in 1961, is passed on the right. A dual carriageway passes out through the industrial zone of Bizerte and then through military land. After 9km the route forks left in the direction of Menzel Bourguiba, passing through the village of (8km) Louata before reaching the marshes of **Lac Ichkeul**. The road passes over the **Tinja river**, which connects Lac Ichkeul to Lac du Bizerte, and over the railway twice before reaching a (1.5km) junction on the outskirts of Menzel Bourguiba, an industrial town with an ironworks. Keep straight on in the direction of Mateur, skirting the marshy edge of Lac Ichkeul. On the far side of the lake, the steep slopes of Jebel Ichkeul rise up from its northern shore to a summit of 508m. After crossing the (4km) railway there is a track immediately on the right which leads into the nature preserve of Lac Ichkeul.

The **Parc National de l'Ichkeul**, as the preserve is known, is protected by UNESCO as a wetland on the migration route between Africa and Europe. Aquatic birds including flamingoes, widgeons, pochards, shovellers, coots and white-headed ducks all touch down here, while other wildlife, including wild boar, deer, porcupine, hyenas, jackals, hares and foxes, inhabit the mountainside. The track heads through the parkland for 6km, where water buffalo graze, and in springtime storks can be seen. The park gates are at the end of the track on the right, where there is a ticket office (open daily, 08.00–18.00). The track continues from here for a further 3km along the base of Jebel Ichkeul and up through olive groves to a small natural history museum, and a birdwatching platform, the best period being between November and February.

From the Parc National de l'Ichkeul return to the RN11 and continue in the direction of Mateur. After 9km turn right onto the GP7. The road crosses the Oued Joumine river which drains into the marshes of Lac Ichkeul before reaching Mateur (1km). Along with Beja, **Mateur**, an agricultural town, is known as the 'gates of the Barbary' having been ruled by Berber tribes for most of its history. The nomadic lifestyle of the Berbers is rich in tradition but has little architecture, as is testified by Mateur, which is not endowed with any fine buildings, but has a lively Friday market, where you may see Berber women wearing their traditional costumes.

From Mateur follow signs to Tabarka on the GP7, crossing the Ras el Ain river. The road winds through grain fields, passing through the village of (8km) **Ghazela** where there is a petrol station (the last until Sejenane). After the Oued el Gous river the road climbs up into the hills, a patchwork of olives, grain and thistles.

At 3km further on is the turning right to **Cap Serrat** (40km), where there is an attractive sandy bay and a small village, although it is a lengthy excursion with the last 16km on a dirt track.

The GP7 continues through the hills to the hamlet of (2.5km) **Rekoub** and winds on up to (2.5km) **Jefna**, a hamlet at the summit. From here, the road starts its tortuous descent, crossing over the railway and then the (4km) Oued Melah river. After 10km the road joins the valley of the Oued Mograt river which gradually opens out into a plain, at the edge of which is the village of (6.5km) Sejenane.

Sejenane, a Berber village, is well-known for its pottery. Most of it, which is made mainly by women, consists of white-glazed animals, figures and vessels, decorated with simple dark red lines. There are pottery shops either side of the wide square at the village centre.

From Sejenane, the GP7 traverses the plain to the cork forests at the other side and crosses over the (14km) railway.

Just after the railway a tortuous excursion can be taken to the coast to **Sidi Mechrig**, reached by a 17km dirt track. There is a large sandy beach here overlooked by the scant remains of a Roman bath.

The GP7 continues past an open cast zinc mine to the mining villages of (1.5km) **Tamra** and (1.5km) **Sidi Driss**, after which the road joins the Sejenane river valley which is lined with cork oaks and oleanders.

A (1km) right turn leads to **Cap Negro**, a coastal excursion of 20km. The track, which is really only suitable for four-wheel drive vehicles, leads to a coral factory that formed part of the trading station ceded to the French by a commercial treaty in 1666. It was reclaimed in 1741 by Ali Pasha and is now the seat of the National Guard. Nearby there is a small but good sandy beach.

The GP7 crosses the railway on a narrow (1.5km) bridge and passes a cemetery, set in an olive grove where traditional Berber grave chambers, *haouaret*, have been found dating from the 2C BC. The domed tombs on the right side of the road are the burial places of marabouts. The road then crosses two rivers, the Oued Hamma and the Boudzenna, before reaching (6.5km) Nefza.

Nefza is a small Berber town with very little to keep you except for a lively Wednesday market where you stand a good chance of seeing traditional Berber costume.

> Jewellery is an important part of Berber costume, and pieces are passed on from generation to generation. Typically made from silver, it is decorated with stones which once would have been semi-precious, such as yellow amber; today this has been replaced by plastic. Silver is used in preference to gold because it is '*baraka*' or brings good luck, as does henna which Berber women use lavishly.

After passing through the main street, leave the town by turning right at the junction with the clock. The GP7 continues to wind through the hills, where, just after crossing the (8km) Oued Melah river, there is a right turn to **Plage**

Zaouaria, a sandy beach, which is reached by making a 13km excursion on a small road through the pine forest.

The road continues through eucalyptus and cork, olive and oleander, for 6km before entering the Jendouba district. From the hamlet of (2km) **Ain Sobah**, the GP7 starts its descent to the coast. At (13km) **Ras Rajel** it passes a **Commonwealth War Cemetery**. The 500 soldiers buried here lost their lives during an assault on Tunis, which after a month's bitter fighting ended in stalemate on 24 December 1942 with all transport ground to a halt in deep mud. The turning to Tabarka airport is also at Ras Rajel.

After a further 6.5km, the GP7 joins the coastal plain. The road follows the banks of the Oued el Kebir river before crossing over it into (3km) Tabarka, the centre of which is reached by turning right along Avenue Habib Bourguiba to a gardens presided over by the seated statue of Bourguiba.

TABARKA

Tabarka, just 13km from the Algerian border, is a small fishing town gradually being surrounded by tourist developments. A yacht marina is being built at the harbour with arcades of shops, restaurants and hotels, and along the coast there are numerous large hotels. The centre, however, remains untouched, with its red-roofed buildings looking across a sandy bay to a romantic ruined castle.

- **Bus station**. SNT and SNTRI, Rue du Peuple, tel. (08) 644404. Services to Beja–Tunis, Sejenane–Mateur–Menzel Bourguiba–Bizerte, Ain Draham–Jendouba–El Kef. SRT, Ave Habib Bourguiba, tel. (08) 644097. Services to Mateur–Tunis, Ain Draham–Jendouba, Beja–Jendouba.

- **Louage station**. From the gardens on Ave Habib Bourguiba.

- **Taxis**. From the gardens on Ave Habib Bourguiba.

- **Hotels**. There are hotels both in the town and on the coast, 2km to the south. The cheaper hotels are in the town. The *Mammia*, two blocks up from Ave Habib Bourguiba, is at the bottom end of the market, but is clean and pleasant. The *Hotel de France*, at the north end of Ave Habib Bourguiba, is where Bourguiba stayed when he was exiled here in 1952. It has seen better days but is reasonably priced. *Les Aiguilles*, opposite the Hotel de France, charges more, but has been newly refurbished and is very clean and comfortable. The *Mimosa Hotel*, up on the hill above the town, is the most expensive, but it has a good reputation and offers excellent views. The hotels along the coast are connected to the town by a regular mini-train service. They are all in the upper-price bracket, designed to accommodate package tours, and have swimming pools and other sports facilities. The *Morjane* is one of the largest and has three tennis courts in addition to a swimming pool. Further hotels will open shortly with the completion of the tourist complex, known as Montazah, around the yacht marina.

- **Restaurants**. Fish is very good in Tabarka, particularly the prawns which are served in large portions at reasonable prices. Lobster is another local speciality. Both the *Les Aiguilles* and *Hotel de France* have licensed restaurants and fixed-price menus. There are other restaurants along Ave Habib Bourguiba, including *Les Agriculteurs* at No. 4.

- **Shopping**. Tarbaka has a large concentration of jewellery shops selling coral.

- **Post office**. Rue Hédi Cheker, tel. (08) 644417.

- **Tourist information**. Antenne du Tourisme, 32 Ave Habib Bourguiba, tel. (08) 644491.

- **Medical care**. Hôpital Régionale, Rue de Calle, tel. (08) 644023.

- **Festivals**. International Festival, Coral Market and Université de l'Été, July–August.

- **Entertainment**. Both the Hotel de France and the Hotel des Aiguilles have bars and will serve drinks outside. Next to the Aiguilles, in the direction of the port, there is a men's drinking bar. For beaches there is the sandy bay at the end of Ave Habib Bourguiba, or the wide sandy stretch to the east of the town along the Route Touristique.

- **Children**. Riding along the coast in the mini-train is popular.

- **Sports**. Yachting Club de Tabarka, Port, tel. (08) 644478, and Loisirs de Tabarka, Rue Ali Zouaoui, tel. (08) 6792815, organise deep sea-diving. Club de Chasse, Route d'Ain Draham, tel. (08) 644138, organises hunting in the mountains. An 18-hole golf course, tel. (08) 644321, set in 110 hectares of pine forest, overlooks the coast on Route Touristique.

History

Known as Thabraca in ancient times, Tabarka was founded in the 5C BC by Phoenicians. The name, however, with its 'th' is typical Berber, suggesting it had earlier Berber origins. The Romans kept the same name and developed a prosperous port from where the precious Chemtou marble was exported to Italy. It also exported wood for building, minerals including iron and lead, cereals, olive oil and wild beasts for the circus; all of these came from the rich hinterland which, even during the Byzantine rule of Constantine, remained under Berber control. During the 3C Thabraca became an important centre of Christianity and was the site of a large basilica. Mosaic workshops were established in the town (their output, including many tomb mosaics, can be seen in Salle 5 of Bardo Museum in Tunis).

From the 7C onwards the town was the target of Arab attacks, but rose to importance as a port again in the 16C under the Ottoman corsair, Barbarossa. In 1541, however, it was arranged by Emperor Charles V of Spain that Barbarossa should cede the town to the Genoese banking family, the Lomellini, as ransom for the corsair's deputy, Dragut, who had been captured by the Genoese off the coast of Corsica and had spent the last four years as a galley slave. The Lomellini built a fortress on the Island of Tabarka and in 1542 Charles V gave them the rights to use the port for the trade of coral from the beds off the Tabarka coast. The Lomellini family also traded in slaves, taking 3 per cent commission for holding them prisoner in their fortress. In 1741, to prevent the French claiming the town, the Husainid Bey of Tunis, Ali Pasha, took control, selling the

Genoese into slavery. In 1781, however, the French gained the sole rights to all the coral beds along the coast from Tabarka to Tripoli and by the 19C Tabarka was a popular French resort and hunting centre.

The bay of Tabarka, with its sandy beach and harbour, is overlooked by a **fortress** built by the Genoese in the 16C. It stands at the summit of a small island which is connected to the mainland by a 400m causeway. A road, signposted to the Fort Genois, leads across the causeway and up to the castle walls where there is a car park. From the car park follow the footpath up to the east wall of the fortress, passing beneath an arch that has been cut away. The footpath ends at a blue painted door decorated with black studs which leads into the ruined interior of the castle where there are excellent views. Looking across to the headland on the west side of the bay is the circular tower of **Borj Messaoud**, originally a cistern, but converted into a fortress by merchant traders from Pisa and Marseilles in the 12C.

Back in the town some very scant remains of Roman Thabraca can be seen on the hill above the *Hotel de France*, on Rue de Khroumire. There is a paved area with the low-lying walls of shops at either side. A little further up the hill is **La Basilique**, an ex-basilica, which is only open when exhibitions are held during the summer festival. It was originally a cistern, built by the Romans in the 3C with a capacity of 2700 cubic metres, which supplied both the baths and fountains with water. In the 19C, the missionary order of the Pères Blancs had the cistern converted into a basilica with three aisles. There is a small **garden** at the foot of the basilica walls which contains pieces of stone masonry dating from the Roman era.

A promenade leads from Avenue Habib Bourguiba along the west side of the bay to **Les Aiguilles**, a group of monolithic rocks. Standing to a height of 20–25m, these natural pinnacles have been sculpted by the wind into dramatic shapes. Off the coast, on a very clear day you may see the volcanic island known as **La Galite**. Measuring 5.3km by 2km, it is inhabited by fishermen who catch lobster, and is surrounded by six small islets, the largest of which, **Galitons**, is inhabited by monk seals. There are no regular ferry services, and if you wish to visit, a visitor's permit must first be obtained from the ministry.

On the road to Ain Draham, 8km from Tabarka, there is a cork museum, the **Musée du Liège**, (open summer, daily, 08.00–12.30, 14.00–17.30, winter, 08.00–12.30, 14.00–18.00). It is situated on the premises of a cork factory and gives detailed explanations of how cork is processed and manufactured with examples of the machinery that is used. There are also cork souvenirs on sale.

III MEJERDA VALLEY AND HILLS

8 · Tabarka to El Kef

Tabarka to El Kef via Ain Draham and Jendouba is 121km. Initially mountainous, the roads improve in the Mejerda valley, where excursions can be made to ancient Bulla Regia and Chemtou. There are two direct buses to El Kef, and four buses to Jendouba, from where there are ten buses a day to El Kef.

Leave Tabarka by the Ain Draham road, the GP17, by following signs to the Musée du Liège from the main roundabout on Avenue Habib Bourguiba. Heading south across the coastal plain, the road crosses over the Oued el Kebir river which has its source in Algeria, the border being 10km away. After 6.5km the road starts its tortuous ascent through the Khroumerie Hills, passing through the hamlet of (2.5km) **Khadharia**. The woods covering the hills are mostly cork oak, and you will see signs of the bark having been harvested from the lower trunks. During the summer season objects made from cork are sold at the roadside.

The road passes very close to the Algerian border at the village of (10km) **Baboucha** which lies above a eucalyptus forest on the strip of neutral territory that divides the two countries.

From here, an excursion of 10km takes you along the border to the Roman spa resort of **Hammam Bourguiba**, in the Ouled Barbar valley, once a retreat of the ex-President. A three-star hotel, treatment centre and chalet complex has been built over three natural hot springs which rise at a temperature of 50°C.

The GP17 continues to wind up above Baboucha, where lions were hunted up until the 19C, to (4km) **AIN DRAHAM**. This mountain resort, 800m above sea level, with its steep-roofed chalets surrounded by fir trees, first became popular in the French colonial era for hunting. It is still used as a hunting centre (mostly for boars, the last panther having been shot in 1932), but serves mainly as a retreat from the heat of the coast. When it is 40°C on the coast it is typically only 28°C in the mountains. During the winter, it is one of the few places in Tunisia where snow falls. Due to the cooler temperatures, **hiking** is quite popular, particularly to the **Col des Ruines ridge**, 500m in the direction of Tabarka and left for a kilometre, from where a footpath climbs the ridge to the summit. A more challenging hike is up the 1014m **Jebel Bir**. The footpath starts from the town centre and leads up through an ex-barracks to the summit from where one can see west Algeria and the Oued el Kebir valley.

At the centre of the resort, street cafés surround an elegant minaret with a green tiled top. The outskirts, with their recent developments are less picturesque, but there are several hotels and numerous villas for rent.

From Ain Draham, follow the GP17 in the direction of Jendouba. The road heads down, passing a (3km) **spring** and a (2km) **sports complex** before climbing up to a colonial-style hunting lodge surrounded by oak trees, the (2km) *Hotel des Chenes*, which is on the left. As the road starts to wind down, the turning to the (1.5km) **Ben M'Tir dam** is passed on the left.

The GP17 continues to wind down through cork oak forests to (11km) **Fernana**, a sprawling village named after a revered cork oak that once stood here, which was said to have had oracular powers. Amongst other predictions it was able to tell the local inhabitants the amount of revenue they should declare for tax purposes.

Continuing along the GP17, the mountains diminish as the Mejerda river approaches. After 15km the road meets the MC59 which goes left for the ruined city of Bulla Regia (3km) and right for Chemtou (16km) with its Roman quarries.

The excursion to **Chemtou** is along a narrow, undulating road that deteriorates into a rough, stony track for the last 2km. The **Site Archeologique du Chemtou** is signposted on the left, 150m down a track which ends at the foot of the quarries.

History
The hillside was first quarried in the 2C BC by the Numidian King Masinissa, who is said to have discovered the marble while building an altar on the summit of Jebel Chemtou. The marble was first imported to Rome in 78 BC although a Roman settlement was not established here until 27 BC. Colonia Augusta Numidica Simmithus, as the settlement was known, remained a quarrying centre (providing marble for Augustus' forum in Rome and Hadrian's Villa, Tivoli), up until the decline of the Byzantine Empire in the 6C. Factories were built on site to process the marble, cutting it into slabs for facings, and carving columns and small statues. During the 19C the quarries were once more put to use and it is only recently that they have been totally abandoned.

A bridlepath leads up the hill into the bowl of the **quarry**, where in Roman times the precious *antico giallo*, or Numidian marble, was extracted and shipped from Tabarka to Rome, or sent by boat down the river to Carthage. Overlooking the quarry are the ruins of a **19C church**, which has an arched door below a circular window. From the south-west side of the church there is a good view of Roman Simmithus, the remains of which extend to the deep banks of the Mejerda river. The piers of a **2C Roman bridge** dating from the reign of Emperor Trajan, which carried the main road from Tabarka to El Kef, can be seen in the river. The bridge itself was washed away by floods in the 4C. Nearby the bridge are the walls of a **Roman watermill**, which was used for grinding corn.

The foundations of the **Numidian altar** lie on the hill summit above the quarry. Dating from the 2C BC, it was either commissioned by King Masinissa or his son Micipsa, and was originally adorned with Hellenistic statues. It stood to a height of 10m, on a base that measured 12.15m by 5.64m. During the Roman era it was the site of a temple to Saturn which in the 4C was transformed into a basilica. Little remains of these structures but there are good views, and the faint outline of an amphitheatre can be made out at the east end of the Roman town.

The **labour camp** where Chemtou marble was manufactured and the workers lived is unexcavated and lies to the north of the hill-top sanctuary. Once surrounded by high walls, it covered an area of 4 hectares, and had workshops and housing arranged around a series of courtyards.

Returning to the track at the foot of the quarry, resume the MC59 and continue south-west for a further 200m to the ruins of a large **baths** and the nearby piers of an **aqueduct** that supplied the water.

Continue for a further 200m along the MC59 to the **theatre** walls on the left. It is one of the few free-standing Roman theatres in North Africa, but only a small portion of the seating remains.

Just south of the theatre is the large apse of a **nymphaeum**, opposite which stands one of the piers of the aqueduct, built to supply water to the town when the local source dried up. A little further south is another apse which is part of a vast **basilica**, last used in the 6C. The basilica stands on the site of the Roman **forum**, which has recently been excavated, revealing a row of small chambers along the north side and a large circular recess at the centre.

The unexcavated ruins of **Thuburnica**, a colony established by Roman veterans in the 1C BC under Marius, lie 14km west of Chemtou, along the MC59. Before considering the excursion, however, be warned that road conditions on the MC59 deteriorate and necessary provisions, including water, should be carried. Spread amongst olive trees, the most impressive ruins are a two-storey mausoleum, two triumphal arches and a 3C temple dedicated to Mercury. There are also the remains of cisterns, baths, an aqueduct and a Byzantine fortress.

BULLA REGIA
Bulla Regia, 3km from the GP17 crossroads, is outstanding for its excellently preserved underground villas, built by the Romans to escape from the summer heat. The site (open summer, daily, 07.00–19.00, winter, daily, 08.30–17.30), set at the foot of the parched slopes of Jebel Rebia (627m), includes a museum, which is on the right, along with a car park.

History
The site dates from the 4C BC when a settlement was built here over the springs of Bulla. It was named Bulla Regia in the 2C BC under the Numidian King Micipsa, who ruled one of the three Numidian kingdoms laid down by the Romans following the death of King Masinissa in 148 BC. By the 1C AD, rid of the Numidian rulers, the city was Romanised and granted the status of a colony by Emperor Hadrian. The cultivation of olives and corn brought wealth to the inhabitants, who, according to the inscriptions uncovered in the underground villas, were mostly of Punic origin. Wealth apparently also brought corruption; passing through here in AD 339, Augustine complained of the moral turpitude of the population and of lurid performances in the theatre. Further evidence of this was found in 1906, when an iron collar was found around the neck of a female skeleton inscribed: *adultera meretrix: tene me qvia fvgavi a Bvlla Regia*

(adulterous prostitute: hold me, because I have run away from Bulla Regia). The city survived until the fall of Byzantine Africa in 647, after which it was never inhabited again.

The ****MUSEUM** holds finds from the excavations which were started in the early 1900s under the Institut National de Tunis and the École Française de Rome. The **first room** has a relief of a Numidian warrior dating from the 2C BC, and portraits taken from coins of the six Numidian kings from 202–45 BC. The **second room** contains **two statues** of 3C Bulla Regians, one of which is headless. The 2C **funerary urn** of Flavia Spica and the 4C circular mosaic depicting Medusa's head are also of note. Adjoining the museum is a small shop selling postcards and books, and there is a café in the garden alongside.

The ****RUINS** lie on the opposite side of the road. Inside the gates on the right is the massive structure of the **Baths of Julia Memnia**. The baths, named after the local dignitary who commissioned them in the 2C, are centred around the frigidarium, a large hall with pools at either end and blind arcades decorating the walls. Along the north and west sides are raised walkways, once porticoed and lined with shops. The whole structure is supported on barrel vaults, constructed of terracotta pipes, a technique peculiar to North Africa. The vaults are constructed with interlocking tubes of terracotta,

BULLA REGIA

0   100 yds

0   100 metres

Maison d'amphitrite

Maison de la Nouvelle Chasse

Maison de la Chasse

Maison de la pêche

Necropolis

Excavator's debris

Spring

Temple of Apollo

Basilicas

Forum

Capitol

Temple of Apollo

Byzantine Fort

Maison du Trésor

Cisterns

Baths of Julia Memnia

Market

Theatrre

Cisterns

Monument in opus reticulatum

Curch of Alexander

South Baths

Museum

striated to make the mortar adhere. Their use avoided the need for scaffolding and produced vaulting that was both quick, easy, light, and had insulating properties.

A footpath, signed 'quartier des maisons', heads north of the baths for 80m to the first of the underground Roman villas, the **MAISON DU TRÉSOR**, on the left. It is named after a hoard of 7C Byzantine gold coins that was found here. From the north side of the house, 17 steps lead down into its cool underground quarters, made up of a mosaic paved corridor, off which are three rooms. The central room, the **triclinium** or dining room, is the largest, measuring 6.70m by 4.60m. It has a fine arched doorway and a geometric floor mosaic around which the seating would have been arranged. The small rooms to either side are less deep, but have their own ventilation ducts and windows. The room to the west of the triclinium was a **bedroom** and the space in the mosaic pavement shows the position of the bed.

Continue for 200m north of the Maison du Trésor along a paved section of road to the main housing area. On the left are the poorly preserved remains of the **Maison du Paon**, which is named after a mosaic of a peacock that was found here. A 120m detour south-west of Maison du Paon takes you to the ruins of two 6C **basilicas**, the largest of which has broken marble columns at either side of a wide central aisle and a full immersion **baptistery font** in the shape of a cross.

Back at Maison du Paon, 50m to the east there is a large mound of excavator's debris which offers good views of the site from its summit. Much of the debris probably came from **MAISON DE LA CHASSE**, a grand villa built 225–250 AD, which stands between the mound and Maison du Paon. The ruins above ground are extensive but hard to make out, with the exception of the main **courtyard** which is surrounded by **red columns**, and measures 8.20m by 9.70m. It is open at the centre to allow light into the rooms below, which are reached by 22 steps that lead down to an exceptionally well-preserved **lower courtyard**. Around it stand nine Corinthian columns with lotus leaf carved capitals, while off the west side a pair of fluted columns flank the entrance to the largest room, the **triclinium**. A richly coloured **mosaic** fills the centre, with plain black-and-white mosaics that would have been covered by seating and tables along the sides. The ceiling is finely vaulted with terracotta tubes, and on the left there is a well. The rooms either side of the triclinium and also off the west side of the courtyard were **bedrooms** and have mosaics that show the positions of the beds.

Adjoining the north side of Maison de la Chasse, forming part of the same insula, is **MAISON DE LA NOUVELLE CHASSE** which has a series of well-preserved **geometric mosaics** in the rooms above ground. Steps lead down into a hallway where there is a niche above an **inscription** in the mosaic floor. The main room, which has a poorly preserved hunting mosaic, is flanked on either side by tiny vaulted chambers.

Head east of Maison de la Nouvelle Chasse along the paved road to **MAISON DE LA PÊCHE**, the oldest house on the site. Steps on the right lead up into the peristyle which is scattered with broken columns. Below it is a **subterranean courtyard**, reached by 18 steps and a **ramp**, which is surrounded by cool walkways and has a **semicircular mosaic basin** on its west side where a fountain once played. In front of it is the **triclinium**, its entrance flanked by a pair of pillars, and its floor decorated with **mosaic** of cupids fishing, riding dolphins and playing the lyre.

From Maison de la Pêche, head north for 120m to ****MAISON D'AM-PHITRITE**. Very little remains above ground but there are fine mosaics in the rooms below. Dating from the Antonine era (138–193), 23 steps lead down to a vaulted hallway which has a **mosaic portrait** of a woman in the centre of the floor and a small niche facing the main room, the triclinium. Flanked by pillars, the **triclinium** contains an excellent mosaic, **the triumph of Venus**, also called Amphitrite. She is depicted riding a sea horse and wearing a halo, while cupids hold her crown, jewel box and mirror. There are rooms to either side of the triclinium, and also two small rooms off the other side of the corridor, all of which have geometric mosaic floors.

Return to Maison de la Pêche and continue along its east side to the end of the insula, from where a footpath leads off left to the site of the **spring** around which the city was founded. The source is now housed, along with a pump, in a stone hut with a circular window, but in Roman times a monumental fountain stood here. From the spring, continue for a further 100m south to the **forum**. Restored in 285, it is now a grassy area, measuring 39m by 26m, overlooked by the crumbling remains of a **basilica** on its east side. Along the north side, preceded by a ditch, is the large paved courtyard of the **TEMPLE OF APOLLO**, which is the earliest structure to survive in Bulla Regia, dating from AD 34. It was rebuilt in the 2C in the North African style and consists of a large courtyard with a small sanctuary off one side. The sanctuary is partly built into the hillside and has broken columns along its façade. **Statue pedestals** with inscriptions stand at either side, but the marble statues of the divine triad— Apollo, Ceres and Aesculapuis—are now in Salle VI of the Bardo Museum.

From the south side of the forum, which is raised by five steps, a paved road leads past the market area on the right. Raised above the road by four steps, the **market** consists of a large paved area scattered with Corinthian capitals that would once have formed part of the market porticoes.

Continuing south along the paved road, the very scant remains of the baths, used by theatre performers in the 4C, are passed on the left. The **THEATRE** is opposite, to the south-east. Built during the reign of Marcus Aurelius (161–180), the present structure dates from the 4C which was when Augustine was said to have preached to the local community here. The huge piers of the outer walls are pierced by two vaulted passageways which lead into the **auditorium**. 60m in diameter, the auditorium is divided into eight sections, but only the lower rows of seating remaining. The **floor** of the orchestra, which has its original Chemtou marble paving, has a **bear mosaic** set into it.

Head along the paved road that leads west from the theatre. On the left are two vast clearings containing various traces of temples, including one which dates from the 2C and was dedicated to Isis. The paved road continues westwards, past the Baths of Julia Memnia with its portico, back to the entrance. Continuing west, beyond the entrance, the paved road passes beneath an arch to a row of barrel-vaulted **cisterns** on the right. From here one can see the well-preserved walls of a Byzantine fortress to the north, which is now used by excavators for storage. To the south of the cisterns, on the opposite side of the MC59, one can see the low-lying walls of the **South Baths**. To the west of the baths are the remains of the **Church of Alexander** which was destroyed by fire.

From Bulla Regia return to the GP17 and continue south in the direction of **Jendouba** which lies on the bank of the Mejerda river. This small provincial town has some basic accommodation and is the centre of public transport in the region.

The GP17 bypasses the town and continues south across the valley bed in the direction of El Kef. The road joins another large river, the Oued Mellegue, which after 12km is crossed by a narrow iron bridge. From here the GP17 climbs up to a plain, at the centre of which is the Baraj Oued Mellegue dam. The village of (14.5km) **Nebeur**, surrounded by olive groves, lies on the edge of the plain, and the road from here climbs for the next 5km. The descent offers fine views across low-lying hills before meeting a (9km) crossroads; here you turn right onto the GP5 which passes through (4km) **Zaafrane** before climbing up towards the rocky mountain of Dyr el Kef and the city of (14km) El Kef.

9 · El Kef

The city of **EL KEF**, crowned by a kasbah, lies on the southern slopes of Dyr el Kef (1084m) at an altitude of 800m, overlooking a vast plain. The plain, formed by the Mellegue river, extends to the Algerian border which is 42km away. The city has the unsettled atmosphere of a border town, somewhat cut off from the rest of Tunisia, and feels neglected. Were the city better cared for, it would be a top destination on tourist itineraries as it has many fine historical buildings.

- **Bus station**. SNTRI, Rue Monji Slim. Services every hour to Jendouba and Tunis. Other destinations: Ain Draham, Bizerte, Gafsa, Kasserine, Maktar, Sbeitla, Tabarka.

- **Louage station**. From the bus station, frequent services to Tunis, Sousse, Jendouba and Kasserine.

- **Hotels**. El Kef has few hotels and restaurants. A luxury hotel is to be opened in the kasbah, but until the project is completed, the best hotel is the *Sibla*, a modern block on Rue Monji Slim, which is dominated by a busy bar. The *Hotel Auberge* on Avenue Habib Bourguiba is worse and also has a noisy bar. The *Hotel de la Source* on Rue Moncef Bey is in the same category, as is *Hotel de la Medina* on Rue Farhat Hached, although it is cleaner than the others.

- **Shopping**. Monoprix, west end of Rue Monji Slim, 500m from the centre. Thursday market on Avenue Habib Bourguiba selling spices and textiles.

- **Post office**. Rue Monji Slim.

■ **Tourist information**. There is no official tourist office, but the ASM (Association for Protection of Medina) office on 7 Place de l'Indépendance helps tourists where they can.

■ **Festivals**. Festival du Chanteuse Saed, May–June. Festival de Jugurtha, biannually, summertime. Festival de Sidi Bou Makhlouf, July.

History

The site of El Kef was inhabited in neolithic times as tools discovered in the vicinity testify. However, the Carthaginians were the first to build here, establishing a fortress town in 450 BC, named Sicca. In 240 BC, Sicca was drawn into the Mercenary War, when Carthage, unwilling to pay their mercenaries after the great losses incurred by the First Punic War, sent the soldiers and their families to the garrison here with the promise of payment to follow. Payment never arrived and the mercenaries revolted, organising themselves into an army to attack Carthage which led to the three-year Mercenary War.

Following the fall of Carthage, Sicca, was annexed by Numidian royalty and remained under their control until the victory of Caesar at Thapsus (46 BC). Augustus made Sicca a colony of veterans in 27 BC, renaming it Sicca Veneria. The name 'Veneria' comes from the famous temple in which the Romans adapted the religious rites of the Carthaginian goddess, Ashtarte, to suit those of Venus. According to the historian Polybius, there was sacred prostitution at the temple and magic rites of fecundity.

During the 2–3C, Sicca Veneria prospered, becoming the seat of a bishop in 256. In the 6C the fortress was rebuilt by the Byzantines, but failed to repel the Arab invasions of the 7C which led to the town's destruction.

The modern part of El Kef was built by the French under the Protectorate on the site of ancient Sicca Veneria which was razed to the ground in the process. The town lies either side of a gulley, at the head of which is the site of the **spring**, known as **Ras el Ain**, upon which the ancient city was founded. Steps lead down into the spring enclosure from the base of the square minaret of Sidi Hamed Gharib mosque.

North of the Sidi Hamed Gharib mosque, a gate on the left leads into the remains of **Roman baths**. The **hexagonal frigidarium** is the best-preserved part of the baths and the pool which was once clad in marble is largely intact. It is surrounded by arches, four of which are in perfect condition. Other rooms are less well preserved, as stone from the baths went into the construction of the ruined **Byzantine church** which overlooks the frigidarium. Dating from the 4C, it has a wide apse with an ambulatory.

Opposite the gate into the baths, on the other side of the road, is a paved area above the **cistern** that once supplied the baths with water. Steps lead down into the cistern which has a high vaulted ceiling supported on 54 square pillars.

Returning to Sidi Hamed Ghareb mosque, cross over to **Rue Moncef Bey** which leads up from the right of *Hotel de la Source*. This narrow street of cobbled steps winds steeply uphill for 300m past a low bastion to **Place Sidi Bou Makhlouf** at the foot of the kasbah walls. Recently restored, Place Sidi Bou Makhlouf is the old centre of the city. On the left is a low square building, **Jamaa el Kebir**, which has Roman masonry built into its walls. It dates from the 4C and was converted to a mosque in the 8C, although now it is deconsecrated and houses fragments of Roman carved stones and stelae.

Steps lead up from the left side of the mosque to the **KASBAH** which is currently undergoing restoration. Planned as a cultural centre and luxury hotel and restaurant, it has two distinct sections. The **lower area** is the original Byzantine fort built with Roman stones on natural rock foundations, which was reconstructed in 1813 by Hammouda Pasha to house troops installed to defend the town against Algeria. The **upper part** which is much larger was built in 1740 by Ali Beyin. The steps wind around to a **horseshoe arch gate** which pierces the outer walls and climb up past a row of **barrel-roofed cisterns** on the left to another gateway (currently closed) which is flanked by Roman statues and has Roman Corinthian capitals across the lintel. The route then continues up past a **prison** on the left to a white stone arch which gives access, via a vaulted passage, to the restored **central court-yard** of the upper part of the kasbah. There is a large **vaulted hall** on the east side, once used as a mosque, which is filled with columns, many of which have antique capitals. A ramp leads up from the east corner of the courtyard to a bastion. There are excellent views from here of the town, the plain beyond, and the fortress walls which climb up the hill behind enclosing the upper reaches of the city.

Returning to Place Sidi Bou Makhlouf, the **Mosque of Sidi Bou Makhlouf**, at the northern end of the square, is the seat of the Aissaouia brotherhood that was founded in Morocco in the 16C. Tourists must content themselves with the white walls of its exterior, its pair of fluted domes and its pretty octagonal minaret. The inner courtyard, which you can in fact see into from the kasbah, is surrounded by antique columns.

A narrow road follows along the east wall of the Sidi Bou Makhlouf Mosque and continues for 250m to the lower walls of the **Belvedere Park** which contains the ex-President's residential villa, a modern white building on the hill-top. A brief detour (right) leads to the **Zaouia of Qadriya**, which is also known as the Zaouia of Sidi Mizouni, a Koranic school, on the corner of Rue Ibn Khaldoun, which was founded by the Qadriya brotherhood in 1834. It has a charming shady **courtyard** with the school off one side. The school is covered by a large **dome** with four smaller ones at the corners. Standing next to it is a square, tower-like **minaret**, built in the Andalucian style with double openings at the top. Go back along the road and follow the Belvedere Park walls northwards for 100m to a roundabout which has a garden and cannon at its centre. On the west side of the roundabout is the ****REGIONAL MUSEUM OF POPULAR ART AND TRADITIONS** (open summer, daily, except Mon 09.00–12.00, 16.00–19.00, winter, daily, except Mon 09.30–16.30), which is housed in an 18C zaouia. Founded by the Er Rahmania brotherhood in 1784, the whitewashed building with its two large domes surrounds two inner courtyards. Off the first courtyard on the north-west side is a large domed room containing the simple **tomb** of Ali ben Aissa

(1901–56), a descendant of the brotherhood's founder. The **dome**, decorated with intricate plasterwork, has the 99 names of God painted around its base and saints' names in the spandrels. The exhibits in this room include **local marriage costumes and jewellery**. From the other side of the courtyard, steps lead up to another domed room, the **nomad room**, which has a large Bedouin tent at its centre and a door at the far side leading to the second courtyard. A vaulted passage off the left side of the courtyard has a collection of **local pottery** dating from the 18–20C and leads through to a series of exhibitions including a **traditional kitchen**, a display of medicinal plants and various instruments ranging from hairdressing to circumcision tools. A small annex holds dyeing and weaving materials, as well as a forge and a 19C grain mill. Returning to the courtyard, the last room in the museum is dedicated to **horsemanship** and has a collection of saddlery.

From the museum, a road leads uphill for 200m to **Bab Ghedive**, the Gate of Treachery, so-named as this was where the French entered the town in 1880. In the wide grassy area outside the walls are 11 underground cisterns dating from the Roman period, each measuring 28m by 6m.

The final monument of note in El Kef is the church of **Dar el Kous** which lies 50m south of Rue Farhat Hached. Dedicated to St Peter, the church dates from the 4C and was used by the French community until independence in 1956.

A 14km excursion from El Kef, most of which is on unpaved roads, takes you to ****HAMMAM MELLEGUE**, Roman baths set above the banks of the Mellegue river. Take Rue Monji Slim down the hill, out through the suburbs of El Kef and past a military camp before turning right onto Rue 740, a stony track signposted to Hammam Mellegue which is a further 12km west. The road eventually makes a hair-raising descent of 2.5km to the baths.

Built over a natural hot spring which issues from the ground at 40˚C, the baths are still in use. There are two barrel-vaulted buildings, each containing original **Roman pools** which are rectangular and have steps leading down, one for men and one for women. Pools that are not in use, including one that is octagonal, lie amongst the adjacent ruins. The baths are mainly used during the summer when large Tunisian families camp down here for their

Hammam Mellegue, Roman baths

holidays. There are no fixed opening times, but the guardian and his family live in the barrel-vaulted house next to the baths, and will open up at any time.

A much longer excursion, involving some 80km each way, can be made from El Kef to the ancient ruins at **Haidra**. Located at an altitude of 900m, close to the Algerian border, the remains of Roman Amaedara include a triumphal arch, a two-storey mausoleum and the faint traces of a theatre. There is also a Byzantine citadel and numerous ruined churches.

10 · El Kef to Tunis

It is 165km from El Kef to Tunis on the GP5, a main road running along the Mejerda valley. It passes three archaeological sites, of which Dougga is the largest and deserves at least a morning's visit. There are eight buses a day from El Kef to Tunis, as well as a frequent louage service.

Leave El Kef by the GP5 which forks left at the bottom of the hill for Tunis. After 29km the road enters the olive-lined valley of Oued Tessa, crossing over the river just before (10.5km) **Mediene**. The road continues to head north-east, passing through (3km) **Bordj Messaoudi**, before climbing between the Teboursouk Hills to (7km) **El Krib**. This small agricultural town, centred on a cattle market, lies next to the ancient settlement of Mustis, on the left as you head out of El Krib, past a **triumphal arch** which marks the west boundary of the ancient city.

MUSTIS

Mustis (open, daily, 07.00–19.00), set on the edge of a thistle-covered plain at the foot of a barren hill range, was founded by the Roman General Marius who settled here with his veterans after the Jugurthine War at the end of the 2C BC. First uncovered in 1959, the city stretches over an area of 14 hectares, of which only 5 hectares have so far been excavated.

From the site entrance, head to the **triple arch**, to the left of which is a carved **Gorgon's head**, said to bring good luck. The arch leads through to an arcaded street, which is scored with carriage ruts and has the remains of shops along the right side. Along the left side is the east wall of the terrace of the **Temple of Ceres**, which was built in AD 116. Climbing up onto the temple platform, a good number of its columns remain standing, but the façade, which was lined with statues, is no longer preceded by steps, these having been removed by the Byzantines in order to build a fort.

Head north along the paved road, past the circular stone base of an **olive press** on the left. The road ends at the base of the citadel, now the site of the **Byzantine fort** built with Roman masonry. A footpath climbs up to the fort walls, which stand above head height, to a square portal which has an inscription stone citing the history of Mustis on its left. Inside the walls, on the right, are three large vaulted **cisterns**. The first two are used as storage space for

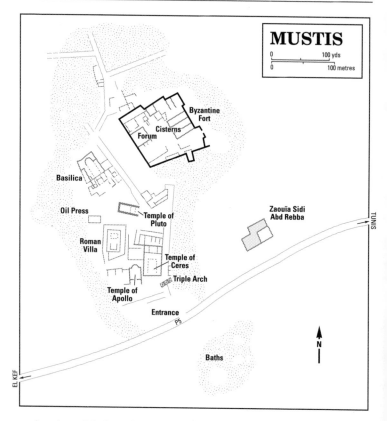

archaeological finds, including a Roman sarcophagus in the first cistern, and sections of mosaic removed from the basilica in the second. The third cistern has been excavated to reveal its original capacity. Along the back wall of the fort are the remains of garrison housing, and inside the left wall is a remnant of the **forum** which is lined with Roman statue pedestals.

Head west of the fort, crossing over a paved road to the ruins of a 6C **basilica**. Its three aisles are marked by the bases of columns, preceding the wide apse which has small carved crosses at either side. To the left of the apse there is a **baptistery** which contains a circular font of Carrara marble set into the floor with two steps leading into it.

Below the basilica to the south are the remains of an **oil press**. Opposite the press to the east is the small **Temple of Pluto** which was built in AD 117. The base, which is made of finely cut stone, is well preserved. Immediately to the south of the temple are the remains of a **Roman villa** with broken columns in each corner of its atrium and a central courtyard which is built over a cistern.

Follow the path south between the ruins of housing, past a fine **inscription stone** on the right, to the **Temple of Apollo** on the left. Built in AD 117, the temple is preceded by three steps which lead up to a small paved atrium in front of the well-preserved inner sanctuary. The sanctuary, with its finely cut stone walls, has an apse, to the right of which is a small door for a priest.

Back at the site entrance, there are various pieces of carved masonry, including a very worn **relief** depicting the sacrifice of a sheep, and a pair of **sphinxes** seated on top of an inscription. There is also a water channel set in the ground here which would originally have crossed over the modern-day road to the unexcavated **baths** on the other side.

From Mustis, continue to head in the direction of Tunis along the GP5 to the outstanding remains of ancient Dougga.

Temple of Ceres, inscribed column

DOUGGA

The site (open dawn to dusk) is set amongst olive groves on a steep slope of the Teboursouk Hills. There are two approaches to the site, one from the bottom of the hill and the other from the top. The bottom entrance, signposted on the left 13km from Mustis, is at the end of a 3km road, from where one must climb up to the site. To get to the top entrance follow the GP5 for a further 6km before turning left into Teboursouk from where the 7km road to the top is signposted. The road ends at a car park below the theatre, which is the starting point of the itinerary. There is also a ticket office and a café here.

History

Dougga, known as Thugga in ancient times, was originally a Numidian principality which later became subject to Carthage. With the weakening of Carthaginian power, the Numidian King Masinissa, an ally of Rome, took control in 155 BC. Following Caesar's victory at the Battle of Thapsus in 46 BC, Dougga was integrated into the Roman Province of Africa Nova. In AD 205 Septimius Severus made Dougga a municipality, giving its mostly Numidian inhabitants Roman citizenship. In AD 261 the city was made a colony and renamed Colonia Licinia. The city was at its most prosperous from the reign of Diocletian (284–305) to the end of the 4C, after which it began to decline; however, the city was never completely abandoned and archaeologists had to work around the inhabitants when they began excavations in 1899. In 1911, when the writer L. Grant visited the city, he remarked: 'immediately below us, just outside the theatre, lay the squalid little Arab village of Dougga, which unfortunately occupies much of the site of the old town'. The villagers are now rehoused in Nouvelle Dougga.

The **theatre**, which is within a stone's throw of the upper car park, was built in AD 168 with a diameter measuring 63.5m. It could hold 3500 spectators, and has a stage measuring 37.75m by 5.5m, raised on a light vault of terracotta tubes which probably increased the resonance of the actors' voices. Little remains of the stage proscenium, but the series of niches for statues are in good condition. The seating, which is well preserved, is built into the hillside to a height of 15m and offers excellent views.

From the theatre, a Roman paved road heads west for 150m, past four pillars on the left which mark the 2C **Temple of Augustan Piety**, to the central square, **Place de la Rose des Vents**. The square takes its name from the 3C circle, or rose, set into the paving, which is inscribed with three concentric rings and the names of the 12 winds: septentrio (north), aquilo, euraquilo, vulturnus (normally south-east but here east), eurus, leuconotuus, auster (south), libonotus, africus, favonius (west), argestes, and circius. The square, which was completed c AD 180–192, was commissioned by Quintus Pacuvius and his wife, Nahania Victoria (a mixed Roman and Numidian name), to celebrate the donor's elevation to an honourable priesthood.

Above the three curved steps along the east side of the square, a **mosque** stands on the site of the 3C **Temple of Fortune**, below which are the remains of a **market-place**. Built in the 1C, it was converted to a meat market in the 2C, but was plundered for its stone in the 6C to build a Byzantine fort. Along the north side of the Place de la Rose des Vents, steps lead up to the base of the **Temple of Mercury** which was built 180–190. A row of columns, one of which stands to its original height, precedes a courtyard, at the back of which are three chambers.

Standing against the west wall of the Temple of Mercury is the very well preserved **Capitoline Temple**. Built from local limestone in AD 166, during the joint reign of Marcus Aurelius and Lucius Verus, the temple is dedicated to Jupiter, Juno and Minerva. It has a grand portico made up of six Corinthian columns, the flutings of which have been damaged by villagers who believe them to be a charm against scorpions. They support a remarkably intact pediment, with an inscription to the trinity and to the two people who commissioned the building. Beneath the portico, a high doorway with a carved lintel leads into the inner sanctuary. Measuring 13m by 14m, the sanctuary is enclosed by stone walls that stand almost to their original

Capitoline Temple

height, with three niches along the back wall where statues of the gods would have stood. The arched central niche holds the head from the marble statue of Jupiter, which was originally 6m tall.

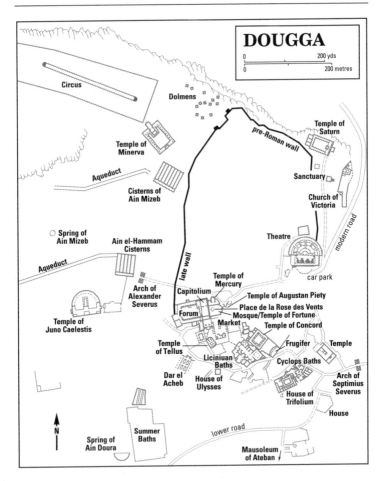

DOUGGA

0   200 yds

0   200 metres

Circus

Dolmens

Temple of Saturn

pre-Roman wall

Temple of Minerva

Sanctuary

Aqueduct

Cisterns of Ain Mizeb

Church of Victoria

Spring of Ain Mizeb

Ain el-Hammam Cisterns

Theatre

Aqueduct

late wall

car park

modern road

Temple of Juno Caelestis

Arch of Alexander Severus

Capitolium

Temple of Mercury

Temple of Augustan Piety

Forum

Place de la Rose des Vents

Mosque/Temple of Fortune

Market

Temple of Concord

Temple of Tellus

Frugifer

Temple

Liciniuan Baths

Cyclops Baths

Dar el Acheb

House of Ulysses

Arch of Septimius Severus

House of Trifolium

House

N

Spring of Ain Doura

Summer Baths

lower road

Mausoleum of Ateban

From the west side of the Temple of Mercury, nine steps lead down into the **forum**, which was converted into a fortress in 540 and remains enclosed by the Byzantine walls. It is surrounded by column bases and Corinthian capitals, the remains of red marble porticoes which once stood here.

From the back of the Capitoline temple, a paved road leads 150m west to the ****Arch of Alexander Severus**. This impressive gateway was erected between 222 and 235 in celebration of new privileges granted to the city. It is identical on both sides, with large rectangular niches in the upper walls for bronze statues, and pilasters, the fluting of which has been damaged.

A short distance beyond the gate, set in an olive grove, are the **Ain el Hammam cisterns**. There are five chambers, each one measuring 33m by 3.3m, covered by barrel-vaulted roofs which have partly collapsed. They stored water that was carried by aqueduct from a spring 12km away and were used to supply the summer baths.

A deviation 200m north takes you to another group of cisterns, made up of seven chambers, measuring 34m by 5m each, making a total capacity of 9000 cubic metres. Just to the north of the cisterns are the remains of the **Temple of Minerva**. Built 138–161, little remains except for a row of columns, one of which stands to its original height and still has its Corinthian capital. The thistle-covered hill-top on which the temple stands was where the Carthaginian settlement was built. Sections of the **pre-Roman wall**, made up of Cyclopean masonry, lie in the vicinity of the temple. There are also **dolmens** dotted about the hill-top which date from the 1C BC.

Return to the Arch of Alexander Severus, and follow the path down the hill for 100m to the ****Temple of Juno Caelestis**. Built during the reign of Alexander Severus, between 222–235, the temple is set within a semicircular enclosure, which has a diameter of 52m, and looks out over ancient olive groves. The semicircular wall surrounding the temple is lined with a colonnade in good condition with part of the inscription along the architrave remaining on the east side. The temple is raised on a platform at the centre of the enclosure and has six columns complete with their entablature across a portico that once stood three columns deep. It stands over the site of an earlier temple dedicated to Tanit which was built to face south so that the star of Hammon would light up the shrine. It is more than just coincidence that the enclosure takes the form of a crescent, the symbol of Tanit.

From the Temple of Juno Caelestis, follow the footpath east through the olive groves for 150m back to the site of the forum, from where the lower part of the city can be explored. Steps lead down to the **Temple of Tellus**, which is due south of the forum. Dating from AD 261, the courtyard in front of the temple is said to have been used as a slave market. The sanctuary has three niches in the end wall, which once contained the statues of Tellus, Pluto and Ceres.

Some 50m east of the Temple of Tellus is the **Temple of Concord**, part of a complex of three temples commissioned by a wealthy local family, the Gabinii, between 118–138. Enter the temple through the side entrance flanked by small Corinthian columns. From the paved courtyard a series of seven steps leads up through a columned portal to the narthex which has an apse at the east end. The second temple in this complex, dedicated to **Liber Pater**, the Punic wine god Shadrach, adjoins the south-east corner of the Temple of Concord. It was constructed in AD 293–305, and like Vespasian's forum of peace in Rome, it comprises an open peristyle of eight by seven columns, of which only the bases now remain. It is dramatically positioned above the plain and looks over the third temple in the complex, which is dedicated to ****Frugifer**, the town's tutelary deity. The temple resembles a theatre, with six of the original 30 rows of seats remaining, overlooking a small stage where religious pageants were presented.

On the south-west side of the temple complex are the extensive ruins of the ****Liciniuan Baths** which were used as the winter baths. Built in the 3C, the baths are in good condition and are entered through the original entrance on the north side of the building. The steep flight of steps leads into a colonnaded courtyard, where there are sections of the original mosaic flooring. The frigidarium, at the centre of the baths, is very impressive and has triple arcades at either end and tall windows looking out over the plain. The gymnasium, off the east corner, has many of the columns of its portico still standing, and looks down onto the House of Trifolium (see below).

West of the Liciniuan Baths is the **House of Ulysses**, one of the best-preserved houses on the site. Dating from the reign of Gallienus (AD 253–268), it surrounds a central courtyard on two floors. The mosaics after which the house is named are now in Bardo Museum.

To the west of the House of Ulysses is a monumental building of unknown origin which is known as **Dar el Acheb**. Thought to have been a temple, it was built in 164–166.

The base of the **Temple of Parthian Victory**, built under Caracalla in 214, lies along the west side of Dar el Acheb.

Returning to the House of Ulysses, head eastwards for 100m to the **House of Trifolium**, said to have been the city brothel. Built in the late 3C, it is the largest house yet discovered at Dougga. Its numerous rooms, one of which has three apses arranged in the shape of a trefoil, surround a central courtyard with a garden at its centre.

The **Cyclops Baths** lie along the Trifolium's east side. The baths are named after a mosaic of a Cyclops that was found in the frigidarium and is now in the Bardo Museum. The remains are scant except for some very well preserved latrines just inside the entrance. A paved road, which has a gaming board for marbles or pawns carved into one of its slabs, leads downhill from the baths for 100m to the **Arch of Septimius Severus**. It was built in AD 205 when Dougga was made a municipality by the Severan Emperor. The arch is mostly ruined, although the niches can still be seen where statues once stood.

Return up the paved road and take the first left turn which leads downhill for 200m, past the ruins of a house on the left (which has the remains of a mosaic paved courtyard), to the three-storey ****MAUSOLEUM OF ATEBAN**. This exceptional monument stands on a six-stepped base and is made up of three sections. The **middle section**, decorated with fluted Ionic half-columns, is topped by three steps, surmounted by carved reliefs of a chief in a chariot drawn by horses on his last terrestial journey. Statues of horses stand at each corner. The **top section** is crowned by a pyramid which has sirens carved at each corner to ward off the souls of the dead. The mausoleum dates from 202 BC when the Numidian King, Masinissa, joined Scipio to fight Hannibal at Zama, and contained the remains of Ateban, who, the inscription tells us, was the son of Iepmateth, son of Palu, a Numidian chief. The inscription, which was written in Libyan and Punic, is now in the British Museum, having been removed by Sir Thomas Reade in 1842.

A footpath leads up the hill from the monument for 130m and emerges at the west side of the House of Trifolium. From here, follow the road back up to the theatre; although you may first want to explore further downhill towards the lower car park, passing the 4C **House of Eros and Psyche** on the left, before reaching the Hammam Ain Doura, the **summer baths**, which were built at the end of the 2C.

From the theatre, a paved road leads northwards for 200m to the **Temple of Saturn**. It was built in 195 during the reign of Septimius Severus but reconstructed 223–235. Standing on the site of an earlier temple dedicated to Baal (36–37 AD), it lies at the edge of the pre-Roman settlement. A row of four columns, two of which are complete with Corinthian capitals, line the vestibule. Joining it is a courtyard surrounded by the remnants of a portico and in traditional North African style, an inner sanctuary consisting of three apsidal cellae. The central cella contained a huge statue of Saturn in front of which a pair of footprints indicated where worshippers should stop.

To the south of the temple, built against a rocky bluff, are the scant remains of a **sanctuary** dedicated to Neptune. To the south-east of the temple, steps lead down to a small **hypogeum** which dates from the 4C and is filled with sarcophagi from the nearby Christian cemetery. At one end of the cemetery, to the east of the hypogeum, stand the remains of a Christian church, dedicated to **Victoria**. It dates from the 5C and is constructed with stones that were removed from the theatre and other nearby monuments.

From Dougga, return to the GP5 via Teboursouk, and follow signs to Tunis. The road winds through the Oued Khalled valley for 13km to ****AIN TOUNGA** which stands on the Roman site of Thignica, at its height in the 3C when it was granted the status of a municipality under Alexander Severus. The ruins lie at the foot of Jebel Louej (466m) on the right side of the road, just beyond a modern water tower.

A track leads from the road to the well-preserved **Byzantine fortress**, which was built in the 6C. It has five square towers: the best preserved, on the south-east side, standing almost to its original height, has an arched window in the upper wall and a slender arched door at its base with a Latin inscription on its keystone. A footpath heads east of the fort to a simple **triumphal arch** which leads through to the **residential and commercial quarters** of the city, currently under excavation. To the east is the site of a large **temple**, strewn with the fragments of its monolithic columns, and behind it, built into the hill are the remains of a wall that once enclosed a **theatre**. None of the seating is visible, but the stage is scattered with broken pieces of columns. Below the theatre, to its west, are the ruins of the **baths**, which have large apses at either end and are lined with columns.

The GP5 continues through gentle hills in the direction of Tunis for 8km to **TESTOUR**. Set above the Mejerda river, the town occupies the site of Roman Tichilla which was granted to Andalucian refugees in 1609. The town centre is signposted left off the GP5 opposite the **Mosque of Sidi Abdul Latif** which has an Andalucian minaret decorated with faience tiles. At the centre of the town is the **Great Mosque**, which was built with the arrival of the Andalucians in the 17C. Its tower-like minaret is a classic Toledo model, apart from the decorative top which was added in the 20C. A traditional festival of Andalucian music is held every June outside the walls of the Great Mosque.

Continuing along the GP5, at the outskirts of Testour, the road passes by the **Zaouia of Nasser el Baraouachi**, identified by its green conical roof. Built in 1733, the zaouia contains a Koranic school and the tomb of a Jewish saint, Es Saad Rebbi Fradji Chaoua, who was born in Fez and died in Testour in the 16C.

A short distance beyond the zaouia, there is a left turn to the **Baraj Sidi Salem**, a vast dam on the Mejerda river. The GP5 continues in the direction of

Tunis, passing through (6km) **Essloughia** with its Andalucian-style minaret before crossing over the (2.5km) Mejerda river. After a further 7km the **Mejez el Bab War Cemetery** is passed on the left. It is the largest Commonwealth cemetery in Tunisia, containing 3000 tombs and a memorial to 2000 British soldiers. The town of **Mejez el Bab**, a further 5km, was founded by Andalucians in 1611 on the site of ancient Membressa, the only remains of which are the pieces of Roman masonry used in a bridge over the Mejerda river.

The GP5 leaves the Mejerda river and crosses a plain where there are extensive vineyards to (26km) **Borj el Amri**. The town has a reasonable hotel, *The Maghres*, near the ruins of Roman baths where there are 4C mosaic floors with marine themes.

The GP5 continues past the (3km) **Massicault Commonwealth War Cemetery** on the left, which holds over 1500 graves, and passes into the (13km) Tunis region before climbing a low range of (3km) hills at the other side of which lies the vast sprawl of Tunis. The city outskirts begin after a further 3km. Follow signs to El Ouardia until you meet the ring road and then continue in the direction of La Goulette and (10km) Tunis city centre.

IV CAP BON PENINSULA

11 · Tunis to El Haouaria

It is 110km from Tunis to El Haouaria on the tip of the Cap Bon peninsula. The route follows the autostrada, the only stretch of motorway in Tunisia, which connects Tunis to the south coast, before taking the narrow, winding road around the peninsula itself. There are three buses a day from Tunis to El Haouaria via Korbous.

Leave Tunis along Avenue de la République which heads south of the TGM station under a flyover. The goods' station is passed on the right, shortly after which the *autostrada* is joined in the direction of Sousse. After 7km turn off the *autostrada* and follow the road through an area of heavy industry to (8km) **Hammam Lif**. Spread at the base of the rocky-topped Jebel Bou Kornine (576m), this industrial town is built on the hot spring of Ain el Ariane, which was first exploited for its medicinal properties by the Carthaginians who used the water to cure nasal infections. In the 18C, the Ottoman Beys had their winter residence here, the baths of which is now part of the *Hotel des Thermes*.

Follow the GP1 alongside the railway line, through (2km) **Bou Kornine** which has a thermal cure centre located on its central, palm-lined square. At (7.5km) **Borj Cedria** turn left onto the MC26 in the direction of Soliman. A wide marshy expanse extends for 3km to the sandy beaches of the **Borj Soliman Cedria zone touristique**, which run from here to the north of Soliman. There are several tracks crossing the marsh to the beach, but the main one takes you to the hotels around **Plage Ejjehris** which is signposted on the left after 5.5km.

The MC26 continues for a further 2.5km to **Soliman**. The town is named after an Ottoman landowner, but owes its prosperity to Andalucians who settled here in the 17C, bringing with them new farming techniques. The only remnant of the Andalucian town is the tiled mosque which was built with the antique columns and capitals of nearby ancient Gumis.

Continuing north-east of Soliman in the direction of Korbous, 1km outside the town there is another track to the Borj Soliman Cedria beach. The MC26 continues through (5km) **Marja**, where esparto grass mats are sold at the roadside, to the (3.5km) left turn for Korbous on the MC128. This very narrow road is cut into the rocky coastline of the **Costa del Sol**. After 3km the road touches down at the narrow beach of **Sidi Rais**, before heading up through a rock-hewn tunnel. Just over the summit, which is reached after 3km, is the small thermal establishment of **Ain Oktor** and the three-star *Oktor Hotel*.

The MC128 continues down for 3km into a narrow creek, at the mouth of which is the thermal spa of **Korbous**. Known to the Romans as Acquae Calidae Carpitanae, Korbous has long been frequented for its hot mineral waters which rise from the ground at a temperature of 50–60°C. The site was abandoned after the Arab conquest, but regained popularity in the 19C when Ahmed Bey built a pavilion here. The pavilion is now the **Office du Thermalisme** which is a hotel and treatment centre offering cures for rheumatism, arthiritis, respiratory conditions and skin maladies. Also popular is the **Turkish bath** or hammam, which is covered by a silvery dome. To the left of the hammam there is a terrace and café overlooking the small rocky beach in the bay below, while hugging the cliff above the resort is the three-star hotel *Les Sources*.

The road leaves Korbous, past the Office du Thermalisme, and continues along the coast for 2km to **Ain el Atrous**, where there is another hot spring which runs into the sea. The rocky beach is overlooked by an outdoor café which supplies picnic-style grills for its customers to cook their meat on. The MC128 winds up from here for 2.5km before heading down into the fertile hinterland of the peninsula. After 8km, turn left at the T-junction back onto the MC26, which heads through an undulating landscape of olive groves, vineyards and grain fields. After 16km, the sea comes into view and there is a sign on the left to **Plage Rtiba**, from where a footpath leads through an olive grove to the sand dunes that back this excellent beach. The village of Rtiba, which is 1.5km further along the MC26, has a small white mosque and simple barrel-vaulted houses which look across to the Island of Zembra (see below). At 3km beyond Rtiba, there is another track to the beach, signposted *plaj*.

Continue north on the MC26 to the turning on the left to **Sidi Daoud** (22km). This small village, 3km off the road, is a centre of tuna fishing and has a canning factory. Nets are laid in spring to catch the tuna on their way to their spawning ground. La Matanza, the slaughtering of the fish, takes place in the port between April and July. It is a tradition that dates back to Roman times, having been brought here by inhabitants of Sicily.

El Haouaria, 6.5km further along the MC26, is set below the great mass of the Cap Bon headland which is a nesting ground for falcons. Falconry provides one of the main livelihoods in the village. Falcons are caught or taken from their nests in February or March and trained for a month, to be used by hunters who come for the shooting season which starts in the spring. The end of the season is celebrated in June with a festival of falconry. There is one smart hotel in the village, the *Epervier*, which caters for hunting parties; otherwise there is little to keep you here.

The main attraction of El Haouaria is the Roman quarries at the tip of the peninsula, which are reached by following the signs to 'Les Grottes'. The road winds from the village for 2km, past the *Les Grottes* falconer's club on the right which has a restaurant and bar, to a large car park at the sea edge. At the far side of the car park there is a café and restaurant, the *Daurade*, with a terrace looking out to sea. To the right is the ticket office for **Les Grottes quarries** (open summer, daily, 08.00–19.00, winter, daily, 08.30–17.00). The soft orange limestone in the hills was first extracted by the Carthaginians who established quarries that continued to be used in Roman times. The stone was cut away in blocks and then hauled up a shaft using a pulley system before being loaded onto ships bound for Carthage. There are said to be 90 caves quarried in the hills, many of which are interconnected. Some of the redundant quarries were used as a barracks in Byzantine times and have the remnants of cooking areas and wells. The largest cave, down the footpath to the left of the ticket office, is known as **Ghar el Kebir**. A camel has been carved from the soft stone at the cave entrance, which opens into a vast area where the stone has been cut away in the shape of a pyramid.

Carthage Room, Bardo
Museum, Tunis

Old port and kasbah,
Bizerte

La Maison de la Chasse,
basement, Bulla Reggia

La Maison d'Amphitrite,
basement, Venus mosaic,
Bulla Reggia

Theatre, inscription, Dougga

Zaouia Sidi Abid El Ghariani,
Kairouan

Citadel. Chenini

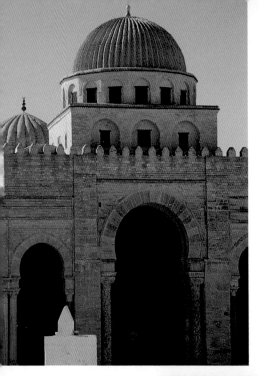

Great Mosque,
Kairouan

Great Mosque,
the double portico,
Kairouan

Schola des Juvenes, Mactaris

Haddada Hotel, Ksar
Haddada

Potter, Younes El Ghoul,
Guellala

Kasbah, Museum of
Antiquities, Sousse

Garlic sellers, medina,
Sfax

The beach below the quarries looks across to two islands, known in Roman times as 'Aegimuti'. The largest of the two, **Zembra**, which covers an area of 5 square km, was once a quarantine station for pilgrims en route for Mecca, but is now a protection ground for the monk seal. The smaller island, **Zembretta**, has a lighthouse.

12 · El Haouaria to Hammamet

It is 94km from El Haouaria to Hammamet, via the Punic remains of Kerkouane, Kelibia, Korba and Nabeul. There are three mini-buses a day from El Haouaria to Nabeul, from where there is a bus every half an hour to Hammamet. There are up to 10 louages a day, from El Haouaria to Kelibia, which is connected by a regular louage service to Nabeul.

Leave El Haouaria by the MC27 which passes through the farming villages of (4km) Echraf and (3km) Dar Alouche, after which it is a further 5.5km to the left turn for Kerkouane (also spelt Kerkouenne and Karkouan). Follow the narrow road for 2km to the coast where there is a parking area next to the site.

KERKOUANE
Kerkouane (open summer, daily, 08.00–18.00, museum closed Mon, winter, daily, 09.00–16.00, museum closed Mon) is one of the few Punic settlements not to have been built on by the Romans. Wandering around the low-lying walls of the closely packed town one can imagine the peaceful daily life here in Punic times.

History
Discovered in 1952 by Pierre Cintas, Kerkouane, or Tamezret as it was known, was founded in the 6C BC. There may have been a 'Libyan' settlement here already which was then taken over by Phoenician settlers, possibly fleeing Nebuchadnezzar's attack on Tyre in 574. Excavations have revealed that the main forms of livelihood were fishing and the manufacture of a purple dye made from the molluscs of murex shells. Vast piles of discarded shells have been discovered on the site (5000 molluscs were needed to make 1 gram of dye). Remains also suggest that the economy included potters, sculptors, glass-makers, stone-cutters, weavers and jewellers. Following Regulus' invasion in 248 BC, the city was gradually abandoned, never to be inhabited again. In the 2C BC Scipio made certain of this by razing the city to the ground.

To the right of the entrance there is a good site ****MUSEUM**. In the courtyard that proceeds it is a collection of 4–3C BC **pottery** excavated from the necropolis, which is 1.5km north of the site, and **limestone stelae** of the same era. A pair of 4C BC **sandstone capitals** from a villa at Carthage flank the museum entrance. In the **first of the museum's four rooms** there are further finds from the Punic necropolis, including **red and black pottery** imported from Magna Graeca (southern Italy) and amphorae, one of which dates from the 6C BC and depicts Minerva between two warriors. The **second room** holds more pottery and a red ****sarcophagus** made from wood. It is the largest piece of Punic sculpture so far discovered and has the goddess Astart, who oversees the peace of the dead, carved on the lid with a bracelet on one of her arms. The **third room** has **statuettes** found in the sanctuary and **moulds** from the town potteries. The **fourth room**, which is reached via the first room, has a collection of small objects including **jewellery, coins, fishing weights** and **bronze arrowheads** dating from the 7C BC.

From the museum, proceed through the site gate, to the left of which is the ticket office. A path leads from here, between flower-beds where rock plants are arranged in the symbol of Tanit, to the edge of the site. Once covering an area of 50 hectares surrounded by a double defensive wall, only a relatively small part remains. Much of the east side of the town has disappeared into the sea where the low cliffs have been eroded. What remains is something of a maze (the walls of the houses having been restored to knee height) on the original town plan. Some of the houses, which were generally made of poor materials, skimmed over with a layer of painted stucco in either white, grey or red, have adjoining storerooms, otherwise they are uniform in style. Each has an entrance from the street which leads through a corridor into a small court-yard where there is a well and a drain. Around the courtyard are the rooms, which are paved in red mortar with pieces of crushed brick, broken pottery and white marble set into it. The bathroom is a prominent feature in the houses, each having a distinctive hip bath.

On **Rue de Sphinx** at the centre of the excavations are the remains of the **House of the Sphinx** which had 10 rooms, one of which was a glass-blowers' workshop. Amongst the finds excavated here were a skull, a nursing bottle, a fresco imitating marble and a pebble mosaic depicting a stag and griffin in the reception room. From here **Rue du Temple** leads to the remains of a **sanctuary**. It has a monumental entrance with two frontal pilasters, of which only the bases remain, a vestibule, and a chapel or tabernacle preceded by an altar in the middle of the courtyard. It also had a sculpture workshop attached to it. One of the **best-preserved houses** lies just inside the modern sea wall. The lower part of several sandstone columns surround the courtyard from where steps lead up to the bathroom with its pink plaster tub.

From Kerkouane, return to the MC27 and continue north for 12km where there is a left fork for Kelibia.

KELIBIA

This small town is both a fishing port and a centre of wine-making, producing a distinctive dry Muscatel. The town is rather spread out and lacks a real centre, but is overlooked by a fine fortress and has good beaches nearby.

- **Bus station**. Near the main roundabout with its modern mosaic fountain and broken column. Regular services to Nabeul and Menzel Temine–El Haouaria–Tunis.

- **Taxi and louage station**. Same place as bus station. Regular *louage* services to Nabeul and El Haouaria.

- **Hotels and restaurants**. There are two reasonable hotels in the town next to each other on Avenue des Martyrs, the road that leads to the port. *Hotel Florida* is the older of the two and is dominated by its bar; *Hotel En Nassim* has recently been rebuilt and upgraded. Both hotels have restaurants, which are the main eating places in town apart from the *Relais Touristique* which specialises in fish food. The *Mansoura Hotel*, built on the cliff top 2km north of the town above a sandy bay, rents out chalets only, for a minimum of a week. *Hotel Mamounia* is a similar set up, on the beach 3km south of the town, but has a swimming pool and watersports facilities.

- **Shopping**. Magasin Générale, a supermarket chain, on Avenue des Martyrs. Weekly fruit and vegetable market, Mondays.

- **Post office**. Avenue des Martyrs.,

- **Entertainment**. Long sandy beach, Kelibia Plage, 3km along the right fork from the main roundabout. Wide white sand bay, Kelibia Blanche, 2km to the end of Avenue des Martyrs, left in the direction of Manshoura, then first right, signposted 'plage'.

History

The town is built on the ancient remains of Clupea, which dates from the 3C BC; then, not unlike today, the town had a port and made wine. The Carthaginians sold their wine to the Barbarians, buying in wine from Rhodes for their own consumption. In 310 BC the site was invaded by Agathocles of Syracuse, and then by Regulus in 256 BC. It was razed to the ground by Scipio's legions in 146 BC in the final throes of the Third Punic War. From the debris, the Byzantines built a fort, which was to be their last stronghold in North Africa.

The remains of **ancient Clupea** are along **Avenue des Martyrs**, the left hand of the two roads that lead from the roundabout to the coast. Follow Avenue des Martyrs, past the right fork for the port, to an enclosure on the left behind a wire fence. An excavated pit marks the site of a **temple**, preceded by nine steps. The area is scattered with fallen columns, finely carved sections of architrave and two large capitals decorated with acanthus leaves.

Return back along Avenue des Martyrs and take the first right turn to the remnants of a **Roman villa** on the left. Hemmed in by ramshackle housing and strewn with litter, steps lead down past a deep well, into the ruins of the villa which dates from the 4C. There are a series of rooms with mosaic floors depicting hunting scenes amongst others, and a courtyard surrounded by the bases of columns. Off one side of the

Byzantine Castle, Kelibia

courtyard there are three square vats hewn from natural rock, once used for dyeing wool. Opposite the vats there is a well-preserved semicircular mosaic of fish, sea creatures and shells.

From the Roman villa, the road continues up the hill to the fine ****BYZANTINE CASTLE** (open summer, 08.00–19.00, winter, 08.00–16.00) at its summit where there is a car park. From the car park a stepped ramp leads up to the castle walls which are pierced by a **small arched doorway**, inside of which is the ticket office. A pathway continues up to the **inner walls**, which are built of Roman masonry, to a tunnel which leads through to a large enclosure. At the centre of the enclosure are the remnants of the **Punic fort walls** made of megalithic blocks of stone which are built over a cistern, hence the four nearby well-heads. Gravel paths thread their way through undergrowth, where Roman pillars and Corinthian capitals poke through, to a walkway which runs along the walls between the eight strategically placed bastions. On top of the **east bastion** there is a lighthouse, a squat white tower with a black lantern, which was built in the 19C by the French. The views are panoramic with the port to the south-west and Kelibia's two white sand bays to the north.

A circular route can be made back to Kelibia by continuing from the car park, through a lower parking area where there is a **Turkish café** with fine sea views, down the gravel drive from the castle's north walls. After 350m the drive meets the main road, where you can either turn right to return to the town, or left to continue up the hill to the site of a **Punic necropolis**. The road winds up a ravine to the hill summit where the green gates of *Hotel Mansoura* are on the right, and a track is signed on the left to the necropolis. Cut into a rocky outcrop at the back of a small factory are a cluster of tombs with doors hewn from the stone, connected by carved rock steps; not easy to find.

From Kelibia follow the MC27 in the direction of Menzel Temine which is 10km south-west. Just before reaching the town, the **tomb of Sidi Bou Salem** with its three domes is passed on the right. **Menzel Temine** is a small market town with little of interest apart from its mediocre hotel and a Monoprix supermarket.

The MC27 continues to head south along the Cap Bon peninsula, crossing the wide River Oued Chiba, which empties into the sea here after 18km. To the south of the river, a **marshy lagoon** extends all the way to Korba (7km); during the spring it is a good place to see flamingoes. **Korba** stands on the site of Roman Curubis, of which little remains apart from some cisterns and part of an aqueduct. The town has banks and shops but can otherwise be bypassed. From the roundabout at the town centre continue straight over in the direction of Nabeul. On the way out of Korba on the left is a Club Méditerranée, and after a further 3km there are signs to a **beach**.

The MC27, which is well-surfaced from this point, follows along the marshy coastline to (16km) **Behri Khiar** where there is an unmarked junction at which traffic is expected to give way. After a further 4.5km the road passes through **Dar Chaabane el Fehri** where locally quarried stone is carved. Within the next kilometre the **coastal developments** around Nabeul begin with the Hotel Lido Ramses.

NABEUL

Nabeul lies at one end of Tunisia's most visited stretch of coast which extends southwards for 10km to Hammamet. The town, the largest on the Cap Bon peninsula, is dominated by souvenir shops and yellow calèches waiting to take tourists to the beach which is a kilometre or so away. It is a convenient place for shopping, being better organised than most towns. But it lacks character and gets stiflingly hot in summer due to its position inland from the sea.

■ **Railway station**. Ave Habib Bourguiba, tel. (02) 285474. Line to Tunis, but services erratic.

■ **Bus station**. Ave Habib Thameur. Regular services to Kelibia, Hammamet and Tunis. Other destinations include Kairouan, Sousse and Zaghouan.

■ **Taxi and louage stations**. From Ave Habib Thameur (bus station).

■ **Hotels**. There is a wide range of accommodation in Nabeul, from the dozen or so two- and three-star hotels on the lido to the smaller pensions in the town.

■ **Restaurants**. Plenty of eating places in the town, including western fast food and snacks.

■ **Post office**. Ave Habib Bourguiba.

■ **Tourist information**. Commissariat Regional, Ave Taieb M'hiri, tel. (02) 286800.

■ **Shopping**. ONAT have a sales centre (where prices are fixed by the government) for regional crafts, including pottery and textiles, on Ave Habib Thameur, nearby which is a concentration of pottery shops. Camel market every Friday on Ave Farhat Hached; local pottery and souvenirs are also sold.

■ **Children**. Playground inside the small park on Place du 7 Novembre next to the museum. Horse and camel rides on the beach.

■ **Sport**. Watersports facilities and tennis courts at the big hotels on the lido.

■ **Beaches**. The town centre is 1km inland from a long sandy beach, which stretches from the lido at the northern end of town to the ancient site of Neapolis at the southern end. It is accessible by private roads to the various big hotels, or from the road to Neapolis.

■ **Festivals**. Festival des Fleurs d'Orangers, end March–early April. Summer festival, July–August, in the open-air theatre of the Foire de Nabeul on Ave Habib Bourguiba.

History

Nabeul stands on the site of ancient Neapolis which was founded in the 5C BC when it served as a port for the Greeks of Cyrene, being less than two days and one night by boat from Sicily. It was conquered by Agathocles in the 3C BC and then taken by the Romans at the end of the Third Punic War when it was given the lowest possible status of a tribute.

In the 2C the town prospered once more, being made a colony and renamed Colonia Julia Neapolis. After the 3C it became the see of a bishop, and there was also a small Jewish community. Following the Arab invasions in the 7C, however, the town declined and was described by a 12C traveller as being abandoned. During the 16C Andalucians settled in the area and the town became known for its potteries which produced distinctive green and yellow glazes.

Finds from the archaeological excavations of Neapolis and other sites on the Cap Bon peninsula are housed in the town's **MUSEUM** (open Tues–Sun, 09.00–16.00), which is near the roundabout with a giant pottery jar, in Place du 7 Novembre. The **first room**, off left, has Punic objects dating from the 7–4C BC, many of which are from Kerkouane. In the **second room** there are Punic sculptures to the Goddess Tanit, and in the **third room** there is a collection of Roman oil lamps and fragments of mosaics.

The **RUINS OF NEAPOLIS** are reached by following Avenue Habib Thameur out of town in the direction of Hammamet. The road crosses over the river, Oued Souhil, and continues for 750m to the *Hotel les Jasmins* where there is a left turn signed **Neapolis**. After crossing over the railway, turn left, and continue for 200m to the green gates on the right which lead into the ruins (open daily, dawn to dusk).

Follow the footpath from the site gate and turn left to the remains of a grand **peristyle villa** which was discovered in 1965 when foundations were being dug for a hotel. Dating from the 4C, it has a large mosaic paved **courtyard** with the bases of curvilinear fountains off the north and west sides. Along the east side of the courtyard, there are four rooms with **mosaics** of aquatic birds and fish decorating medallions. Off the north side of the courtyard, across the paved road, are the remains of a **sanctuary**, where there is a small raised room with the bases of columns either side of the entrance and an altar at the back. The word 'Artemonis' is set into the white mosaic floor suggesting that the building was associated with the Artemisian Games.

Head back along the path, but instead of returning to the gates keep straight on and then bear left to the south-west corner of the site where there are the remains of a **garum manufactory**. Garum was a sauce, widely used in Roman times, made from small fish, or the guts of large fish, which were dried in the sun or in an oven, and then preserved under salt. During the excavations several amphorae were uncovered still full of the garum paste. There are **six containers** where garum would have been stored and one large vat, all of which are sunk into the ground.

From Nabeul continue to head south along the MC28 for a further 10km to Hammamet which lies at the heart of a vast *zone touristique* where hotels, none of which are more than three or four storeys high, are spread along the beach for at least 5km to either side.

HAMMAMET

Hammamet, with its fine sand beaches and historic medina, is descended upon by tens of thousands of tourists every summer. Its popularity began at the turn of the 20C when the Roumanian millionaire George Sebastian built a luxurious villa here which now serves as a cultural centre. Hammamet was subsequently visited by writers and artists including André Gide, Paul Klee and Frank Lloyd Wright. Paul Klee wrote in his diary in 1914: 'The city is magnificent, right by the sea, full of bends and sharp corners. Now and then I get a look at the ramparts!' Despite being inundated with tourists, the centre of Hammamet has retained its charm with the walls of the medina rising up from the water front, and narrow streets lined with whitewashed houses.

■ **Railway station**. Ave Habib Bourguiba. Lines to Tunis, Sousse–El Jem–Sfax–Gabès–Gafsa–Tozeur.

■ **Bus station**. Ave de la République. Regular services to Nabeul and Tunis.

■ **Louage station**. From bus station, regular services to Nabeul.

■ **Taxis**. Place 7 Novembre.

■ **Hotels and restaurants**. There are almost as many hotels in Hammamet as in Tunis. The tourist office hold lists of accommodation. Restaurants are also thick on the ground, with a whole block on Ave Habib Bourguiba, next to the tourist office. There is another cluster of restaurants in the medina with terraces on top of the west walls.

■ **Shopping**. Supermarket chain Magasin Générale have a well-stocked branch on Place 7 Novembre, opposite the medina. On the same square there is a small covered market. The weekly market is held on Thursdays. Bargaining over prices is common. If you are buying a carpet, consult the fixed rates in the tourist office as a guideline.

■ **Post office**. Ave de la République, tel. (02) 280598.

■ **Tourist information**. Antenne du Tourisme, Ave Habib Bourguiba, tel. (02) 280423.

■ **Festivals**. Festival of the Arts in George Sebastian's villa, 3km south, July and August.

■ **Entertainment**. The sandy beaches to either side of Hammamet are serviced by a mini-train which leaves from west wall of the medina and calls in at Nabeul Gare before making the circuit of the *route touristique*.

■ **Sports**. All big hotels have watersports facilities, tennis courts and swimming pools. 18-hole golf course at Bir Bou Rekba, 10km on Sousse road, tel. (02) 282722.

History
Hammamet stands on the site of ancient Pupput which was made a Roman colony under the Emperor Commodus in the 2C. The present-day town, however, is 15C, a period when the fortified medina played an active role in the piracy of the Mediterranean.

The ****MEDINA** dominates the sea front at Hammamet, sheltering a sandy bay on its west side and a large square on the north where a concrete replica of the Eiffel Tower commemorates the French soldiers who died here during the first occupation in the 19C. The **main gate** is through a bastion in the north wall, from where the main drag, a **vaulted street** crowded with souvenir shops, zig-zags through the medina. The first left turn leads to the **Grand Mosque** which was restored in 1972 but has its original 15C minaret. On the east side of the mosque is the whitewashed dome of the **Bains Maures**, a Turkish bath, which has a red and green doorway decorated with black and white stripes.

Return to the main street and keep straight on, following inside the west wall to the ****KASBAH** which is built into the west corner facing the sea. A ramp leads up to the **gate house**, now the ticket office, which leads into the **central courtyard**. Shaded by large pines, at the centre of the courtyard is the **domed tomb** of the marabout Sidi Bou Ali. Stairs lead up to a walkway, the **Chemin du Ronde**, which makes a complete circuit of the walls. From the highest bastion, there are good views over the flat roofs of the medina and the white houses of the town.

In the *zone touristique*, 6km along the road to Sousse, which passes by George Sebastian's villa with its 1960s theatre, are the remains of ancient **Pupput**. There are the ruins of a **villa** with 5C **mosaics** as well as its own **private baths**, and another to the north with early black-and-white mosaic floors dating from the 2C. The site also boasts a good collection of 4C tomb mosaics which date from the Byzantine era when it was an important stronghold.

V THE STEPPE

13 · Hammamet to Kairouan

It is 95km from Hammamet to Kairouan. The A1 motorway runs as far as Enfidaville after which the route follows the GP2. There are two direct buses a day from Hammamet to Kairouan.

From the centre of Hammamet follow Avenue Habib Bourguiba up the hill, turn left at the railway station and follow Avenue des Nations Unies out of town. The road crosses the Oued Batten river before joining the motorway (7km) in the direction of Sousse. After 36km leave the motorway for **ENFI-DAVILLE**, a small market town, 4km off the road. Surrounded by an agricultural estate of 100,000 hectares, the town was built by the French in the 1880s when they purchased the land from a Turkish official, Khaireddin.

The town is well worth visiting for its **museum** which is housed in a deconsecrated church with a clock tower surmounting its newly-cleaned, sandstone façade. The museum (open Tues–Sun, 08.00–12.00, 15.00–19.00), signposted 'musée' from the town outskirts, is midway along the main street. It contains a good collection of Christian mosaics, most of which were removed from tombs. They come mainly from Uppena and Sidi Abich and Pheradi Maius, which are 5km, 3km and 18km north of the town respectively.

PHERADI MAIUS, a Roman settlement now in ruins, lies in a peaceful rural setting, overlooking a large olive grove, 18km north of Enfidaville. Take the GP1 for 9km to **Bou Ficha which is on the left of the main road, then follow signs on Rue 640 to Sidi Khelifa which is a further 9km. At **Sidi Khelifa** there is a domed shrine on the left of the road, from where a track leads for 500m up to the ruins which lie scattered around an excellently preserved triumphal arch. From the site gate, follow the track up towards the arch, past the scant remains of **market buildings** on the left, to the better preserved **baths**, also on the left. Excavators have uncovered attractive mosaic floors and pools in the baths, including a large mosaic of a marine scene, dating from the late Roman era. Continue up to the arch, which is preceded by the ruins of houses to the right, and remnants of the deeply rutted paved road. The ****arch**, with its niches, that would once have held statues, is decorated with half-columns that have palm leaf capitals. It leads through to the **forum**, a large flat area paved with white stone slabs. Along the north-east side of the forum are the remnants of **two sanctuaries**, while on the south side is a reconstructed **colonnade**. The remains of a flight of steps lead up from here to a terrace, once occupied by a **temple**. There are some plinths for statues, and other fragments of stone, but nothing substantial remains of the temple. The rest of the city which covers the hill slopes on either side lies unexcavated. The best remaining edifice is the **Temple to Baal** which can be seen from the site gate on the summit of the thickly forested hill to the left. It is constructed of massive blocks of finely cut stone and commands a fine view over the coast, but is a steep climb.

KAIROUAN

From Enfidaville follow the GP2 across marshy steppeland to Kairouan which lies 59km south. The city, founded on an ancient caravan route, is an oasis in the barren plain. The road approaches the crenellated brick walls of the medina, passing the tourist office, the Agence Nationale de Patrimonie, on the right, where it is advisable to stop to purchase the ticket necessary to visit the city's monuments. The ticket, which covers seven monuments, is valid for one day and can only be obtained from this office. From the tourist office, either park along the medina walls, or head south for the modern part of the city by skirting around the medina. The modern part of the city, built during the colonial period by the French, is centred on Place de l'Indépendance.

- **Bus station**. Gare Routière, El Hadjem, Rue Farhat Hached, tel. (07) 220125. Regular services to Gafsa, Kasserine, Sfax, Sousse and Tunis.

- **Louage stations**. Bab ech Chouhada and roundabout on Ave de la République.

- **Taxis**. Place Kasbah.

- **Hotels**. There are not that many hotels in Kairouan and during religious festivals they are fully booked. The *Continental* and *Les Aghlabites*, near the Aghlabid Basins in the north of the city, cater for coach tours. In the French colonial town, around the Place de l'Independance, there are two reasonable hotels, the *Tunisia* on Ave de la République, which is the best value of the two, and the *Splendid* on Rue de 9 Avril. More basic hotels can be found inside the medina walls. The *Hotel Marhala* is the best, and has simple rooms surrounding a courtyard.

- **Shopping**. There is a lively market held every Monday outside the north walls of the medina around Place de Tunis. Carpet shops abound, there being some 5000 weaving families in the city. There are three basic qualities, graded according to the number of knots per square metre: Qualité Supérieure (160,000 knots per m2); Première Choix (90,000 knots per m2); and Deuxiéme Choix (40,000 knots per m2). In the Souk des Tapis everyday except Friday and Sunday, there is a carpet auction at 13.00. For fixed-price carpets, go to the ONAT sales room on Ave Ali Zaouaoui.

- **Post office**. Rue Farhat Hached.

- **Tourist information**. Agence Nationale de Patrimonie, Place des Basins Aghlabite, tel. (07) 226300.

- **Sport**. Swimming pool, Piscine Municipale, Bab el Khoukha.

- **Children**. Children's fairground at the Aghlabid Basins. Small playground near the Great Mosque, below the north-west wall of the medina.

- **Festivals**. Religious festivals held during Ramadan. Mouled festival celebrating the Prophet's birthday. Fantasia Sidi Ali ben Nasrallah, a traditional equestrian festival, September.

History

The city of Kairouan was founded in AD 670 by Uqba Ibn Nafi, a disciple of Mohammed, the Prophet, who, travelling across the desert with his caravan, discovered a spring flowing from the ground here. When he went to drink from the spring he found a golden cup which he had lost at Mecca and took this as a sign he should build a city. According to an account given by En Noweiri: 'Uqba came to a valley filled with trees and scrub, a habitation of wild beasts and owls. So he prayed to God, and said to the beasts: "inhabitants of this valley, begone, and may God have mercy on you, we intend to abide here". When he had thus proclaimed three times, the serpents and scorpions and other unknown beasts began to depart before the eyes of the spectator.'

The site was strategically positioned midway between the Berbers in the mountains and the Byzantines on the coast. However, Uqba lost his life in 682, during the first of three Berber uprisings. Arab power was restored in 694 by Hassan Ibn Al Numan who made Kairouan his capital city. It remained the capital under the Aghlabids, a period when the city was at its zenith, but was abandoned in favour of Mahdia by the Fatamids in 916 after which it was destroyed by the Hilali Bedouin tribe in 1057. In the 13C the city was rebuilt by the Hafsids, and by the 16C it had become the second largest city in Tunisia. The city continued to prosper and as late as the 19C it was still actively involved in the slave trade. It also flourished on the trade brought by pilgrims, which continues to be a major source of revenue to this day.

The **GREAT MOSQUE** (open, daily, 08.00–14.00), in the north-east corner of the medina, is the oldest place of prayer in the Islamic world, making Kairouan its fourth holiest city, after Mecca, Medina and Jerusalem. It is said that seven visits here are equal to one to Mecca. Covering an area of 135m by 80m, the mosque is enclosed by a fortified wall, which is pierced by numerous gates, of which that on Rue Brahim ben Lagleb, in the west wall, is the one used by tourists.

> The mosque stands on the site of the original building founded by Uqba ben Nafi in 670, but was rebuilt in 772–774 by Yazid Ibn Hatim who was governor for the Abbasids of Ifriqiya. It was almost entirely rebuilt by the Aghlabid Ziyadat Allah I in 836. Ifriqiya's fifth Emir, Abu Ibrahim Ahmad, altered the mosque yet again between 856–63. Over subsequent centuries the mosque was restored and renovated many times, but most notably in 1025, 1249, 1294 and 1618 when the Ottomans were in control.

Inside the gate there is a vast **courtyard** which stands over a 3m deep cistern which has seven wells, their sides scored by rope, set into the stone pavement. Water drains into the cistern through the globed basin at the centre which is so-designed to prevent sand and dust from getting into it. Around the courtyard is a double portico which was added by Abu Ahmad, but rebuilt under the Hafsids in the 13C. The numerous columns of the portico are topped by Byzantine and Roman capitals and support horseshoe arches.

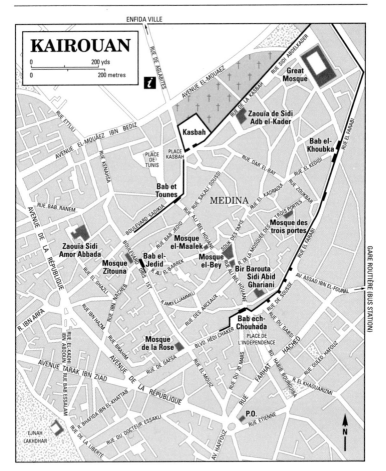

Set into the north wall of the courtyard is the mosque's immense **square minaret** which stands 35m high. The lower section of the minaret is the oldest extant in the Islamic world and dates from the rule of Caliph Hishamm (724–743). The upper section with its grooved dome was added in the 9C, as was the door in the base of the minaret which is surrounded by Roman carved lintels. Along the south side of the courtyard is the **entrance** to the mosque which is preceded by a deep portico, added by Ziyadet Allah I in the 9C. Also of this period is the **fluted dome** over the entrance, which is raised on a drum pierced by 12 windows that rests on a square base. There are 17 horseshoe doors in the façade, the largest of which are the central ones which are carved from cedarwood and date from the 13C restoration. The interior is not open to tourists, but it is possible to peer inside the doors. The 150 porphyry and marble columns in 17 parallel rows are Roman and Byzantine, but have Islamic capitals typical of the Aghlabid period. The **mihrab** stands higher than the original, as a result of Ziyadat's reconstruction when the whole structure was raised by 3m, and much Roman and Byzantine material from nearby sites was incorporated. The mihrab is lined with marble panels, each of which measures 60 by 45cm, brought from Samarra, carved with geometric, vegetal and shell motifs. One hundred and thirty lustre tiles (the earliest-known in the world as they were not new when placed there in 862) from Baghdad decorate the arch which is flanked by columns and capitals taken from a Byzantine church. The Emperor Constantine is said to have offered to buy the columns back for their weight in gold. The **cupola** preceding the mihrab rests on a drum which is encircled by eight windows and is decorated with shell squinches, a feature that was to become a trademark of the Fatimid period. The magnificent **teak wood mimber** to the right of the mihrab, the oldest in the Islamic world, was commisioned by Abu Ibrahim Ahmad.

Before leaving the mosque precinct it is worth walking along the side opposite the entrance to see the gate, **Lalla Rihana**. It was built in 1294 and is the most decorative of the mosque's entrances.

THE MEDINA
From the Great Mosque, head south-west along the **walls** which extend for 3.5km right the way around the medina, and were built in 1706–12, on the foundations of the 11C wall. Below is a **cemetery**, where some of the thickly whitewashed tombs are octagonal and support a gadrooned dome, in a style that dates from the Aghlabid era. Others have minarets modelled on the Great Mosque. Follow Rue de la Kasbah, which is lined with carpet shops, past the grooved dome of Zaouia Sidi Abd el Kader, along the walls to the **kasbah**. Closed to the public, the kasbah has high walls built of small bricks, and stands to one side of a large gateway in the medina walls. A short distance to the south is the busy square, Place de Tunis, off which is another gateway, **Bab et Tounes**, which was built in 1771 by Ali Bey.

Enter the medina, which measures 1km by 500m, through Bab et Tounes and follow the main drag, Rue Ali Bel Houane southwards. After 300m turn left and wander through the **souks**, each of which specialises in its own products. Throughout the medina you will see the local date cakes steeped in syrup, known as *makrouth*. The principal souks are: Souk Er Reba and Souk el Attarine which date from 1674; Souk Es Sekkajine, built at the end of the 17C; Souk dei Calzolai, where N. Davis wrote in 1862 that: 'The yellow leather slippers made here are as famous throughout the East as the red skull-caps made at Tunis', which was built in 1768, as was the Souk de Cisternes. **Bir Barouta**, a well built over the supposed spring found by Uqba, is surrounded by the souks and lies at the northern end of Place Barouta. Topped by a cupola, water is drawn from the well by a camel-powered wheel. It is much venerated by Muslims and is believed to be connected with a similar well in Mecca.

On the east side of the souk area, at the end of Rue de la Mosque des Trois Portes, is the **Mosque des Trois Portes**. The façade, dating from 866, is named after its three doors, one for women, one for men and the other for children. The upper wall of the façade has four bands of Kufic carvings. The lowest one dates from 1440, which was when the fat square minaret to the left of the façade was added. The upper inscriptions date from the 9C and sandwich a frieze of floral motifs.

Return to the main artery through the medina, Rue Ali Bel Haouane, and head towards the south gate in the medina walls, Bab ech Chouhada, turning left 50m before them, down Rue Ghariani. The **Zaouia Sidi Abid Ghariani** is 30m down this road on the right. It is named after the person who lived here in the 14C and who is buried within, although the present building dates from the 17C. A large studded door, set in an arched portal decorated with black-and-white stripes, leads into an L-shaped vestibule. The walls are clad with tiles and fine plasterwork and the ceiling is covered in cedar wood. Steps lead down into a courtyard which is surrounded by a portico of black and white horseshoe arches. Under the portico, the upper walls are decorated with finely fretted plaster, and on the south-west wall there are tiled panels depicting mosques and gardens. A door in the south-west wall leads into a former prayer room, with six columns and a black and white niche, which now contains an exhibition of restoration projects in the city. In the north-east wall, the first of two doors leads into a small room with a richly decorated ceiling that contains the tomb of Ghariani, which dates from the 14C. The second door in the north-east wall off the courtyard leads to an adjoining medersa which is also built around a courtyard with a well at its centre. The courtyard is surrounded by columns, many of which have fine Byzantine capitals. A staircase leads up from the west corner of the courtyard to the first floor of the main courtyard where there are wooden balconies and a series of rooms that house the offices of the medina restoration association the A.S.M.

Returning to Rue Ali Bel Haouane, continue through the south gate, **Bab ech Chouhada**, which was built in 1772. It overlooks a wide square, to the south of which is the modern part of the city, where there are cafés, restaurants and hotels surrounding the Place de l'Indépendance.

OUTER KAIROUAN

The remaining monuments in Kairouan lie outside the medina, off the ring-road, Avenue de la République and are perhaps rather distant to be visited on foot.

From the main roundabout in the modern city, follow Avenue de la République northwards for 900m, and turn right onto Rue el Gadraoul. After 100m turn left onto the small square in front of the **Zaouia of Sidi Amor Abbada**. Covered by five grooved domes, it was built in 1860 and contains the tomb of the marabout, Sidi Amor Abada. The tomb room now houses a small museum, the Museum of Popular Art and Tradition, which amongst other objects of the 19C has some enormous wooden tables inscribed with Kufic script.

Continue northwards along Avenue de la République for a further 700m to the **Mausolée Abi Zomaa** (open daily dawn to dusk). The mausoleum contains the remains of Abi Zomaa who was a companion of the Prophet. It is housed in a complex, the **ZAOUIA OF SIDI SAHAB**, which is also known as the Barber's Mosque. After the Prophet's death in 685, Abi Zomaa is said to have carried three hairs from his beard: one under his tongue, another under his right arm, and the third next to his heart. The building, which is a popular pilgrimage destination, dates from the 14C although it was largely rebuilt in 1631–65 by the Muradite Emir, Hammouda Pasha, and restored in the 19C.

The entrance leads into a spacious **courtyard** with brick walls and white-washed arches. In the north-west corner stands an elegant **minaret** with tiles decorating the upper part in the Andalucian style. A door on the left side of the courtyard leads into a tiled inner courtyard of an adjoining **medrese**, which was built by Mohammed Bey in 1685. It is surrounded by delicate columns, some of which are twisted, topped by Byzantine capitals. Off the west side, a black-and-white horseshoe arch leads into the **prayer hall** where brick arches are supported on columns.

Return to the main courtyard and head through the door to the right of the minaret into a charming **tiled vestibule** where fine plasterwork decorates the upper walls. Steps lead from here into a long **rectangular courtyard**, open to the sky, which is decorated with panels of Tunisian tiles and stucco work. Off the far end, a marble portal leads into a small square room, covered by a delicately patterned plaster dome. The room leads through to the last and most ornate of the **courtyards** in the complex, where marble columns support arcading with heavily carved spandrels, off the south-west side of which is the **tomb room of Abi Zomaa**. Preceded by a marble doorway, the tomb is surrounded by an ornate grille, and the room is covered by a plasterwork dome, which is gadrooned on the outside.

From the Zaouia of Sidi Sahab, Avenue de la République becomes wider and heads east in the direction of Enfidaville. After 600m there is a large car park on the left, in front of the **Aghlabid Basins** (open daily dawn to dusk). Restored in 1969, the basins were originally built by the Aghlabids to supply their palace, which stood behind the Great Mosque, with water. The water was carried by aqueduct from a spring 30km away. Two of the original 14 basins remain, the largest of the two having 64 sides and measuring 130m across its widest point. It is strengthened by round buttresses inside and out and has a central pier which the ruler used for watersports. The smaller basin has a diameter of 37m and was used as a filter.

RAQQUADA

The Aghlabids' other palace, **Raqquada**, built outside Kairouan so that the Aghlabids could escape criticism of their dissolute lifestyle, can be visited by a 14km excursion south of the city. Surrounding a large courtyard, the palace had a series of semicircular towers supporting the outer walls. It had an underground cistern, as well as nearby free-standing cisterns, and an artificial lake, 182m long, which was reinforced with buttresses similar to those in the reservoir at Kairouan. A few hundred metres from the ruins is the **National Museum of Islamic Art** (open Tues–Sun, 09.00–16.00). It houses finds from the excavations of Raqquada, including 9C ceramics and jewellery. Also of interest are the 10C manuscripts of pages from the Koran and a collection of Fatimid and Zirid coins.

14 · Kairouan to Sbeitla

The route from Kairouan to Sbeitla heads westwards to the ancient site of (105km) Mactaris, from where excursions are made into the Dorsale Mountains, before turning south to (88km) Sufetula via Sbiba. Accommodation along the way is limited. If excursions are made into the Dorsale Mountains, an overnight stay in El Kef would break up an otherwise long day. Buses bound for El Kef from Kairouan stop at Maktar, from where occasional louages leave for Sbeitla.

From Kairouan, take the GP3, which leaves the city from alongside the Zaouia Sidi Sahab, in the direction of Maktar. At the crossroads in (10km) **El Batten**, turn left in the direction of Tozeur, passing through the village of (13km) **Chebika**. At the next crossroads, after a further 6km, turn right and follow signs to (22km) **Haffouz** on the GP12, a quiet road which heads over the barren foothills of the Dorsale Mountains. Turn right at Haffouz to Maktar, following the El Kerd river through a desolate landscape, before climbing up onto a rocky spur of the Dorsale Mountains, where, 32km from Haffouz, the road passes through an impressive outcrop of **eroded rock**. The road emerges from the tunnel in the village of **El Garia**, from where it is a further 5km until the right turn (which has no sign) to Kesra.

   KESRA, hugging a cliff face at a height of 1075m, lies 3km off the main road. At the edge of the village is a large graveyard and a **koubba**, the tomb of a marabout. On the hill summit above the village are the scant remains of a **Byzantine fortress**, the stone of which has been plundered to build the terraces on the steep surrounding terrain. The village stands on the Roman site of Chusira, but nothing remains apart from the odd chunk of masonry built into the walls of the local houses, which, not unlike their Roman predecessors, are built round courtyards. The GP12 winds through the modern outskirts of Kesra where there is a reasonable hotel, Hotel des Chasseurs, passed on the left.

   After 17km the road climbs up above a vast corn-growing plain to **MAKTAR**, which stands at an altitude of 950m. This agricultural town, built by the French in 1887, is a centre of corn farming. It has one very basic hotel, the *Mactaris*, near the roundabout, which has a simple restaurant, and an area of small shops laid out on a grid system of streets on the hill slope, with the bus station at the top.

MACTARIS

The ancient site of **Mactaris (open summer, daily, 08.00–17.30, winter, daily, 08.00–17.00) is just below the town near the main roundabout. Before reaching the site, to the left of the roundabout is a **triumphal arch**. Once the main entrance to the city, it was described by N. Davis in 1862 as: 'The first attractive object in approaching Maktar from the part we entered it, is a stately triumphal arch, built on a slight eminence, at the foot of which there is a small olive grove, and close to it a spring of delicious water. A spot better adapted for a tent cannot possibly be conceived.' The arch, currently under restoration, is known as Bab el Ain, but also as the tophet gate, as a Punic tophet, with 85 stelae which are now in the Bardo, has been found next to it. A few steps further brings you to the car park and site entrance.

History

Mactaris was originally the site of a Numidian fortress which protected the region of the Massyle kings against Berber incursions. In 146 BC, with the fall of Carthage, many Punic refugees took shelter here, and in 46 BC the city, which was by then inhabited by a mixed Punic–Numidian population, was incorporated into the Roman province of Africa Nova. The city prospered, becoming a regional capital over 62 other towns, and was made a colony in 180 under Marcus Aurelius. An inscription on stone to a local agricultural worker, the Reaper of Mactaris, now in the Louvre, gives an insight into the flourishing economy and social mobility of the population. It says that the Reaper came from a poor family and worked in tropical conditions from infancy as an itinerant reaper. He rose to foreman, and managed to save enough money to buy his own property and was later elected to the town council, rising from 'hayseed to censor'.

Mactaris remained inhabited until 1050, with the city was looted by the Hilali Arab invaders.

The **MUSEUM**, at the site entrance, has a collection of **neo-Punic stelae**, indicating how Punic culture survived among the inhabitants of Mactaris as late as the 3C. The museum also has a collection of Roman sculpture and masonry, amongst the most important of which is an **inscribed architrave**, dedicated to Domiziano from the Juvenes school. Other finds include **oil lamps** from the Roman to Byzantine era, coins and a **6C tomb mosaic** with an inscription.

From the museum, head through the garden, past the ticket office on the right, and up a well-preserved **paved Roman road** which is lined with bases of columns and capitals at either side. After 500m, off to the left, are the scant remains of a Punic temple dedicated to **Hathor Miskar**. The temple, which was reconstructed in the 2C, is built over a shrine which dates from the 1C BC. It was here that the longest Punic inscription in Tunisia, an inventory of 47 lines inscribed on ten columns, was discovered. To the east of the temple are the ruins of the **House of Venus** which is named after the 2C mosaic found here. The house covered an area of 500 square metres, and in addition to the **Venus mosaic**, a bird mosaic was found in a bedchamber, and a marine motif mosaic with lobsters and octopuses in the dining room.

Continue up the paved way to the ****forum** which was first built in 116 and then enlarged in the 3C. Raised on a stepped platform, this rectangular paved area is surrounded by the remnants of its porticoes and is scattered with pieces of masonry. On the south side of the forum stands the very well-preserved ****Arch of Trajan**. It was built at the same time as the forum in 116 and is complete with its inscribed dedication to Trajan which reads: 'Conqueror of the Germans, Armenians and Parthinians in honour of the town's promotion to the status of municipium'.

Head through the arch down to a small square, **Place Sévériènne**. A short distance straight ahead are the remains of a 5C church, the **Hildeguns Basilica**, which was built to inter the remains of a Vandal who converted to Byzantine Christianity. It originally had three naves with a baptistery behind the main apse. The remains, including a few broken columns along the central aisle, are rather confusing as they are built over the ruins of Roman housing. Continue beyond the Hildeguns Basilica for 200m to the **Great South Baths**. Built in the heyday of the late 2C, the baths are modelled on those of Carthage, but have survived in a better state of preservation with the walls still standing 20m high in parts. The small stones used in the structure are Byzantine and date from the 6C when the baths were converted into a fortress.

Return to Place Sévérienne, and turn left down a paved road, which heads eastwards for 150m to the scant remains of the **Punic Forum**. Once over-looking the forum, the base of the **Temple of Liber Pater**, also known as the Temple of Bacchus, is on the right. It was commissioned by the city's fullers (clothes' cleaners) in 180 and had a double crypt. A little further on, to the west, are the remains of a curious semicircular building surrounded by arches and facing an apse. It is of unknown origin and was named by the excavators in 1911 as the **Châtelain**. To the north-west are the insignificant remains of the **North Baths** which date from the 6C Byzantine era. There is another baths complex to the south-west known as the **Thermes du Soffite Capitolin**. Erected under Marcus Aurelius at the end of the 2C, the baths were later converted into a Christian basilica.

Off the west side of the Punic forum are the charming remains of the ****Schola Juvenes**, a clubhouse built in AD 88, for a paramilitary group of men of Romanised Punic families; the names on the inscription, which is now in the site museum, include Datus, Felix, Fortunatus, Saturninus, Rogatus and Victor. The members, as well as defending the city, were said to have collected taxes and it is thought that the **Quadrilobe Building** to the south was used for collecting and distributing moneys for the city. During the Byzantine era it was converted into a church and the central clubroom is now an apsidal chapel with mosaic floors and columns lining the central aisle, and an altar constructed from a Punic stele.

A Roman and Byzantine **necropolis** lies to the south-west of the Schola where there is a **pyramidal mausoleum**, similar in style to the Numidian tomb at Dougga, although this one is thought to be Roman.

Return to Place Sévérienne and turn left down a 600m track which leads back to the car park, passing on the right the remains of an **amphitheatre**, just before the museum. At the back of the museum is the stepped base of a **temple** which was later converted into a church in the 6C.

In the Dorsale Mountains to the north of Maktar there are numerous Roman ruins. A selection of these, namely Kbor Klib, Ksour Toual and Elles, lie within a 100km round trip excursion from Maktar.

The excursion starts by taking the GP12, which leaves Maktar from along-side the museum, in the direction of El Kef. The road heads downhill to a vast rolling plain of cornfields. After 20km turn right in the direction of Siliana and proceed for 13.5km to a ridge, where just before the summit is an unsigned track on the right which leads to the ruins of **Kbor Klib**. The track, which is covered in sea-shell fossils, ends after 100m at the well-preserved walls of a **Roman monument** measuring 15m by 40m, and now 6m high, which was built to celebrate the triumph of Caesar over his foreign enemies in Gaul and domestic enemies (Pompey) at Thapsus. Divided by two blind alleys, the left fork of which has particularly fine stonework, the monument originally had a frieze which incorporated Macedonian devices such as Artemis on a shield and a cuirass on pikes. These were references to Caesar's enemies, the vanquished Ptolemies, who were descended from the Macedonian, Alexander the Great. It was erected in this isolated spot as it was considered bad taste to gloat over victory in a civil war.

Return to the road and continue to the summit of the ridge, on the far side of which, after 1km, the mausoleum of **Ksar Toual** can be seen on the left. The monument, which is two storeys high, lies in a field 50m from the road. A typical **Roman mausoleum**, its walls are decorated with pilasters and it has a doorway with carved lintels in the base. Inside, the niches, columbaria, used to hold lamps and ashes, and are still visible.

Head back to the GP12, and continue for a further 3km in the direction of El Kef to the village of Vieux Sers. Turn left onto a pot-holed road which finally ends after 11km at **Elles**, a remote village which relies on a spring for its water supply. From the spring, head up the first left fork to a stepped platform, catalogued as number 18, which is covered by vast stone slabs that form burial chambers. Dating from the 2C BC, the **mausoleum** was built for the Numidian nobility. Following the track around the bend to the hill-top, there are numerous other, less well-preserved **burial chambers**. The **best-preserved mausoleum**, however, is to the right of the village, and is catalogued as number 29. It has an impressive façade of megalithic stone slabs and contains seven chambers.

From Maktar, head southwards, leaving the town on the road to Rouhia, which climbs up to a pass after 11km. It descends the other side into a vast plain, meeting a crossroads after a further 11km. Turn left at the crossroads onto the MC71 in the direction of **Rouhia**, 12km south. This small village, surrounded by young olive groves, has a few shops straddled along the road. Continue south on the MC71 through the large village of (7km) **Jediliene**, which lies on the banks of a river of the same name, to (7km) Sbiba.

Sbiba, a small agricultural backwater, is built on the site of ancient **Sufes**. Apart from having a Punic name, little is known of the city and its history, except for the incident that has come down to us through St Augustine. The saint wrote to the authorities, accusing them of allowing the city's inhabitants to kill 60 Christians. (The Christians, then a minority, had followed the directives issued by the emperor, a Christian, and smashed a statue of Hercules, the city's god.) Augustine wrote: 'Your crime has stained with blood the temples and public places. You have flouted Roman law, insulted and spoken foul of the emperor. The man amongst you who has killed the greatest number is praised, and you gave him a place in your council.'

The remains of Sufes are scant. The best-preserved structure is a semicircular **nymphaeum** which is at the bottom of the village. It stands in a wire enclosure, amid broken columns and parts of an inscription. Further down the hill, to the east, surrounded by fruit orchards, are the crumbling walls of the former **baths**. The **mosque** in the village also has ancient origins, being converted from a basilica in the 7C.

The MC71 continues across the monotonous steppe for 40km to the town of Sbeitla, the starting point of route 15.

15 · Sbeitla to Gafsa

The route starts with a tour of Sbeitla, before heading south for 128km to Gafsa. There are two buses a day direct from Sbeitla to Gafsa. Alternatively, regular services depart for Kasserine from where there are louages to Gafsa.

SBEITLA

Sbeitla is a small town straddled alongside the main road on a high plain at an altitude of 537m. It is mainly of interest, not for anything in the town itself, but for the very impressive nearby ruins of Sufetula, a Roman city built of a striking ochre-colour stone.

- **Railway station**. Rue Habib Thameur. Lines for Kasserine and Kairouan–Sousse.

- **Bus station**. On road to Kairouan. SNT services to Maktar, Siliana and Tunis. Other destinations: El Kef (via Sbiba), Gafsa, Kairouan, Kasserine, Sfax and Tozeur.

- **Louage and taxi station**. From the bus station.

- **Hotels**. There are two decent hotels, both of which have swimming pools although they are not always filled. The more expensive of the two is the *Sufetula* which enjoys excellent views of the Roman ruins. The *Bakini*, which is more affordable and very adequate, is in the town on Rue du 2 Mars 1934. At the cheap end of the market is the *Ezzohour* at the bus station.

- **Shopping**. There is a permanent food market off Ave A. Belhaouane, and a general market held every Wednesday.

- **Post office**. Rue Farhat Hached.

History
Sufetula, with its Punic name, undoubtedly has Punic origins, but as yet there has been no archaeological evidence to prove this. The ruins seen today are of the prosperous Roman city, founded by either Vespasian or Flavia, which became a municipality in the 1C. The cultivation of olive trees and the export of oil to Italy was central to the city's economy as was its strategic position on the north trade route. So affluent was trade that the city, built on a grid network of streets, covered some 50 hectares. In 646, the pretender to the Byzantine throne, Gregory, transferred his capital here from Carthage in order to defend it against Arab invasions. Although protected by a fort, measuring 20m by 20m, which was only accessible by a ladder over its double walls, the city fell in 647 when the Arab leader Abdallah ibn Saad attacked with 20,000 men, defeating and killing Gregory. The city was thereafter abandoned and according to an account of 1862: 'Till within the last few years these ruins were the haunt, and stronghold, of the banditti of the Maajer Arabs, under the command of Sheikh Ahmed Belaarem.' The first excavations took place between 1906 and 1922. Archaeologists continue to work on the site but as yet only one third of the city has been uncovered.

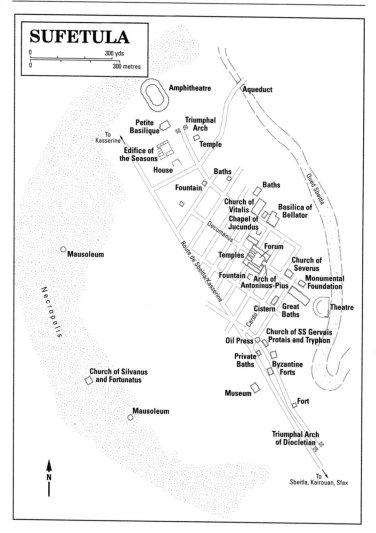

SUFETULA

0 — 300 yds
0 — 300 metres

Amphitheatre
Aqueduct
Petite Basilique
Triumphal Arch
To Kasserine
Temple
Edifice of the Seasons
House
Baths
Fountain
Baths
Church of Vitalis
Basilica of Bellator
Chapel of Jucundus
Decumanus
Forum
Temples
Church of Severus
Route de Sbeitla/Kasserine
Fountain
Arch of Antoninus-Pius
Monumental Foundation
Mausoleum
Cistern
Great Baths
Theatre
Cardo
Church of SS Gervais Protais and Tryphon
Oil Press
Private Baths
Byzantine Forts
Church of Silvanus and Fortunatus
Museum
Necropolis
Mausoleum
Fort
Oued Sbeitla
Triumphal Arch of Diocletian
N
To Sbeitla, Kairouan, Sfax

The ruins of **Sufetula** (open daily dawn to dusk) are next to the main road,
to the north of the town. The **museum** (open daily, 09.00–16.30), which is
on one side of the road, contains finds from the site and the surrounding
region. To the left of the door there are **three Roman statues**: a torso of
Diana, a bust of Creperia Innula and a headless female statuette from Sbiba.
In the second room there is a fine mosaic of the Triumph of Venus. This room
also contains a collection of **Roman oil lamps**, pottery and coins. There is an

unusual collection of square **Hafsid coins** dating from the 13–14C, as well as Byzantine inscriptions from the 5C and an inscribed **circular altar table**.

The site entrance is opposite the museum on the other side of the road. Inside the gates turn left onto a **Roman paved road** which passes between a pair of 7C **Byzantine forts**, their walls built with large blocks of Roman masonry. A little further beyond on the left there are the remains of **private baths**, a series of rooms with mosaic-lined pools. The paved road ends at an **oil press** which was built in the 10C in the middle of the street, as good an indication as any that Sufetula was a shadow of its former self. Raised above the road, to the right of the oil press, are the ruins of the **Church of Sts Gervais, Protais and Tryphon** which was consecrated in the 6C. The foundations and doorway, which are all that remain, are made from Roman masonry.

Byzantine olive press

Turn right at the church and follow an irregularly paved road which heads northwards passing tombstones and a large **cistern** on the left, before reaching the ruins of a late 4C **monumental fountain**, of which only the lower section of five pillars remain. Turn left at the fountain, descending four steep steps onto a paved road, to the right side of which tall piers mark the site of the **Church of Severus** with its broken columns lining the aisles. It was built by the Donatist community, probably as their cathedral, on the site of a 3C temple. The five aisles stand on the temple courtyard and the quadrilobed baptistery occupies the cella.

From the church head west, past the low walls of **market buildings**, to the forum which is approached by the magnificent ****Arch of Antoninus Pius**. This triple bay arch, according to its inscription, was built in 139, but was never completed as is testified by the unfinished surface of the four Corinthian columns across its façade. The ****forum**, a paved area measuring 67m by 40m, was built at the same time, although the enclosing wall, which stands up to 4m high in places, was built by the Byzantines. It is surrounded on three sides by the remnants of shops and colonnades, while the fourth side, that facing the arch, has ****three temples**. Unlike at Dougga and other cities, where one temple was dedicated to the triad of gods, here there is one temple for each. The **central temple**, which is the largest and was the most decorative, is dedicated to Jupiter. It is not preceded by steps, but was entered through the **sister temples**, originally connected by arches at either side, dedicated to Juno and Minerva, both of which had porticoed entrances topped by pediments (only that on the left has been restored). The **interiors** are well-preserved, with niches, and recesses for beams in the upper walls. The temples are also well worth viewing from behind, where the **back wall** of the Jupiter temple is complete with its pediment and decorative half columns.

Head north of the forum for 100m to the walls of the Byzantine **Basilica of Bellator**, which was built in the 4C as the city's cathedral, on the site of an earlier temple. To its west is a former baptistery which preserves the original font and the four surrounding columns. Two still have their Corinthian capitals but the canopy has long gone. The baptistery was converted to a **chapel**, dedicated to the Bishop Jucundus, who was buried in the apse after he was martyred by the Arian Vandals.

Further to the west is the **Church of Vitalis**, which was built as the new cathedral. It has five aisles, in which the mosaic pavement remains in parts, and two apses dating from different periods. In the adjoining **baptistery** there is a very fine immersion font decorated with mosaics. Other fragments of mosaics remain in the series of surrounding rooms which probably belonged to the **Bishop's residence**.

From the Church of Vitalis, continue north-west along a roughly paved road for 200m to a well-preserved 3C **fountain** on the left of the road. Raised on a paved area which is preceded by three arches, it has a rectangular basin with four pilasters decorating its back wall.

Continue past the fountain, joining a grassy track which leads for a further 250m to the north-westernmost extent of the city. On the left is the **Edifice of the Seasons** which has a large central courtyard surrounded by the remnants of columns and a series of rooms off the north and south sides. The largest room is the **dining room** which has a wide apse where a mosaic of the four seasons (now in the Bardo Museum) was found. To the left is a smaller room with apses at either end which would once have had a fountain at the centre.

Capitoline Temples of Juno, Jupiter and Minerva

On the right of the grassy track are the remains of a **temple** of which only the cella has survived. The track ends at the base of a 3C **triumphal arch** dedicated to Severus. Beyond the arch on the left is the **Petite Basilique** which is built on a Roman peristyle house, the central courtyard of which is still visible with its column bases. A further 100m beyond this there is a mound, at the far side of which lies the great grassy bowl of an **amphitheatre** which is dotted with square column bases.

The remaining monuments lie at the opposite end of the site. Return to the Church of Severus and follow the paved road down the hill past the ruins of the **Great Baths** on the right. Built in the 3C, the caldarium and frigidarium occupy two large rooms at the centre of the complex, one of which has well-preserved **pools** at either end. Both are surrounded by remnants of columns and have mosaic pavements. On the south side there is a colonnaded **palaestra**, and a series of small rooms linked by arches and doorways with traces of the hypercaust system visible in places.

Continue down the paved road to the remains of the **theatre** which is built above a river, the Oued Sbeitla, dry for most of the year. Dating from the 3C, only a small section of the seating has been preserved and the stage is likewise dilapidated. Seven columns raised on a low wall mark where the stage buildings once stood.

Return to the site entrance, from where the excellently preserved **Triumphal Arch of Diocletian** is visible 300m away, in the direction of Sbeitla town centre. It once stood on the road to Hadrumetum (Sousse) and marked the southern extremity of the city. Built in the 3C, it is decorated with Corinthian columns and rectangular niches that would have held statues.

Leave Sbeitla by heading back along the Sbiba road for 5km and then forking left onto the GP13 in the direction of Gafsa. The road heads across a barren plain to the right of which rises the mountainous mass of Jebel Chambi (1544m), the tallest mountain in Tunisia. It was made a National Park area in 1981, protecting gazelles, moufflons, hyenas and birds of prey. It was through a pass here in the mountains, in February 1943, that the Axis powers launched an offensive against the Americans, causing the loss of 100 lives.

After 19km, the GP13 passes through the village of **Bouzguem**, which is built on the banks of the wide muddy river, the Oued el Htab. Crossing the river, the road follows the railway and after a further 7km it approaches Kasserine, passing a cellulose factory on the left, the Société Saccherie du Centre, which uses local esparto grass for the production of paper.

KASSERINE is unattractively sprawled along the main road. It has two or three hotels, including the *Hotel Pinus* on the right, banks, shops and a market on Thursdays where baskets and mats made from esparto grass are sold. Nearby, however, are the **Roman ruins** of Cillium.

CILLIUM

The first ancient relic is a **mausoleum**, which stands below the GP13 on the right, 2km beyond the town centre, just before the road forks left to Gafsa. Dating from the reign of Marcus Aurelius, is stands on three storeys, 14m high. The epitaph carved on the side, 110 lines long, is dedicated to Flavius Secundus and his family, for whom the mausoleum was built. A statue of Flavius once filled the niche in the topmost section, which was originally surmounted by a pyramidal roof.

The main part of ancient Cillium is further along the GP17, the road to Gafsa, which passes under the railway and past the Hotel Cillium. A yellow signpost 300m after the hotel marks the track to the *Site Archéologique* (open daily dawn to dusk).

History

Cillium was founded as a castellum during the Flavian period and promoted to a municipality by Trajan. It was the wealthy centre of an olive oil-producing area which fell into decline along with Roman Africa, the trees being torn up when they became subject to taxation under Islamic rule.

The best-preserved edifice is the 3C **triumphal arch** which lies 350m from the gate. Restored under Constantine in 312, it has a well-preserved inscription on one side. At the highest point of the site, 150m south-east of the gate, now surrounded by prickly pear cactus, are the ruins of a podium. It once supported a Roman temple which had a colonnaded enclosure in front. A statue base found here with 'genio' inscribed on it suggests that this is the remains of the **capitol**. A further 100m south-east, the remains of a **theatre** look out across the Oued Derb river. Built during the reign of Flavius, the cavea, which is 53m in diameter, could hold 2500 spectators. Only eight rows of seats are left standing, but they are in good condition, as are the stage buildings with their niches for statues.

The site is otherwise unexcavated with stones strewn all over the sandy soil giving little indication as to what once stood there. The brick structure to the west of the capitol is believed to be a **Byzantine baths**, nearby which are the walls of a **Byzantine fortress** built from huge blocks of Roman masonry.

The GP17 continues south-west through a region of high, arid steppe with a series of ridges which run between the Dorsale Mountains and the Gafsa range at the north end of the Sahara. After 27km turn left onto the GP15 which continues southwards in the direction of Gafsa. The road crosses the railway line, 2km beyond which it passes a vast area of fallen masonry, the site of ancient **THELEPTE**. The ruins cover both sides of the road for the next 5km. Thelepte, originally known as Thamesmida, was an important settlement during the Byzantine era, when numerous basilicas were built here. In a large area of **Byzantine housing**, all of which was razed to the ground, is the home of St Fulgentius. Born in 467 of a senatorial family, Fulgentius was appointed procurator of the town, but gave up the post in order to become a monk. He was exiled by the Vandal Arians to Sicily and Sardinia from where he wrote a series of essays against the Arian creed. The best remains, however, are the **Roman theatre** and the **baths** near the banks of the river, to the right of the road.

At the southernmost point of Thelepte, the GP15 passes through **Feriana**, a busy town with a weekly market on Thursdays, a hotel, banks, shops and petrol station. The road crosses a series of rivers which are dry for most of the year and after 22km passes through **Del Abbes** and heads towards the Gafsa mountain range. The province of Gafsa is entered after a further 9km on a stretch of road which is often dusted with sand. The village of **Ennadhour**, a further 12km, is set in the Gafsa foothills, through which the road heads, passing an oasis of palms on the left, before reaching Gafsa after a further 18km.

VI GAFSA AND THE CHOTT

16 · Gafsa to Tozeur

The route takes in Gafsa, then heads south-west into the Saharan region, crossing the Chott el Jerid, a vast salt lake. It is 93km from Gafsa to Tozeur, via Philippe Thomas, and there are no petrol stations along the way. Also check on road conditions before setting out as the road can be covered with drifting sand. There are seven buses a day from Gafsa to Tozeur, and at least as many louages.

GAFSA

Gafsa, the administrative and economic centre of the Jerid region, is a large town with a busy market area and a palmery of some 100,000 trees. The dates produced here are of inferior quality but other fruit, grown in the shade of the palms—apricots, citrus fruits, figs and particularly pistachios—are first rate. There is not a great deal to see in the town, but it is a peaceful place with the atmosphere of an oasis.

- **Railway station**. Gafsa Gare, 2km from the town centre on Gabès road. Lines for Tozeur, Gabès, Sfax–El Jem–Sousse–Hammamet–Tunis.

- **Bus station**. Ave Habib Bourguiba, tel. (06) 221587. SNTRI run services to Tunis. STN operate buses to Kairouan, Tozeur and Nefta. Other destinations are Kasserine, Sfax, Gabès.

- **Louage station**. On road to Gabès. Regular services to Gabès, Kasserine, Metlaoui, Sfax, Tunis.

- **Taxis**. Place du 7 Novembre.

- **Hotels**. The most expensive hotel in town is the *Hotel Mamoun*, on the road to Gabès, which is used by tour groups. Next in price is the *Hotel Jugurtha* which is near the public gardens and the *Hotel Gafsa* on Rue Ahmet Snoussi. At the cheaper end of the market there is the *Tunis Hotel* on Place du 7 Novembre.

- **Shopping**. General market every Wednesday. Main shopping street in souk area, Rue Kilani el Metoui, runs east of the kasbah.

- **Post office**. Avenue Habib Bourguiba.

- **Tourist information**. Antenne du Tourisme, Place des Piscines Romaines, tel. (06) 221664.

- **Children**. Zoo, 6km north on GP3 in direction of Tunis.

History

The area was settled as far back as 10,000 BC, by a Stone Age people, whose artefacts have been unearthed by archaeologists in the surrounding region. The culture, known as Capsian, took its name from the ancient city of Capsa which stood on the site of modern Gafsa. Capsa was founded after the Roman General Marius arrived in 107 BC and destroyed the original Numidian settlement along with its inhabitants. The act marked the end of the Jugurthine War, and allowed Marius to settle his veterans on the site in a new Roman colony. It became a municipality under Hadrian and was later fortified by Soloman, the Byzantine Emperor Justinian's general, in 540. The town fell into Arab control in 668 but was not totally destroyed, and Latin continued to be spoken up until the 12C. During the Hafsid era, the Byzantine fortifications were renovated, and in 1556 the corsair Dragut took control of the fort. The defensive walls were destroyed in 1943 by the explosion of an Allied ammunition store.

The **kasbah** is on Avenue Habib Bourguiba, the main street in the modern part of the town. Originally a Byzantine fort, the kasbah was rebuilt in its present form by the Hafsids in 1434. Its defences were strong enough to repel Dragut's attack in 1551, although it succumbed when he returned with larger forces in 1556. It has been pristinely restored, but although it is possible to walk around the outside of the **walls** which are interspersed with towers, the interior is not open to the public. Following the road along the right wall of the kasbah you will find a **crafts centre** where apprentice weavers can be seen at work making *haouli* (carpets) and *ferrachia* (covers in highly coloured geometric designs of Berber origin).

Continue south along Avenue Habib Bourguiba to the **arch** at the end of the road. A short distance beyond the arch on the left is a small **museum** (open summer, daily, 08.00–12.00, 15.00–17.00, winter, Tues–Sun, 08.00–16.30). It contains several 4C mosaics, the largest of which, **Athletic Games of Pugilat**, is set in the floor. The museum also has finds from Capsian sites, including a large collection of Stone Age flints.

Continue downhill from the museum to a charming square which is built around **two Roman pools**. Built as cisterns, they are 4m deep and linked by an underground channel. The water issues from a natural hot spring at a temperature of 31°C. The larger of the two, the men's bath, measures 19m by 16m, and has an inscription on the east wall dedicated to Neptune and the nymphs. The pool is also known as Ain Es Saqqain, meaning the 'source of the Christians'. Men and children bathe in the water here while women tend to use the privacy of the **hammam** which is just off the square.

From Gafsa, head west on the GP3, turning left at the main crossroads in the town, in the direction of Metlaoui. The GP3, a narrow road, often heavy with traffic, heads along the base of the Gafsa Mountains, which rise to the right, bare and gullied. There are no signs of humanity until **Philippe Thomas**, 37km from Gafsa, where factories and housing spread along the road.

Philippe Thomas, a Frenchman, discovered phosphates in the region in 1885. In 1895, the French opened a factory here, the Compagnie des Phosphates de Gafsa, producing phosphate fertilisers. The fertilisers were exported to France via Sfax which was connected by a narrow gauge railway in 1899. The industry thrives to this day, being the fourth largest producer of phosphates in the world.

Metlaoui, where phosphate is mined at a depth of 5–8m, is signposted on the right, a further 3km along the GP3. The town was built at the end of the 19C by the French. From here the **Lézard Rouge**, a train dating from colonial times which was presented as a gift in 1940 to the Bey of Tunis, can be taken up the **Seldja Gorge**, which is 10km to the west of the town. The gorge ranges in depth from 150–200m and offers some spectacular scenery. The narrowest point is named the Coup du Sabre. It is so-named after the legend which recounts that it was hewn out by the Berber prince Al Mansour with his sabre, while running away with his sweetheart, Leila. The gorge can also be reached by road. Follow the mining track to the west of the town which leads for 5km to the gorge entrance, from where a footpath continues on the right along the railway line.

The GP3 heads south across an undulating landscape which becomes increasingly desert-like with barriers built along the road to stop sand drifting. After 16km the road approaches the salt lake of **El Gharsa**, crossing the reedy Oued el Melah, 3km further on, which drains into it. Palmeries, like mirages, appear after a further 14.5km. **El Hamma du Jerid**, 10km further on, lies at the centre of a large palmery, and is built on the site of a Roman thermal spa, Acquae Tacapitanae. A **brick hammam** has replaced the original Roman baths where the sulphureous water, recommended for rheumatism and skin conditions, issues at 47°C. In 1912 Norman Douglas wrote: 'A pious legend runs to the effect that this water of El Hamma used to be cold, but that an Arab marabout was persuaded to spit in it and lo! it suddenly became hot and mineral.'

The GP3 leaves El Hamma, passing a popular restaurant on the left, before continuing for a further 11km across the desert to Tozeur, which is the starting point of Route 17.

17 · Tozeur and Nefta

The oases of Tozeur and Nefta are 23km apart, on the stretch of land that separates the Chott el Jerid and Chott el Gharsa. The road between the two towns is reasonable and protected from drifting sands by palm fences. Five buses a day ply back and forth between the two towns, and at least as many louages.

TOZEUR

Tozeur, on the edge of the Sahara, is baking hot and very dry in summer. Like the desert sand, the town is predominantly yellow and is built from small bricks made of sand and clay, a technique that was first used in 8C Syria and Iraq. Despite the tourism attracted to the town by its proximity with the Sahara, and its airport, local life is relatively unspoilt. Local women still wear their traditional black *haik* with its pale blue stripe, and the market-place is filled with fodder and esparto grass brought in from the palmeries by donkey. The town stands in a large oasis of 196 springs, covering 1000 hectares, which supports 20 small villages. The dates grown here, *deglet en nour*, are the best in Tunisia and have been exported for centuries. Accounts from the 17C tell of a thousand camels a day leaving the town loaded with dates. The climate, which gives the dates their quality, has its drawbacks and the streets are often dusted with blown sand. Sandstorms are not uncommon; one which blew for 72 hours in 1857 when French legions were posted here 'threw some of the French detachment off their horses, and finally obliged the whole company to stamp up and down for 24 hours in the twilight of raging sand for fear of being buried alive. It submerged several hundred palm trees of the Tozeur oasis up to their crowns, and they are 60–100ft high.'

- **Airport**. International Airport of Tozeur, 2km on Nefta road, tel. (06) 450388.

- **Airline companies**. Tunis Air, Ave Farhat Hached, tel. (06) 452127.

- **Railway station**. Line for Gafsa–Sfax–Sousse, but station currently out of operation.

- **Bus station**. Ave Farhat Hached. Services to Gabès, Gafsa, Kairouan, Kebili, Nefta and Tunis.

- **Louage station**. Opposite bus station. Regular services to Degache, Gafsa and Nefta. Other destinations include Tunis and Jerba.

- **Hotels**. There are several smart hotels catering for tour groups, including the *Continental* and *Oasis* on Ave Abou el Kacem Chebbi, and the *Ras el Ain* and others in the *zone touristique* to the west of the town. The *Jerid* on Ave Abou el Kacem Chebbi is less prestigious. In the bottom bracket there is the *Residence Warda*, a clean family-run pension, on Ave Abou el Kacem Chebbi. There is also the *Splendid* and *Essada* in the town centre.

- **Shopping**. Monoprix on Nefta road. General market Tuesday. Covered market on Place du Marché.

- **Post office**. Place du Marché, tel. (06) 451166.

- **Tourist information**. Syndicat d'Initiative, Ave Habib Bourguiba, tel. (06) 450034. Bureau du Tourisme, Ave Abou el Kacem Chebbi, tel. (06) 454503.

- **Medical care**. Tourism assistance, tel. (06) 454999.

- **Festivals**. Oasis Festival, December.

- **Entertainment**. Café in the tourist complex, Dar Chraiet.

- **Children**. Pony traps and camels can be hired on Ave Abou el Kacem Chebbi. Medina of 1001 Nights, a living museum in the tourist complex, Dar Chraiet. Sahara Zoo, 2km south of Ave Abou el Kacem Chebbi, tel. (06) 450003. Si Tijani zoo, 1km north of Ave Farhat Hached.

History

Thusuros, as Tozeur was originally known, was a Roman outpost, marking the south-west extremity of the empire; it survived through Byzantine times, when Christian Berbers defended it against the Arabs. Like the rest of the country it eventually fell to the Arabs in the 7C and was resettled, becoming an important town on the desert trade route under the Hafsids in the 14C. Through trade in dates, Negro slaves, gold and ivory, Tozeur grew rich, only to be devastated in the 16C by a cholera epidemic which wiped out half of the population. However, the town re-established its trading reputation and in the 18C prospered on the bartering of dates for slaves. Dates continue to be a main source of income in the town, second only to tourism.

The town is centred on **Avenue Habib Bourguiba**, where there are tourist shops in the **brick arcades** along either side, which sell the attractive local flat weaves and baskets. Roughly midway along, there is a square off one side, the **Place du Marché**, also known as the Place Ibn Chaabat. On one side of this bustling square is the entrance to the **covered fruit and vegetable market** and on the other a **fountain**. From here it is possible to explore the oldest part of the town, which dates from the 14C, by heading east along **Rue des Jardins**. Although peaceful now, this quarter, known as **Ouled el Hadef**, was a dangerous place up until the mid 19C, as it was in conflict with the neighbouring Zebda quarter, which lies along the west side of Avenue Habib Bourguiba. There is a modest museum in Ouled el Hadef, on **Rue de Kairouan**, the **Musée Sidi Bou Aissa** (open Tues–Sun, 09.00–12.00, 14.00–17.30) which is housed in the koubba, or tomb room, of Sidi Bou Aissa. It is dedicated to social and domestic life in the pre-desert region, and includes exhibits concerning the marriage ceremony, costumes, textiles, ceramics, weapons, oil lamps and coins.

Tozeur's ****palmery** is made up of some 200,000 palm trees, each of which is up to 20–25m high, with a trunk 60–80cm in diameter and leaves 4–5m long.

A palm tree usually has a life of 100–150 years and starts to produce fruit after the fifth or sixth year. The flowers, of which each tree has seven or eight, need to be artificially pollinated, a procedure that takes place beween April and June. The fruit starts to mature in September, from which time the trees are often covered in plastic to protect the dates from parasites, and from rain and dust blown from the Sahara. During autumn, the dates are harvested, in great bunches, which usually weigh between 6–8kg. Sometimes, between April and October, the sap from the tree is collected (up to 5 litres a day) to make palm wine, which is known as *laghmi*. However, there is the chance that the tree will not bear fruit for the next few years, so this is generally only done on trees with poor quality fruit.

In the shade of the palms, other plants and fruit trees flourish, and you will see signs on Avenue Abou el Kalem Chebbi, alongside the Hotel Continental, to the lush **Paradise Garden**. The garden is on the edge of the palmery and is particularly impressive in spring when there is a great variety of flowers in bloom. Continuing into the palmery, the track comes to the small village of **B'del de Har**, which stands on the foundations of ancient Thusuros. The only remnant of note is the **Roman base of the brick minaret**, adjoining a mosque, which was built between 1027 and 1030. The mosque interior has a

fine mihrab, decorated in the Hispanic-Maghreb style, which dates from 1193, but most of the structure is more recent. In the cemetery next to the mosque is the **tomb of Ibn Chabbat** who died in 1282 and is remembered for his important work on the irrigation and the cultivation of palms. The irrigation system he planned for Tozeur, a series of water channels, *seguias*, is still in use to this day.

The track continues to another small village, **Abbes**, at the far side of which, on the left, is the **tomb** of a marabout, Sidi Ali Bou Lifa. It is shaded by a giant Jujube tree, which is said to have been planted by the marabout himself.

To reach the **belvedere**, return to **Avenue Abou el Kacem Chebbi**, and continue westwards out of town, keeping straight on where the road divides just after the *Jerid Hotel*. Follow the signposted track, which ends after 2.7km, near a rock outcrop, from the summit of which there are **outstanding views**, taking in the palmery, Tozeur, and on the horizon the Chott el Jerid and the Sahara.

Return to Avenue Abou el Kacem Chebbi and continue up the hill through the *zone touristique*. On the left is ****Dar Chraiet** (open daily, 08.00–23.30), a tourist complex surrounding two courtyards which contain shops, self-catering flats, cafés, a restaurant and two museums. The **first museum**, in the first courtyard on the left, contains an **ethnographic collection**. It covers the period from the 18C to the 20C and includes a series of traditional rooms, such as the *notaire's* office and a women's reception room. In a gallery downstairs there is a re-creation of the house of Aboul Chabbi, a local poet who died in 1934. The **second museum**, in the second courtyard, is a living museum, called the **Medina of 1001 Nights**, and is a Disneyland-type version of the popular legends.

From Tozeur follow the RN3 alongside the great shimmering expanse of the Chott el Jerid for 21km to Nefta.

NEFTA

Nefta, a small but spread out town, lies either side of the main road, Avenue Habib Bourguiba. On the left side is the souk area and the French-built part of the town; on the right is the Corbeille, a palmery filling a natural bowl in the landscape.

■ **Bus station**. Ave Habib Bourguiba. SNTRI run a daily service to Tunis. SNT run four buses a day to Tozeur. Other destinations include Gafsa and Kairouan.

■ **Louage station**. Ave Habib Bourguiba. On right, 100m beyond bus station.

■ **Hotels**. Like Tozeur, Nefta is developing its *zone touristique* with large hotels, including the *Hotel Sunoa*, which caters for tour parties. The *Sahara Palace*, at the top of the Corbeille, is a colonial haunt. The *Mirage* further along the road is less pricey as is the *Touring Club Hotel Marhala* on Ave Habib Bourguiba.

■ **Shopping**. General market every Thursday on Place de la République.

■ **Post office**. Ave Habib Bourguiba.

- **Tourist information**. Syndicat d'Initiative, Ave Habib Bourguiba, tel. (06) 430236.
- **Festivals**. Date Festival, November and December.

History

Nefta stands on the site of Roman Nepte, of which there are no remains. Never a populous town, Nepte was an outpost on the road that ran along the provincial border from Biskra to Gabès. The present-day town contains 24 mosques and boasts tombs of about 100 marabouts, making it the second most important religious centre in Tunisia. It was here that Sufism was first introduced to Tunisia, the shrines of the marabouts rapidly becoming major pilgrimage attractions. The shrines are still well-attended, particularly that of Sidi Bou Ali, who was born in Morocco and came to Tunisia in the 13C to resolve a disagreement over religion.

There is a fair amount of walking between sights in Nefta and if you are without transport you may wish to hire one of the *calèches* or camels which are in abundance here.

A good point to start a tour is the top of the **Corbeille**. To arrive there, take the first right after the tourist information office. Follow the road to the top of the hill and continue along it for a further 400m, following signposts to **Saharan Circuit**, as far as the *Café de la Corbeille* (just before the *Mirage Hotel*) on your left. From the café there are good views of the Corbeille which is a 30m deep, palm-filled depression with a gully at its head from where a hot natural spring, one of 152, issues. Literally translated, Corbeille means 'basket' or 'theatre circle'. Next to the café is the **Zaouia de Qadriya**, also known as the Zaouia of Sidi Brahim, after the Sufist who is buried within. A footpath leads eastwards along the edge of the Corbeille passing five mosques, the oldest of which is **Sidi Salem**, the Great Mosque, which dates from the 15C.

Return to Avenue Habib Bourguiba and head into town from the tourist office, passing the post office on the left. This is a good point from which to explore the **oasis** which covers 1100 hectares and has over 400,000 palm trees, 70,000 of which produce the top quality date (*deglet en nour*). The numerous springs supply 700 litres per second and support the lush vegetation of the palmery. According to legend, the first dates were planted here by Sidi Bou Ali, whose **tomb** is in the oasis. The room containing the saint's relics is covered by a finely decorated dome and next to it is the house in which Sidi Bou Ali is said to have lived.

To visit the **commercial centre** of the town, return to the tourist office and take the road right, on the opposite side of Avenue Habib Bourguiba to **Place de la République**. This attractive square is surrounded by **brick arcades** and the streets are filled with small shops.

From Nefta a 10km excursion can be made to El Oued, from where the first road on the left leads to the edge of the **Chott**. Absolutely flat and covered with a glaring salt crust, the Chott is an impressive sight, as are the mirages seen here in the heat of the day. There is also a mineral market, **Le Marché**

des Roses du Sahara, which sells sand roses. These are crystals of gypsum, formed over many years by dew or rain dissolving the gypsum in the sand and then evaporating.

It is also possible to make excursions further into the Sahara, either with tours organised by travel agents in the town or through the tourist office.

18 · The Chott–Douz–Gabès

From Tozeur on one side of the Chott, to Kebili on the other, it is 90km. The road, built in 1986, is raised on a causeway, none the less it suffers from drifting sand during windy weather, at which times visibility can be dramatically reduced. There are no petrol stations along the route. From Kebili the itinerary makes an excursion south for 28km to Douz, a road which is also difficult in high winds. Returning to Kebili, the route heads east for 122km to Gabès. There are three buses a day from Tozeur to Kebili, from where there are four daily to Douz and one a day to Gabès. There are also louages operating between Kebili, Douz and Gabès.

Leave Tozeur by the MC106 to Degache, which lies 11km north-east, alongside the Chott. **Degache** is the largest of a number of villages scattered around the series of small oases known as the El Oudiane. As you enter the village there is a good **camp site** beneath trees on the right and opposite is a **municipal swimming pool**. The centre of the town, which is marked by a square **minaret** built of brick, has a fair selection of shops and banks. The palmeries are planted with olive, orange, lemon and fig trees, all of which produce top quality fruit.

Continue through the town on the MC106 for 2km to where there is a date factory on the right. Nearby stands a small 9C **mosque**, thickly whitewashed and covered by domes. It is built on Roman foundations and has a small brick minaret. At the edge of the village of **El Mahassen**, 3km further on and set back from the road, is another whitewashed building with a small dome, the **Koubba of Sidi Mohammed Krissani**. The MC106 continues through the oases for a further 3km to the edge of the **Chott**, which, covering an area of 5000 square km, is the largest salt lake in the Sahara.

> Before the road crossing the Chott was built, the journey was extremely hazardous. An Arab author says, 'A caravan of ours had to cross the Chott one day, it was composed of 1000 baggage camels. Unfortunately one of the beasts strayed from the path and all the others followed it. Nothing in the world could be swifter than the manner in which the crust yielded and engulfed them.' In ancient times, the Chott may have been known as Lake Triton. Herodotus of Halicarnassus refers to it in his '*Histories*' according to which, the people who live on the west of the lake were known as the Maxyes and were 'a people who grow their hair on the right side of their heads and shave it off on the left. They stain their bodies red and claim to be descended from the men of Troy'. Lake Triton also featured in the story of Jason and the Argonauts when their boat was blown off course and ended up lost in the shallow waters. Triton appeared and

asked for the bronze tripod Jason had on board, in return for which he would show him the channel and let them get away in safety. Jason did as he was asked and Triton showed him the course to steer in order to clear the shallows.

As you cross the Chott, you are very likely to see mirages where distant vehicles seem much closer, or hover above the horizon. Either side of the causeway the sparkling salt crust disappears into the distance, interspersed with occasional pools of pink mineral-rich water. After 14km, where there are pans in which salt is collected, the Chott becomes more sandy, but it is another 32km before the first palms are reached at **Debabcha Oum**. From here there are a string of villages along the road. (5km) Farnassa has a large hotel, the *Hotel des Dunes*, while after (7km) **Oumsommia**, there is a ruined ksar on a rock outcrop to the left of the road. After another 6km the villages end and the road continues across open country with small palmeries to **Telmine**, 9km southeast. The oasis at Telmine was the site of Civitas Nybgenorium, a Roman outpost in the 1C, which was granted the status of municipality under Hadrian and renamed Turris Tamalleni. The site was eventually destroyed in 1205 by the Almohads, and the only remains of the ancient city today are **two large basins**, known as Belaat el Hedid, which were restored in 1780 by the Bey of Tunis.

After a further 3km the road enters **Kebili**, the administrative centre of the region of Nefzaoua, which has been Berber territory since 1C BC. The centre lies to the right of the road, where there is a market every Tuesday, which up until the 19C traded in slaves captured from the Sudan. The road to Douz, the MC206, climbs up a slight hill, forks right, and then right again before heading out through Kebili's suburbs. On the edge of the town, the **Fort des Autriches**, a hotel overlooking the desert, is passed on the left, and a military camp sprawls along the road on the right. After the military camp, there is a tourist store and a right turn signed to **ancienne Kebili**, which lies in the palmery.

The MC206 crosses the desert to **Rahmat**, a small village in a palmery 6km from Kebili. **Jemna**, a further 7km south, stands at the edge of another oasis, beyond which desert stretches the remaining 15km to Douz.

DOUZ

Douz, a small Saharan town, is a good base from which to make excursions into the desert, either by camel or jeep, with the help of the local Syndicat d'Initiative. The town also has an informative museum that focuses on life in the desert and the history of the local Nefzaoua tribe, one of the best-documented Saharan tribes in the region.

■ **Bus station**. Ave 7 Novembre. SNTRI run one bus a day to Tunis, and two daily to Gabès.

■ **Louage and taxi station**. From bus station. Frequent *louages* to Kebili; less regularly to Gabès and Tozeur.

■ **Hotels**. A number of big hotels, including four in the three-star bracket, have opened up in the *zone touristique* which lies between the palmery and the edge of the Sahara, a couple of km east of the town centre. The *Sahara Douz* is one of the most luxurious with both an outdoor pool and an indoor pool filled with water from a natural hot spring. By contrast there is the very simple *Hotel Bel Habib* in the town itself, to the north of the main square. On the Zaafrane road, 15km east of Douz, is the *Nomad Hotel*, a distinguished campsite hiring out Bedouin tents.

- **Shopping**. *Chaussure Bedouine* (desert boots), are a speciality of Douz and are sold from the various shoemakers on the main square and the street that leads south of it. There is a market every Thursday, at which camels are bought and sold on Ave 7 Novembre.

- **Post office**. Ave Taip Meheri.

- **Tourist information**. Syndicat d'Initiative, Rue Farhat Hached, tel. (05) 470351 (closed Fri–Sat afternoons).

- **Festivals**. Douz Sahara Festival, December.

- **Entertainment and Children**. Camel rides can be taken for up to one hour across the desert from the *zone touristique* (negotiate the price before setting out). Take bottled water and something to protect your head from the sun.

History
Douz has been the base of the largest semi-nomadic tribe of the Nefzaoua clan, the Mherazig (which currently numbers around 15,000 people), for as far back as anyone can remember. The Mherazig only marry within their tribe and are a proud and independent people.

The **main square** in the town is surrounded by eucalyptus trees and white arcades, beneath which are small shops selling Berber-style jewellery, traditional shoes and clothing suitable for the desert. Heading south out of town, past the main roundabout with its camel statue, is the Syndicat d'Initiative on the right. On the left, 150m further south, is the ****MUSÉE DU SAHARA** (open Mon–Thur, 08.30–13.00, 15.00–17.45, Fri and Sat, 08.30–13.00). The museum, which is purpose-built and surrounds a central courtyard, is dedicated to **Bedouin life**. The **first room** has branding tools, giving you an introduction to the symbols used by each tribe (and even by each family in the case of Douz), saddlery and Saharan plants. There are 120 different plants, 15 of which are eaten by camels for their medicinal properties. The **second room**, which is an open courtyard, contains a Bedouin tent, complete with a hanging butter churn made of skin, a method of making butter that is 5000 years old. When nomads are travelling in the desert they can live on fresh camels' milk and the creamed fermented milk diluted with water for months at a time. The tent, positioned to face Mecca, has a red cloth which is used as a division between the male and female quarters. Also in the courtyard is an oven for distilling the medicinal plants used to treat camel illnesses. The **third room** contains a loom and a good collection of textiles, all of which are woven with the tribes' symbols and colours. The **fourth room** has further textiles, mainly kilims, many of which are woven with camel fleece. There are examples of the fleece and dyes, weaving tools and a loom made of palm wood. There is also a collection of head coverings worn by women; white for girls, red for young women and black for older women.

From Douz, an excursion can be made 15km west to **Zafrane**, a small village with a palmery of 35,000 trees, at the edge of the **Grand Erg Oriental**, the east part of the Sahara. To get there, follow the road from the *zone touristique* in the direction of El Faouar. At the entrance to the village a track crosses the desert on the left to a vast **collection point for camels**. There can be up to 600 camels here at any one time. Short excursions (up to one hour) can be made to the **dunes** that typify the Erg. Longer excursions must be arranged through the Syndicat d'Initiative either in Douz or Zafrane.

From Douz, return along the MC206 to Kebili, from where the GP16, a good road with little traffic, proceeds east in the direction of Gabès, with the smooth barren slopes of the Jebel Tebega on the right and the flat expanse of the Chott el Fejal on the left. **Limagues**, 15km east of Kebili, its houses built of ochre stone blending with the landscape, stands on the edge of a palmery. On the right, a small **whitewashed mosque** with a squat minaret marks the centre of the village. Further on, just outside the village, the domed **koubba** of a marabout is passed on the left, set back from the road at the edge of the palmery.

The peaks of the Jebel Tebaga, like crumpled cloth, continue on the right as the road heads over undulating barren land. After 11km it crosses the Zigzaou river, on the east bank of which is a palmery and a hamlet. There is another palmery, 7km further surrounding the village of **Borj Saidane**. A small **fort** with one round tower and one square is passed on the left of the road. It was built here by the French and is now used by the National Guard.

The province of Gabès is entered after 4km, an empty flatness, broken only by the occasional desert plant, stretches ahead as far as the eye can see. After 17km, signs of life start to appear, and after a further 14km there are fruit orchards. The agriculture is supported by irrigation from the Oued el Magroun, a wide river, which is crossed after 8km.

EL HAMMA (10km) is surrounded by both fruit orchards and palmeries, which are fed by a natural spring which was used by the Romans as a **spa**. The sulphureous water rises from the ground at a temperature of 47°C and is said to be beneficial for rheumatism and skin disorders. The **hammam** on the right of the road in the centre of the village is recent and offers basic accommodation in the *Hotel Thermes* alongside. The streets around the hammam, which have arcades along either side, are filled with market stalls every Monday. There is a permanent market area on the left, behind the post office.

The GP16 continues east, crossing Oued T. Kouri 4km outside El Hamma. After 7km, a **spring** is passed on the left, next to which a café sells the *haute water*. About 2km beyond the spring, the landscape changes from sandy desert to red earth dotted with olive groves, and after another 5km the road enters the industrial outskirts of Gabès, which is some 14km distant.

VII THE DAHAR

19 · Gabès to Matmata

It is 45km from Gabès to Matmata, where the rolling coastal plain rises into the gentle foothills of the Dahar Mountains. There are at least six buses a day from Gabès to Matmata as well as a louage service.

Follow the main road, the GP1, in a southerly direction through the outskirts of Gabès. After crossing the Oued Gabès river there is a roundabout, from where Matmata is signposted. The Matmata road, the MC107, passes through (7km) **El M'Dou** where there is a cemetery crowned by the domed tombs of two marabouts to the right of the road, and a small stone mosque to the left. (16km) **Nouvelle Matmata**, which is centred around a mosque with a blue and white minaret, lies at the edge of the rocky foothills of the Dahar.

The **Dahar hills** are peppered with **troglodytic dwellings**, houses hewn into the soft rock of the hillsides. At first they are difficult to spot, as many are marked only by a small entrance or an external wall, and some by a shaft sunk vertically into the ground. Those close to the road have signs and the owners will, for a fee, conduct visitors on a tour of the house. The restaurant, *Relais Touristique les Troglodytes*, on the left of the MC107 at (11km) **Tijma**, is close to a concentration of troglodytic houses and is a departure point for camel treks to the troglodytic village, El Haddej, 7km west.

EL HADDEJ is reached by a rough track, which taken slowly, is passable by car. The village is not easy to identify as only a small school and a clutch of white cube houses stand above ground. The rest of the village, which was largely abandoned following flooding in 1969, lies concealed underground. The houses are built around open courtyards, which are sunk to a depth of 5–7m into the rock, and were traditionally used by animals, while the surrounding rooms were living quarters. One of the underground houses is known as the **marriage house; here, according to tradition, the bride was viewed and the marriage contract signed. At the edge of the village there is a **grain store** and also **rock carved vats** for storing oil produced in the nearby **olive press**.

MATMATA

Matmata, set in the hills 4km beyond Tijma on the MC107, like El Haddej is partly built underground, where, as a local proverb says: 'the living live under the dead'. It is a small town, straggled along a single high street, that has recently developed into a tourist centre, offering cosy troglodytic accommodation and a few basic facilities, including a restaurant.

- **Bus station**. SNTRI, Place de la Victoire. Daily services to Tamezert and Tunis. Eight daily to Gabès.

- **Louage station**. From the bus station, services to Gabès and Medenine.

- **Hotels and restaurants**. Matmata has two reasonably priced hotels, the *Sidi Driss* and the *Marhala*, both of which are troglodytic warrens, excavated in the dark yellow rock and plastered with lime. They are worth visiting, particularly the *Sidi Driss*, even if you do not intend to stay. On the road to Tamezert there are two more expensive hotels, built in the troglodytic style, *Les Berberes* and *Les Troglodytes*. Tourists passing through usually eat at the simple restaurant in the centre of the village, otherwise there are restaurants in the hotels.

- **Shopping**. Limited to small grocery stores on Ave Habib Bourguiba.

- **Post office**. Ave Habib Bourguiba.

- **Tourist information**. Syndicat d'Initiative, Ave Habib Bourguiba, tel. (05) 230114.

History

The origins of the rock-carved houses in Matmata and the surrounding region are known to go back to the 4C BC when Herodotus recorded the fact that Berbers were living here, and referred to them as troglodytes. The Berbers of the region are amongst the earliest to be recorded and due to the inhospitable environment were able to maintain their autonomy up until the end of the 17C, long after other Berber tribes had been assimilated.

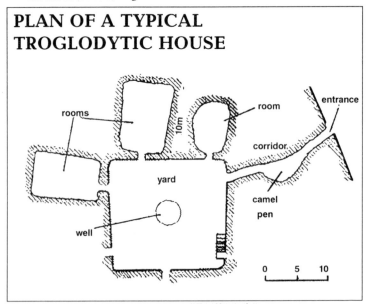

PLAN OF A TYPICAL TROGLODYTIC HOUSE

Matmata's main street, Avenue Habib Bourguiba, dips down past the post office to a tourist office on the left and a simple restaurant on the right. The **underground houses** which lie to either side of Avenue Habib Bourguiba are sunk vertically in the ground to a depth of 6–8m, and sometimes have as many as three open courtyards, each approximately 12m in diameter. Around the courtyards are store rooms, each house having its own cistern and granary, which are filled from above through a hole in the ceiling. Staircases lead up to the living quarters on the first floor.

A 10km trip west of Matmata leads you through troglodytic countryside to the hill-top village of **TAMEZERT**. The road, clearly signed from the centre of Matmata, leads through a deeply gullied landscape, occasionally dotted with a small mosque, indicating the presence, as often as not, of an **underground village**. Excursions can be made down tracks to these, but care should be taken to carry sufficient supplies of water as the sun is intense and the walking strenuous. The road eventually climbs up and up to Tamezert itself, from where there is a **panoramic view** across the countryside, which was chosen for its lunar-like quality as a location for Star Wars. The square at the top of the village has a small café and the houses, partially excavated from the hill-top, have brightly painted blue doors and windows, set in stone façades.

From Matmata it is possible to take a road direct to Medenine, which passes through the picturesque village of **Toujane**. However, at present it is very poorly surfaced and barely passable in places and cannot be recommended. Plans are afoot to rebuild it and it is worth checking with the Syndicat d'Initiative in Matmata to see if it has been completed. Meanwhile it is necessary to return to Gabès before continuing south on the GP1 to Medenine.

20 · Gabès to Tataouine

It is 122km from Gabès to Tataouine, along the main highway, the GP1, which is often busy with heavy traffic bound for Libya. There are three direct buses a day from Gabès to Tataouine, and five buses a day and regular louages to Medenine, from where there are four buses daily onward to Tataouine as well as frequent louages.

Entering Gabès from the Matmata road, turn right past the Sidi Boulbaba museum and then right again at the T-junction (see chapter 9, route 26, Gabès). The GP1 leaves Gabès through the suburb of **Teboulbou** which is surrounded by palmeries. At (14.5km) **Kettana** the local Jerid dates and pottery are sold at the roadside. The road continues, undulating across the coastal plain, through the hamlet of (10km) **Zerkine** to (8km) **Mareth** which is a sizeable town, located just north of the famous **Mareth Line**, a series of defensive emplacements similar to the Maginot Line.

The Mareth Line stretched from the coast south of Mareth to the hills near Toujane. It was built in 1938 by the French to protect against Italian invasion from Tripoli, but later helped the German troops hold back the Allied advance into Tunisia during the Second World War. It fell to the Allies in March 1943, after considerable loss of life, a victory which led to the ultimate defeat of the Axis powers in Africa.

(6.5km) **Arram** is a good point to break the journey with its handful of road-side cafés and eating places. A lot of unofficial money-changing goes on here with travellers to and from Libya. Instead of offering fruit and other wares from the roadside, dealers wave huge wads of money at the passing traffic. There are more roadside cafés at (11km) **Koutine**, just beyond which the road passes between a low range of bare hills into a desolate plain.

   METAMEUR, one of the most easily accessible and best preserved **ksour in the region, lies less than a kilometre off the GP1. The turning is on the right, 13km beyond Koutine, signposted to Matmata. The *ksar*, an extensive fortified granary, presides over a hill-top, and has in part been converted to a simple hotel. A **square**, with a couple of souvenir and kilim shops, precedes the *ksar* entrance, a simple **archway** in the fortified walls. The walls are formed by the backs of a series of **ghorfa**, store rooms approximately 6m deep with barrel-arched roofs.

Ghorfa were originally used by Berbers to store their grain and other food supplies while they moved from one place to another with their flocks. Later, during the Arab invasions, they doubled as forts, or *ksour*, with many of the cells being converted to living quarters or barracks and the outer walls being fortified.

Ghorfa Hotel, Metameur

The *ghorfa* are built next to each other, and are stacked up three or four storeys high, in a honeycomb arrangement. In one corner of the enclosure there is a whitewashed mosque.

A longer excursion can be made to **Ksar Joumaa**. Take the MC113 right, just before entering Medenine, and follow it for 27km to Ksar Joumaa where there is one of the largest fortified granaries in the region and a fine *ksar* dating from 1764.

MEDENINE
Medenine is a large and disorganised town with a busy sheep market at one end, overlooked by an equestrian statue. It provides the basic services, but has little else to offer the tourist.

- **Bus station**. SNTRI, Ave Habib Bourguiba. Daily services to Houmt Souk, Mahdia, Monastir, Sousse and Zarzis. Twice daily services to Gabès, Sfax, Tataouine and Tunis.

- **Louage station**. Opposite the bus station. Services to Djerba (via Jorf), Gabès, Sfax, Tataouine, Tunis and Zarzis.

- **Hotels**. *Motel Agil* is the best of a poor selection.

- **Post office**. Rue 2 du Mai.

History

Up until the 1960s, when Medenine was flattened by bulldozers, the town contained some 25 *ksour* which served as staging posts for the caravans on their way along the trade route into the African interior. The town also had a certain amount of political importance as it was here that the Berber and Arab tribes known as the Ouerghamma Confederation were based, having moved here from Ghoumrassen on the instructions of their marabout Sidi el Assaibi in the 18C.

Only three of the original **ksour** have survived, although not to their original height. They are grouped together and can be found by turning left at the central crossroads onto the Jorf road. After 150m turn left again into **Rue des Palmiers** to the first of the *ksour* which is the best-preserved of the three. It is built on two storeys and contains souvenir and kilim shops. The other two *ksour* are a little further up Rue des Palmiers, and are used as market-places.

Return to the crossroads and continue on the GP19 in the direction of Tataouine, which lies 48km further south.

21 · Tataouine and environs

FOUM TATAOUINE (the town's full name), is Berber in origin, and means place of springs. As a busy market town and an administrative centre, rather severe in appearance, it holds little of particular interest, but is a good base from which to explore the surrounding region, where there are Berber hill villages and 50 or more *ksour* set atop the isolated, flat outcrops that typify the massif here.

- **Bus station**. Rue 1 Juin 1955. Four services a day to Medenine and Ghoumrassen; once daily to Houmt Souk, Tunis and Zarzis.

- **Louage station**. Same as bus station. Regular services to Medenine, Ghoumrassen and Remada. Daily services to Tunis and Zarzis.

- **Hotels**. *La Gazelle* is clean, comfortable and reasonably priced. Try to book ahead if possible, tel. (05) 860009. The *Hotel de la Paix* and *Ennour* are cheap but rough. Otherwise there is the more expensive *Hotel Sangho*, which has bungalow-type accommodation, on the Chenini road, 2km from the town. *Ksar Haddada*, 26km north-west of Tataouine, has simple and reasonably priced accommodation in a converted *ksar*.

- **Shopping**. Market days every Monday and Thursday.

- **Post office**. Ave Habib Bourguiba.

- **Festivals**. Festival des Ksour Saharien, March or April.

History

Like Medenine, Tataouine has a history as a staging post on the caravan route from the Sahara to Sudan. In the 19C it served as a French military base and had a penal colony.

The following three itineraries take in the main sights around Tataouine. The first is a 32km round trip south-east of Tataouine; the second is a 47km round trip south-west of Tatatouine; and the third is a 53km round trip north-west of Tataouine.

The **first itinerary** takes the GP19 in the direction of Remada which is a large village (90km) with a palmery and an old slaughter house. Follow the Remada road for 3km, before turning right, opposite a grey and white mosque, onto the road to Maztouria. The road winds between houses for 2km, after which the abandoned *ksar* of **Beni Barka** comes into view at **Mestegrut** where there is a large domed mosque. Founded in the 14C by a Libyan tribe from Djebel Nefousa, the *ksar* has a panoramic setting atop Gebel Abiod.

From Beni Barka continue on the road to **Maztouria**. From here a dirt track leads for 11km to **KSAR OULED SOULTANE**. The road is poor, but the *ksar* warrants the effort. Sited on a hill-top, surveying the countryside for kilometres around, it is the best-preserved building of its kind in the region. It is surrounded by a perfect circular wall and contains *ghorfas* which stand four storeys high in places. It is divided into two courtyards, one dating from the 15C and the other from the 19C, which are connected by a passageway, built with the trunks of palm trees.

The **second itinerary** leaves Tataouine on the GP19 in the direction of Remada. After 10km the road passes through the village of **KSAR OULED DEBBAB**, named after the impressive *ksar* which stands on the rocky escarpment above. Pass through the village and take the first, unsigned road on the left which winds up to the **gateway** at the north end of the *ksar*. Now abandoned, the *ksar* was converted to a hotel in 1967, but closed down in 1981. It contains two **parallel streets** divided by a block of **grain stores** running down the centre. At the north end there is a **mosque** with a simple dome and an adjoining **terrace** that looks across the village to the ridge of mountains on the far side of the bleached plain.

Return back through the village of Ksar Ouled Debbab in the direction of Tataouine and take the first left turn to Douirette on Rue 1007. After 6km fork right and continue for a further 6km through an arid landscape dotted with **palms**, each of which marks a plot of land. The road approaches a rocky hill, the summit of which is 609m high, where there are the crumbling remains of a fortress. **EL DOUIRAT**, a pure Berber village, lies straddled along a ledge below. El Douirat is reached by a donkey track, 1.5km long, which is fairly steep and difficult to negotiate by car. The village centre is at the **mosque** which is thickly whitewashed and has a fat square minaret. The village houses around it are partly built into the rock and typically have two rooms: the first of which is used for living and the second for storing food. Some also have **ghorfa-style store rooms** built above animal stalls. There are several **olive presses** in the village, which can be located by looking for the dark stains on the rock where the liquid from the olive pulp drains away. The village's modern counterpart, **Douirette**, lies at the foot of the hill and is centred around a whitewashed mosque with a black and white **chequered minaret** which is where the asphalt road comes to an end.

Retrace Rue 1007 back to the main road, the GP19, and continue in the direction of Tataouine.

Two kilometres before reaching the town, take the left turn onto the MC207, which is signposted to Chenini. The road passes the Hotel Sangho before forking (5km) left for a further 11km across the palm-dotted plain to **CHENINI**, another old Berber village, dramatically positioned on a saddle in the hills. To get up there, either climb the footpaths which snake up the hill from the *Café Relais* which is on the left of the MC207, or continue along the MC207 round the bend to the new village on the other side of the col, which involves less walking but is not as picturesque. Many of the old houses built on the hill are partly carved into the rock and are preceded by a **walled court-yard**, known as a *hosh*, which is covered by planks of palm wood to provide shade and shelter for the animals kept there. At the top of the hill, at the centre of the saddle ridge is a small whitewashed **mosque** with a decorative minaret. From here a precarious footpath follows the ridge up to the crumbling remains of the **kalaa**, a fortress built in 1193 to defend against Arab invasions. It was later used as a grain store by the Ouled Debbab tribe. Some of the **store rooms** have decorated plasterwork, with symbols such as rope or dots on the walls and ceilings, which indicate to whom the store belonged. Some of the small store rooms are complete with storage jars recessed into the floor, the stone of which is polished smooth with centuries of use. Local guides will take visitors to see an 11C **olive press** and the **bakery** in the north part of the village.

The **third itinerary** leaves Tataouine by the GP19 in the direction of Medenine. After 6.5km, turn left at the hospital onto the MC121. This narrow road leads through the hamlet of (9m) Horria to (5km) **GHOMRASSEN**. This large village was founded by Berbers fleeing the Hilali Arab invasions in the 10C and their **rock-carved retreats** can still be seen in the cliff spurs all around, although they are no longer inhabited. The present-day village with its neat white houses centres around a square that is surrounded by white-washed arcades. A footpath leads from the square up to the cliff face where houses are carved in the rocks.

Continuing through the village, you pass by a hotel built on a spur of rock, where there are more rock-hewn houses, on the left. Shortly after the hotel are a series of **barrel-vaulted ghorfas**, also on the left.

Follow the road straight through Ghomrassen and fork right 2km from the village centre onto the road to **KSAR HADDADA** which is a further 4km. Overlooked by the silvery dome of its elegant **mosque**, the village is named after the **ksar** here, part of which has been converted into a simple hotel. The *ksar*, which is on the opposite side of the road to the mosque, is entered through the hotel, the entrance to which has its original wooden ceiling made of eucalyptus boughs. The hotel occupies a relatively small part of the *ksar* which is otherwise abandoned, only coming to life in January and February when locals bring their olives to be pressed in the original **oil press** which is still in use.

Return to the GP19, and either head northwards to join route 22, or return to Tataouine.

22 · Tataouine via Gigthis to Jorf

It is 96km from Tataouine to the port of Jorf from where ferries cross to the Isle of Jerba. The ancient site of Gigthis is well worth the short diversion at Boughrara, 20km before Jorf. There is one bus a day from Tataouine to Jorf, from where it continues on to Houmt Souk. Alternatively, take a bus or louage to Medenine, and proceed by louage to Jorf.

From Tataouine, return northwards along the GP19 for 49km to the central crossroads in **Medenine**, and turn right onto the MC108 which is signed Jorf-Bac and Jerba per Bac. After passing the **ksar** on the left, there is a billboard with the ferry times, to the right of the road. The road is fairly narrow, but mainly flat and traffic-free all the way to (27km) **Boughrara**, where there is a right fork for the port. Less than 100m along the fork, on the right, are the ruins of ****GIGTHIS** (open daily dawn to dusk). The ticket office, a small barrel-vaulted building on the left, marks the site entrance.

History
The site of Gigthis, naturally sheltered in the Gulf of Bou Grara, was first established by the Phoenicians in the 6C BC. Their successors, the Carthaginians, were to develop it as a flourishing port and trading post. The Romans, keen to lay claims to such a prosperous centre, focused attacks on the city during both the first and second Punic Wars. The city was finally taken by the Romans in 46 BC. Gigthis continued to expand, becoming an important agricultural centre and port, trading in slaves from Central Africa. During the reign of Antoninus Pius (138–161), it was elevated to the status of a municipality and continued to flourish, reaching its zenith under Alexander Severus in the 3C.

After becoming a Christian city in the 4C, Gigthis was destroyed by the Vandals in 430. It was reconstructed by the Byzantines and passed from them to the Muslims, who further fortified the town. As trade decreased under Muslim rule and the coastline changed, the city dwindled in importance and was gradually abandoned.

From the ticket office, a footpath cuts across the sand, past the scant remains of the **west baths** and **palaestra** on the right, to the centre of the Roman city, the **forum**. Wide steps lead up to the well-preserved podium of the **Capitoline temple** which stands at the west end of the forum. Probably dedicated to Isis and Serapis, the temple is scattered with the broken segments of fluted columns. Around the base of the well-preserved podium are a number of capitals, decorated with finely carved acanthus leaves, which once capped the temple's columns. Along the north wall of the temple are the pedestals of statues, on some of which the inscriptions are still legible.

The remains of the other buildings which once surrounded the forum are less easy to distinguish. The **Temples of Apollo, Concord and Hercules**, on the north side, have remnants of the steps that once preceded the podium, but the **treasury** that originally stood alongside the temples has more or less vanished. The extensive, but confusing ruins at the east end of the forum are the remains of a 4C **basilica**, beyond which a clump of palms marks where the sea once met the **city wall** and the **Quatres Portes gateway**. A sandy beach of some 140m now separates the sea and the ruins of the former **port** which lie to the north-east.

South of the forum are the ruins of a **thermal bath**, where there are remnants of the **mosaic floor**, including one mosaic that depicts a muse. To the west of the baths is a 3C **market-place** which was once surrounded by porticoes and shops with a semicircular enclave at one end, but is now an area of fallen stone and debris. On the hill, west of the market, are the ruins of a series of **small temples**, but again they are in very poor condition, although there are good views of the site from the hill summit.

From Gigthis, return to the MC108 and continue northwards for a further 20km to **Jorf**. The small harbour, with its handful of cafés, stands between low sandstone cliffs. Between 6.30 and 21.00 there are crossings every half hour to Ajim, on the south coast of the Isle of Jerba. There are also hourly crossings between 21.00 and 06.00. The crossing, which takes 15 minutes, is free for foot passengers; there is a nominal charge for vehicles.

Squid pots, Ajim

VIII ISLE OF JERBA

The Isle of Jerba, cited as the mythical Island of the Lotus Eaters where Ulysses and his crew were shipwrecked, has 125km of coastline, and measures only 25km by 22km. The island is virtually flat, the highest point being just 52m above sea-level, and has little vegetation due to the lack of any natural water sources. Water is, however, piped from the mainland and collected in cisterns, of which there are over 2000 on the island. Apart from the cultivation of olives and vines, the main source of income for the islanders is tourism. The island is a popular destination, both for its pleasant atmosphere and good beaches, and as a breaking off point for trips into the Sahara.

23 · Houmt Souk

- **Airport**. International Airport of Jerba-Mellita, 11km west of Houmt Souk, tel. (05) 650509/650233. Daily shuttle service from bus station to airport.

- **Airline companies**. Tunis Air, Ave Habib Bourguiba, tel. (05) 650159.

- **Bus station**. Gare Routière, Ave Habib Bourguiba, tel. (05) 652239/650076. SNTRI operate five buses a day to Tunis; also four a day to Ajim (ferry port), three a day to Zarzis, two a day to Medenine and Sfax and one a day to Gabès. Bus timetables are pinned up in the Commisariat Régional au Tourisme.

- **Louage stations**. From the bus station. *Louage* services are not very frequent. Destinations include Zarzis, Tunis, Medenine and Gabès.

- **Taxis**. From Place Sidi Brahim, Rue de Bizerte and Ave Habib Bourguiba.

- **Hotels**. A wide selection in all price ranges. The coast east of Houmt Souk, along Plage Mehrez and Sidi Bakour, is lined with big hotels and the occasional *pension*. The larger hotels have sports facilities, children's amusements and swimming pools. In the town itself there are a handful of well-priced traditional hotels in *fondouks* with simple but clean rooms surrounding central courtyards. Amongst the most attractive of these is the *Hotel des Sables D'Or*, tel. (05) 650423. The *Hotel Arischa*, tel. (05) 650384, is also to be recommended and has a bar and restaurant in its central courtyard. The *Hotel Marhala* is a little more expensive but tastefully renovated with oleander filling its central courtyard.

- **Restaurants**. There are several small restaurants serving typical Tunisian fare in the town centre. The café on Place Hédi Chaker has an excellent *pâtisserie* and makes good pizza, but is not open in the evening. *Pâtisserie Ben Xedder*, on Place Mohammed Ali, where there are cafés in the centre, is also good.

- **Shopping**. The **Marché Couvert** (covered market) in the town centre has a good selection of fruit, vegetables and spices. On Monday and Thursday mornings a pottery market, primarily aimed at tourists, is held on Place Monji Bali. The souks are also tourist-orientated. Every Sunday, a large market of second-hand clothing, hardware, bedding, fruit and vegetables, is held at the walls of Borj el Kebir.

- **Post office**. Place des Martyrs.

- **Tourist information**. Syndicat d'Initiative, Place des Martyrs, tel. (05) 650019. Comissariat Régional au Tourisme, Route Touristique, tel. (05) 650544.

- **Medical care**. Hospital, Ave Habib Bourguiba, tel. (05) 650018.

- **Festivals**. Festivale d'Ulysses, July–August. Festivale de Guellala (pottery), July–August. International Regatta of Wind-surfing, July.

- **Entertainment**. Big hotels on coast east of town. Bar at *Hotel Arischa* and *Hotel Marhala* in town centre.

- **Children**. A small playground just east of El Borj castle. Horse and cart rides around the town and along the coast.

- **Sport**. Water-skiing, snorkelling, wind-surfing and tennis are the main facilities offered to non-residents from the hotels on the coast east of town.

History

Although there are no significant ancient remains, Houmt Souk is believed to have been settled by Phoenicians in the 6C BC, before coming under Carthaginian control. The city has had a chequered history, which may account for the lack of ancient remains, falling first to the Romans, under whom it was known as Girba. It developed into a strong Christian community which was destroyed by the Vandals but redeveloped by the Byzantines. In 667 Byzantine Girba was conquered by the Arabs, and more or less abandoned. What was left was razed to the ground in the 11C during the Hilali invasions. Europeans, namely the Spaniards, recognised the strategic importance of the island, and in 1284 the Aragonese Admiral, Roger de Loria, was made Count of Jerba by the Pope. The island served the Spaniards as a base for attacks on Muslim shipping in the central Mediterranean until an uprising against Spanish rule in the mid 14C placed it under Hafsid control. For a number of turbulent years the Spaniards struggled to regain control of the island but failed, and after a large and unsuccessful expedition in 1432, gave up the struggle. Under the Hafsids, the island was used as a base by Draghut and other Muslim corsairs for attacks on Christian shipping until 1551, when the Hapsburg navy destroyed Draghut's fleet. They went on to capture the island in 1560, only to lose it shortly afterwards to the Ottomans from Tripoli, who supported Draghut's activities.

The small town of ****HOUMT SOUK**, one of the most picturesque in Tunisia, is centred around a busy **souk area**. Narrow streets lined with clothing boutiques and souvenir shops open out into bright squares with cafés, and two of the main streets, the *qay sarriya*, with their jewellers' and leather shops, are covered by vaults. The town has a relaxed atmosphere and is a charming place in which to spend a few days.

The **Mosque of Sidi Aissa**, east of the souk area, on **Place Jamaa Ghorba**, is also known as the Mosque de Ghorba and the Strangers' Mosque. It has a crenellated minaret which is decorated with bands of Arabic script in black, and surmounted by a high lantern. The minaret is typical of the Wahhabite style that came into being in the 18C with the Arabian Islamic reformer Ibn Abdul Wahhab. Its pronounced central dome, surrounded by cupolas, overlooks an inner courtyard. Outside its west wall there is a small flower garden.

On the opposite side of Place Jamaa Ghorba, a taxi rank abuts the austere walls of the **Zaouia of Sidi Brahim** which is covered by a green tiled dome. This religious school, started in 1674 by the Kharijites, a minority Islamic sect, was not completed until thirty years later under Bey Murad ben Ali. Next to Sidi Brahim is the plastered dome of a **Turkish baths** which is still in use, admitting men in the mornings and women in the afternoons.

Head north of the souk area on Rue Moncef Bey to the whitewashed **Hanefite Mosque**, which was built by the Ottomans. Continue northwards, past a **Catholic church** to the left, an unremarkable white building dating from the 19C, onto Rue T. Mhiri which continues northwards for over 500m to the coastal fort, ****BORJ EL KEBIR** (open daily, except Fri, 09.00–18.00).

History

Originally built in 1289 by the Aragonese Roger de Loria on foundations that dated from Roman times, the castle was largely reconstructed under the Hafsid, Abou Fares. During the 16C the fortress was the setting for the bloody struggles between the Spaniards and the Ottomans, which culminated in the unsuccessful Spanish attack of 1560, after which a pyramid, with a base 11m across, was built using the heads of the Spanish. The site of the pyramid, which was still standing in 1848 when it was ordered to be dismantled by the Bey of Tunis, is now marked by a small monument at the port.

The castle is rectangular, measuring 65m by 53m, and is surrounded by a **moat** that is 10–15m in width. The walls have circular and square towers, and some of the **cannons** that originally defended them are lined up at the entrance in the east wall. The ticket office and small shop

Borj El Kebir

selling publications are inside the **skifa**, a dog-leg shaped hall, which was designed to defend the entrance to the interior. The **inner courtyard** contains pieces of weathered columns and other architectural fragments belonging to the Roman building, as well as remnants of the 13C fort. From the left side of the courtyard, a passageway and stairs lead up onto the castle walls. In the north-east corner is the **koubba of Ghazi Mustapha** who was responsible for enlarging the castle, following the Spanish defeat in 1560. From the south-east corner a walkway leads into the **central keep**, where barrel-vaulted roofs cover a series of rooms now used as an exhibition space for photographs of old Houmt Souk. Steps also lead up to the koubba from the central keep, at the foot of which are piles of cannon balls.

Houmt Souk's museum, the ****CENTRE DES ARTS ET TRADITIONS POPULAIRES MUSÉE RÉGIONALE DE JERBA** (open summer, daily, except Fri, 09.00–18.00, winter, daily, except Fri, 09.30–16.30) is on Avenue Abdelhamid el Kadi which heads east from the Hanefite mosque and is about 400m from the town centre. It is housed in the 18C Zaouia of Sidi Zitouni, a simple, low-lying stone building which was commissioned by the Governor of Jerba, Hamida Ben Ayyed. The ticket office is in a separate building from where steps lead down to the zaouia. Inside the simple stone-carved **entrance** is a courtyard containing a collection of amphorae, which were apparently used as marriage chests due to the scarcity of wood on Jerba. The **first room**, which is covered by a large dome constructed with tubes of terracotta, contains a collection of regional costumes, including the *fut'a*, a wrap for women and the *bakhnug*, a type of shawl. The **second room** has a collection of Jerban jewellery including an interesting display of brooches with descriptions of how women of the Malekite sect wear their brooches on the left side, Berbers in the centre, and Bedouins on the right. Steps lead down to a series of **vaulted rooms** containing pottery and a reconstructed wood-burning kiln. Further steps lead up again to the **last room** which is covered by a large plaster dome. Here there are decorated wooden chests and mirrors and other pieces of woodwork.

The nearest **beaches** to Houmt Souk are along the coast to the east. Leave Houmt Souk along Avenue Abdelhamed el Kadi, which follows the coast on Rue 491 for 7km to the long sandy peninsula, **Rass Rmel**. The beaches, and also the coastal developments, start from the east side of the peninsula. The beach of **Sidi Mehrez** is a further 2.5km and runs into the beach of **Sidi Bakour**. Both beaches are sandy and have very shallow waters which can be reedy. The peninsula, **Rass Tourgueness**, a further few kilometres, marks the westernmost point of the island and has a sandy beach at its tip.

24 · Houmt Souk to Guellala

It is 21km from Houmt Souk on the north coast of the island to Guellala on the south, including the short excursion from Erriadh to the synagogue of El Graiba. The No. 14 from Houmt Souk bus station passes through Erriadh to Guellala.

Leave Houmt Souk following signs to El May and Zarzis. After 5km turn right to (1km) **Erriadh** which, according to legend, was founded in the 6C BC, when Jews settled here, following the destruction of Jerusalem under

Nebuchadnezzar. More Jewish refugees arrived in the 1C, escaping from persecution by the Roman Emperor Titus; centuries later, more Jews arrived, escaping from the Christian reconquest of Spain. There has been a **Jewish community** here ever since, making it one of the oldest in the world.

Follow the road through Erriadh to a left turn, less than a kilometre from the village, for the synagogue, **EL GRAIBA** (open daily, except Sat) which is 500m further on. The road ends at a gate, on the right of which is a **fondouk** (hostel) for pilgrims, and on the left the **synagogue**.

The synagogue serves a dwindling Jewish population, numbering only about 1000, compared to 4000 before the Second World War, when the Germans occupied the island. The German occupation is described by a rabbi of the synagogue:

'In the year 5603 (1943) when the Germans came to our city, they did no harm to the Jews, but on the Sabbath, the 8th of the month of Adar I, some Gestapo officers and soldiers arrived in two cars. They stopped outside the prayer house called the synagogue of the Kohanim, where my father, teacher and rabbi would worship, and sent for him. When he stood before them, they said to him: "On such and such a day the British dropped bombs on the harbour, and we believe that the Jews signalled directions to them; the two Jewish communities are therefore ordered to pay a fine of 50kg of gold and if you do not comply with the order within three and a half hours, we shall blow up the two Jewish settlements and they will become a heap of ruins." They also had a list of rich men, who were to be fetched and shot immediately, if the required sum was not paid. They further informed him that he would now be their prisoner so long as the order had not been carried out. My father was greatly startled and worried and earnestly assured them that compliance was impossible. When he achieved nothing he called a meeting of the leaders of the community, and when he saw that it was impossible to fulfil the demand and the whole community was in danger, he went with them in the car to the holy community of Hara Seghira about 7km away, to inform them of the cruel order, so that they might try to find a way of raising the part due from them. And the Lord miraculously gave him favour in the sight of the two communities, and they relieved themselves of the golden earrings which they had, of their last penny, which they had saved for an emergency, for their old age, for their marriage portions of their sons and daughters. When they saw the great distress in which the holy community found itself, they brought it and, with tears in their eyes, dropped it into the cash-box. Most of the amount was collected, and the Germans took it away, saying they would come back on Thursday to get the remainder. But after the Sabbath the Germans fled and on the following Sabbath the British moved in.' (From *A history of the Jews in North Africa* vol. 2 by H. Hirschberg, pub. by E. Brill in Leiden, Netherlands, 1981.)

The synagogue, which was rebuilt in 1920, stands on the ancient site of a holy stone that tradition claims miraculously fell here from the heavens. Its interior, decorated with blue tiles, dark wood and stained glass, conceals a sacred cavern, inside which is one of the oldest Torah in the world. It is said that the

Torah scrolls, written on gazelle skin, were rescued from the Jerusalem temple in the 6C BC when it was destroyed by Nebuchadnezzar. The cavern is attended by women, many of whom believe they increase their fertility by leaving an egg here overnight.

The synagogue is at its busiest during the Ba'omer festival, which is on the thirty-third day of Passover, and attracts pilgrims from far and wide. During the two-day festival, at which time tourists are not admitted to the synagogue, there is a musical procession to Erriadh, bearing a *menora*, a wooden candle-holder, painted gold and draped with colourful silk cloths.

From El Graiba, return to Erriadh and continue on the road southwards to Guellala. At the (3km) crossroads keep straight ahead and continue for a further 7km to the pottery-making town of **Guellala**. Haribus, as the town was known in ancient times, has long been a **ceramic centre**. The clay is extracted from the nearby Sedouikech Hills, the highest part of Jerba, by shafts up to 80m deep. It is then purified in sea water and left to dry in the sun for 60 days, by which time it has been bleached. The traditional pottery—storage jars, amphorae and squid pots—is fired in wood-burning kilns and is unglazed. In the numerous pottery shops along the town's main streets there is a great variety, most of which is made for the tourist market and is glazed. To see the **local kilns**, of which there are 300 in the town, take the coastal road in the direction of El Kantara. The kilns, built of mud, clay and broken bits of fired pottery, are rectangular, low-lying mounds, being built partly underground.

25 · Houmt Souk to El Kantara and Midoun

It is 28km from Houmt Souk via El May and Cedouikech to El Kantara, the southernmost point of the island. From here the itinerary traces the east coast for 13km before heading inland to Midoun, a further 7km. The entire round trip is 70km. The No. 10 bus from Houmt Souk makes a similar circuit of the island.

Leave Houmt Souk by following the road to El May. Just beyond the Erriadh junction which is 7km south of Houmt Souk, there is a typical Jerban mosque on the left. Thickly whitewashed, the mosque of **Umm et Turkia** has strong **buttressed walls** and a stumpy **minaret** with a traditional rounded top. It dates from the 16C, and was built for the Ibadites, a sub-sect of the Kharijites, who took refuge in Jerba. The road continues south via (4km) **El May**, which is dominated by a modern shopping arcade, through gently rolling countryside where there are numerous **menzel**, the traditional whitewashed farmsteads for which Jerba is known. **Cedouikech**, 8km further south, is a small town with a handful of shops and a lively Tuesday market where farm produce is sold. From Cedouikech it is another 9km through ancient olive groves to **El Kantara** from where a **causeway** dating from Roman times crosses to the mainland.

The route continues northwards along the coast on Rue 941, past the Roman site of **Meninx**, which is on the left of the road just outside El Kantara. Very little remains of the city which was probably founded by Phoenicians in the 10C BC. The best remaining structure is a **Christian basilica**, the baptistery of which is now in the Bardo Museum.

From Meninx, Rue 941 continues along the coastline, which is predominantly flat and marshy, passing a long and thin spit of land, after 7km, at the tip of which is **Borj Kastil**, a simple fortress built by the Aragonese, Roger de Loria in 1285. The coast north of the spit is developed more or less continuously up to Sidi Mehrez, making access to the wide sandy beach difficult for non-residents. The coastal road continues all the way back to Houmt Souk; however, the route heads inland from the resort of (6km) **Aghir** to Midoun which is 7km north-west.

The market town of ****MIDOUN**, surrounded by palms, is neatly whitewashed, its houses, even some of the modern ones, being roofed with traditional barrel-vaults and domes. As the second largest town on the island, tourists come here mainly for the pedestrianised shopping area in the centre which has been purpose-built. Also catering for the town's tourism, every day during the tourist season at 15.30 a traditional **wedding procession** is staged in the town's open-air theatre. On Friday mornings there is a large **market**, much of which is given over to souvenir stalls. The town also has a few historical sights. Ponies and traps ferry tourists around, taking in the thickly whitewashed **Bourguor Mosque**, a kilometre from the centre on the Houmt Souk road, and the **olive oil press** which is 500m from the centre in the direction of Tourgueness.

The standard olive press in the ancient world was a beam press, comprising the trunk of a palm which weighed from 500kg to 1000kg, held between two upright stone orthostats, arbores. After being milled to a pulp, the olives were placed in baskets on the pressing stone, the *ara*, with a wooden cover placed over them on which the ara was rested. The free end of the beam was secured by ropes to a windlass mounted on a counterweight block, a *stipites*, at the lower level in the press room and the beam end was drawn down with handspikes. It weighed around 2000kg so that the pressure would be low, about 3kg/square cm. Oil oozed out slowly and collected in the channel where it was fed off into tanks and skimmed and then decanted. Several grades of oil could be obtained by using water as a separating element.

From Midoun it is 4km to Mahboubine through pretty countryside where women work the fields wearing the traditional local costume, a white *sifsari* and a straw hat with a bright ribbon. ****Mahboubine** is a small unspoilt town with a 19C **mosque**, said to be influenced by Haghia Sofia in Istanbul. The houses are arcaded and have bright blue shutters and the town has a handful of small shops.

From Mahboubine it is a further 7km to El May, from where the main road to Houmt Souk, which is 11km north, is joined.

IX THE LOWER SAHEL

26 · Jorf to Gabès

It is 85km from Jorf to Gabès on easy, flat roads. Five buses a day call at Jorf from Houmt Souk before continuing to Gabès .

From Jorf, the MC116 heads south-west across a barren coastal plain for 46km to join the main highway, the GP1. The GP1 then follows the coast northwards through (4km) Mareth, (10km) Zerkine and (10km) Kettana (see Route 20). Continue north through (13km) Teboulbou, shortly after which the road cuts through the Gabès palmery to the (5km) outskirts of the city where local baskets and ceramics are sold at the roadside.

GABÈS
Gabès is a busy city with a good museum and a popular palmery. It is too big and bustling to be a relaxing place to stay, although not big enough to have much in the way of entertainment. However, its proximity to the coast means there is often a breeze, welcome in the heat of the summer, and the surrounding palmeries offer shade from the sun.

To reach the centre, follow **Avenue de la République**, crossing the Oued Gabès river, before reaching a large roundabout with a clock at its centre. Take the third exit, **Avenue Bechir Drizi**, which leads due north to the central post office and city centre.

- **Airline companies**. Tunis Air, Ave Habib Bourguiba, tel. (05) 270697.

- **Arrival by sea**. Ghannouche Port. Car ferries to Jerba every 20–30 minutes.

- **Maritime companies**. Navitours, Ave Farhat Hached, tel. (05) 271175.

- **Railway station**. Gare de Gabès, Ave de la Gare, tel. (05) 270944. Two services a day to Tunis via Sfax, El Jem, Sousse and Hammamet.

- **Bus stations**. Place Chmama, Ave Farhat Hached, Route de Sfax, tel. (05) 270008. Seven services a day to Matmata, six to Sfax, five to Jerba, four to Tunis, three to Kebili-Douz, Tataouine and Gafsa, two to Sousse.

- **Louage stations**. Same place as the bus station. Destinations include Jerba, Medenine, Sfax and Tunis.

- **Taxis**. Place des Souks, Souk Jara.

- **Hotels**. The *Atlantic* and the *Nejib* at the east end of Ave Habib Bourguiba and Ave Farhat Hached respectively, are the principal hotels in town and are reasonably priced. There are several hotels in the cheap and rough category in the area around the bus station. Alternatively, head to the port, to the south of which are the *Oasis* and the *Chems*, the latter offering bungalow accommodation and a swimming pool.

- **Restaurants**. Most restaurants are to be found along Ave Farhat Hached or the seafront.

- **Shopping**. Souk area around the Jara Mosque. ONAT, 354 Rue Farhat Hached, tel. (05) 270775, government-sponsored local handicrafts, including pile carpets with Berber designs and baskets woven from palm leaves.

- **Post office**. Ave Farhat Hached.

- **Tourist information**. Syndicat d'Initiative, Ave Farhat Hached, tel. (05) 270254.

- **Medical care**. Hôpital Universitaire, Cité Mtorrech, tel. (05) 272700. Polyclinique Bon Secours, Rue Mongi Slim, tel. (05) 271400.

- **Festivals**. Foire Internationale, 1–15 July. Commemoration of Sidi Boulbaba, end of Ramadan.

- **Children**. Calèche rides from bus station through oasis. Zoo des Crocodiles, Chenini.

History

Probably Phoenician in origin, Gabès was a commercial port in Carthaginian times, conquered by the Numidian King Masinissa in 161 BC. During the Roman era, Gabès was a colony, under the name of Tacapae, and marked the southern-most point of the Roman Empire. Destroyed by Barbarians, Gabès was re-established by Sidi Boulbaba in the 7C who is the patron saint of the city to this day. In the following centuries, the city became a centre of silk production and had extensive tanneries. In 1052, however, it was destroyed by Arabs.

Centuries later it was again badly damaged by warfare, this time in the Second World War, when due to its strategic location close to the Mareth Line, it was caught up in the battle between the Germans and the Allies. The city suffered such extensive damage that it had to be largely rebuilt after the war.

The main attraction in the city centre is the **souk area** at the western end of **Avenue Habib Bourguiba**, opposite the **Jara Mosque**, which was built in

The Market, Gabès

1952 and is now overshadowed by a new tower block. The souks lie on either side of **Place du Marché**, a large courtyard and the main market-place. There are stalls selling fruit and vegetables, spices, dried fish, and mounds of green henna for which the city is renowned. Although it is difficult to see at first amid the bustle of the market, the courtyard is surrounded by porticoes which are made up of **ancient pilasters and columns**. The

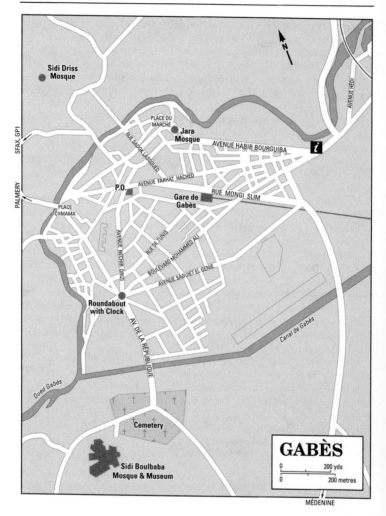

MÉDENINE

various souks each have a speciality, that next to the Place du Marché has a good selection of basketware.

The old quarter of the city, **Petite Jara**, extends to the north-west of the souk area. It is presided over by the **Mosque of Sidi Driss**, which stands on the far side of the river where there is a small palmery. Restored in 1972, it was built in the 11C using **Roman columns** in the interior.

The city's most revered mosque is that of ****SIDI BOULBABA** which stands on a hill, 2.5km from the centre, to the south of the Oued Gabès river. To get there, follow signs to Medenine, and head out of the city along Avenue de la République. Keep straight ahead until the Oued Gabès river is crossed, from where a tall minaret can be seen to the right. Take the first right turn after crossing the river, and then left, up **Rue 6 Octobre**. The road passes the tall minaret and its adjacent mosque on the left, and continues 20m further to the Mosque of Sidi Boulbaba which is on the right. The **mosque**, built on a high terrace above a **cemetery**, is preceded by a stone **portal**, with elegant horseshoe arches resting on sculpted capitals. The portal leads into a **courtyard**, which is built over a cistern and surrounded by porticoes, decorated with faience tiles. The **prayer hall**, covered in **rugs** given as offerings, opens off the courtyard. It contains the **tomb** of the city's founder and patron saint, Sidi Boulbaba, surrounded by a balustrade at the centre of the prayer hall.

The city's ****MUSEUM OF ARTS AND POPULAR TRADITIONS** is 20m back along Rue 6 Octobre, opposite the mosque with the tall minaret. It is housed in a low stone building, originally a medersa, which was built in 1692. Steps lead up to the ticket office just inside the entrance, from where a door leads off right into a **small hall** where maps of Gabès are exhibited. The hall leads through to the **central courtyard** around which the museum is arranged in somewhat dimly lit cells that were once used by students. Working in a clockwise direction, the **first room** contains wools, dyes and a loom. The next **three rooms**, interconnected by arches, have exhibits of woven textiles, including cloaks, blankets and *haiks* with embroidered decorations, and in a corner room there is a collection of local lace. A large **vaulted room**, with four central pillars, originally a prayer and lecture hall, contains local costumes. The series of **five rooms** on the other side of the courtyard are dedicated to local foods and culinary utensils, including mills for grinding, and there is also a fine collection of baskets.

To explore the ****PALMERY**, which covers 2000 hectares and has 300,000 palm trees, head to the bus station at the west side of the city on the road to Sfax. A pleasurable way to tour the palmery, allowing an hour or two, is to hire one of the calèches from here, the tariffs for which are posted in the Syndicat d'Initiative.

Although the palmery produces second-quality dates, only suitable for animal fodder, it is remarkable for the great variety of trees and plants that grow in the shade of the palms, something that Pliny the Elder noted in his *Natural History*.

> 'One finds in the midst of the African sands a town called Tacapae; the soil there is much cultivated and marvellously fruitful. The town extends in all directions to about 3000 paces. Here is found a fountain with an abundant supply of water, which is only used at stated times; and here grows a high palm, and beneath that palm an olive, and under that a fig tree. Under the fig tree grows a pomegranate, and beneath that again a vine. Moreover, beneath these last are sown, first oats, then vegetables or grass, all in the same year. Yes, thus they grow them, each sheltered by the other.'

The palmery itinerary, which follows a narrow and winding tarmac road, starts at the village of **Nahal**. At the centre of **Chenini-de-Gabès**, the main village in the palmery, 9km further on, is a **Roman dam**, rebuilt over subsequent centuries. A little further on, just before entering the village of **El**

Maita, is the **tomb** of the marabout Sidi Ali el Bahlouf. This is a good point from which to walk around the **palmery gardens** which lead down to the Oued Gabès. Returning in the direction of Gabès, the road passes through **Oulad el Haj** and **Chemassa**, joining the banks of the Oued Gabès at **Sidi Merouane**. The road emerges 500m from the starting point of the tour.

27 · Gabès to Sfax

Sfax is on the Sahel coast, 137km north of Gabès. The roads are flat, but traffic can be heavy. Six buses leave Gabès every day for Sfax.

From Gabès follow signs to Sfax on the GP1, northwards through the suburb of **Bou Chemma**. After 32km the road passes through **Akarit**, the scene of heavy fighting in 1943 when the Allies penetrated the Axis defence line along the river, forcing the Axis powers to retreat northwards.

The GP1 continues to head north, with the sea just visible in the distance, into the olive-growing region of the Sahel, where 25 per cent of Tunisia's olive oil is produced.

> The olive trees are planted in wide rows, up to 20m apart, to account for the shortage of water. Rainfall is rare, and a good crop, which requires rainfall in both autumn and spring, is only expected once every seven years. A local saying goes: 'the olive crop if not abundant is little', meaning at least it is something. An average olive crop per tree is approximately 50kg, which after pressing produces 15 litres of oil. The harvest takes place on dry days from mid November onwards, when men wearing lambs' horns on their three middle fingers thresh the trees and collect the olives in a net below.

56km north of Gabès, the road passes the port of **La Skhira** which was first built by the British in the 19C for the export of esparto grass, which is used in the production of paper. The port, now a petrol terminal, lies on the junction with the road inland to Kairouan, after which traffic on the GP1 is less heavy.

After a further 38km on the GP1, there is a track on the right to a 9C Aghlabid fortress, ****Borj Yonga**. The track, signed **Yonca Sidi Ahmed**, leads through olive groves for 3km to the fortress walls. The walls stand on Byzantine foundations and are punctuated by eight defensive towers. To the south of the fortress are the very scant remains of ancient **Junca**. Excavations here have yielded many fine mosaics and architectural fragments now in the Bardo Museum. The ruins to the west of the fortress date from the Byzantine settlement of **Macomades Minores**.

Continue up the GP1 to (48km) **Mahres**, which is a large agricultural town surrounded by olive groves with an outdoor sculpture park centred on a model of a whale's skeleton, next to the water's edge. There are also two sizeable hotels here, north of the centre, catering for local holidaymakers during the summer season.

The GP1 continues through olive groves along the coast, past a (15km) British Gas terminal on the right, before reaching the (3km) **Site Archéologique de Tyna**. The ruins, signposted on the right, are contained within the Parc de Thina, which is an area of rough scrubland. Follow the track for 3km to a **lighthouse** around which the scant ruins of ancient **Thaene** are spread.

History
Mentioned by Pliny the Elder in his *Natural History*, Thaene was raised to the status of a colony under the Emperor Hadrian (117–138) and flourished from the Severan period (193–235) up until the early 5C, after which it was largely abandoned.

The best remaining structure is the **Baths of the Months**, named after its 3–5C **mosaics**, of which only those depicting January, February, April and December remain. The rooms of the frigidarium are on the east side, facing out to sea; those of the caldarium are on the west side. To the north of the baths are the remnants of a **housing area**. Some of the geometric mosaics have been left in situ, but the best have been removed to the Sfax and Bardo museums. To the east of the housing area are the scant remains of a **necropolis** with the remnants of an octagonal mausoleum. Further north along the coast from Thaene are **salt pans** where migrating birds can be seen in season.

SFAX
Sfax, a large city with a genuine walled medina and a good museum, is a further 10km along the GP1. Sfaxians are renowned for their hard work, which is reflected in the city's orderliness, and Sfax thrives on industry. There are some 400 olive presses in the city, producing oil that is shipped directly from the port. Sfax also produces cellulose from esparto grass, perfume and optical glass; the city has two **phospate works**, one of which, established during the French colonial period, is passed on the road as you approach the city. After the phosphate works and over the first set of traffic lights, there is a *war cemetery, where orderly white gravestones surround a cross. There are 1254 soldiers buried here, many of whom lost their lives during the last weeks of the Tunisian campaign, when the Allies drove the Axis forces northwards, taking control of Sfax in April 1943.

Follow the signs to '*centre ville*', forking right onto **Boulevard Farhat Hached** which leads to the *medina walls. The modern part of the city, where **accommodation** and **restaurants** are to be found, is to the south-west, between the medina walls and the port, which is the second largest in Tunisia, after the port of Tunis.

- **Airport**. El Maou, Route de Agareb, 6km on Gafsa road, tel. (04) 241700.

- **Airline companies**. Tunis Air, 4 Ave de l'Armée Nationale, tel. (04) 223691. Air France, Ave Taieb Mehri, tel. (04) 224847.

- **Ferries**. Kerkennah ferry terminal, Ave Hédi Khefacha, tel. (04) 223615. Services to Sidi Youssef, Kerkennah Islands (summer, every two hours, 06.00–20.00, winter, four daily, 07.00–17.00. Buses meet the ferries at Sidi Youssef and go to Remla).

- **Maritime companies**. Maritime Boccara, Rue Alexandre Dumas, tel. (04) 221841. CTN, Chez Navitour, Rue Abou el Kacem Chebbi, tel. (04) 228020.

- **Railway station**. Gare, Rue de Tazarka. Six services daily to Tunis via Sousse; three daily to Gabès.

- **Bus stations**. SNTRI, 2 Rue de Tazarka (opposite railway station). SRT, Gare Routière, Commandant Bgaoui. Six buses daily to Gabès, seven to Tunis, three to Gafsa. Other destinations include Jerba, Matmata, Medenine and Tataouine.

- **Louage station**. Ave de l'Armée Nationale (opposite PTT). Destinations include El Jem, Gabès, Gafsa, Kasserine, Sousse and Tunis.

- **Taxis**. Ave Farhat Hached and Bab Jebli.

- **Hotels**. There is a good selection of hotels in Sfax. At the top of the range is the *Sfax Centre* on Ave Habib Bourguiba, tel. (04) 225700. *Les Oliviers*, 25 Rue Habib Thameur, tel. (04) 225188, is also luxury class but not as pricey. *Le Colisée*, Rue Taieb M'hiri, tel. (04) 227801, and *Thyna*, Rue H. Maazoun, tel. (04) 225262, are classified as two-star hotels. In the one-star category is the *Alexander*, 21 Rue Alexandre Dumas, tel. (04) 221613. The cheapest hotels are to be found inside the medina.

- **Restaurants**. There are a number of cafés and eating places along Boulevard de la République. The most prestigious but not overly expensive restaurant in town is *Le Corail* on Rue Habib Maazoun. In and around the port are smoky bars serving simple food, including grilled fish.

- **Shopping**. Fish and vegetable market at the port. Fruit and vegetable market at Souk el Omrare on the north side of the medina. ONAT, Rue Hamadi Tej, tel. (04) 296826, government crafts centre. Supermarket, Gabès road.

- **Post office**. Ave Habib Bourguiba, tel. (04) 224722.

- **Tourist information**. Bureau d'Information, Place de l'Indépendance, tel. (04) 224606.

- **Medical care**. Hôpital Hédi Chaker, Route d'El Ain, tel. (04) 244422.

- **Festivals**. Foire Internationale de Sfax (trade fair), July.

- **Entertainment**. Night Club, Sfax Centre, Ave Habib Bourguiba, tel. (04) 225700.

- **Children**. Calèche rides around the town. Bumper cars near the railway station. Zoo, Route de la Soukra et d'Agareb.

- **Sport**. Piscine Municipale (public swimming pool), Route de l'Aéroport.

History

Sfax is built over the site of Roman Taparura, the stones of which were used in the construction of the kasbah and mosque in the 9C. By the 10C Sfax, then known as Fakous (Arabic for a type of cucumber), prospered from the production and export of olive oil. Following the Hilali invasions,

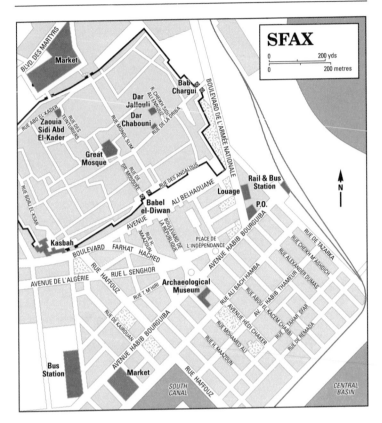

SFAX

0   200 yds
0   200 metres

N

Sfax established itself as the head of a small independent state which survived from 1095–99. Over the next centuries, Sfax was to change hands many times, being taken by the Norman, Roger of Sicily in 1148, and returned to Islamic control in 1159. Islam controlled Sfax over the following centuries, infidels not even being permitted into the city until 1832. When the French arrived in 1880, the Sfaxians resisted strongly in the name of Islam, accepting the French Protectorate in 1881 only after heavy bombardment. Sfax suffered further bombing during the Tunisian campaign which left the French colonial part of the city more or less flattened.

The **MEDINA**, Sfax's main attraction, covers an area measuring 400m by 500m. Its **walls**, which extend for 2km, were built of clay by the Aghlabids in the 9C. Rebuilt in stone over subsequent centuries, the walls were fortified with defence towers and crenellations. The layout of the medina is probably similar to that of the Roman settlement which lies buried beneath it, as unlike any other medina in Tunisia, the streets are arranged on a grid system. This makes finding your way around easier, which is helpful as there are no signs for tourists unlike the Tunis medina.

The main entrance into the medina, **Bab el Diwan**, which has two vast arches, pierces the south walls. Originally built in 1306, it was reconstructed in 1619, 1646 and 1748, and then restored after the bomb damage of 1943. Inside the gate, bear right along **Rue des Andalous** to join the main thoroughfare, **Rue Mongi Slim**, which runs north–south through the medina. Take the third turning on the right, **Rue de la Driba**, which is lined with 18C stone portals, many of which were carved in Gabès. After 150m turn left onto **Rue Cheikh Sidi Ali Ennouz**, 50m along which, on the left, is the ****DAR JALLOULI MUSÉE RÉGIONALE DES ARTS ET TRADITIONS POPULAIRES** (open Tues–Sun, 09.30–16.30). The museum is housed in the former home of a local Andalucian family, after whom the building is named, Dar Jallouli. It dates from the 17C which was when the house was built, contrary to the inscription of 1723 on the façade. It is built of red Gabès stone and sumptuously decorated with ceramic tiles from Tunis and ornate woodwork by local carpenters.

A green studded door leads into an **entrance hall** with a beautifully painted wood ceiling. The ticket desk is on the left and a doorway to a **second hall** is on the right. This double hallway is a typical feature of the *dar*, providing added privacy from the street outside. The second hall leads to a **triple arched loggia** which looks onto a magnificent **inner courtyard** decorated with tiles and surrounded by rooms with carved plaster arched windows. To the right of the entrance is a **store room** containing spices and storage jars. To the left of the entrance are saddles complete with the regalia used on festive days. On the **south side of the courtyard** is a reception room. It is T-shaped, as is typical of the *dar*, and has a richly painted wood ceiling in red and green. The room has showcases of local women's costumes, and a carved screen, on the right, conceals a raised bed. On the **west side of the courtyard** is the kitchen with its cauldrons and cooking utensils, and there is a collection of woodwork in an adjoining room, including screens and coffers, and equipment for turning wood. The **north side of the courtyard** has a reception room, similar to that on the south side. A coffee table is recessed into the end of the room, and a silk curtain, from Mahdia, screens a raised bed. Steps lead up from the **east side of the courtyard** to the **first floor** which has a fine wooden balustrade. The **room on the left** has local costumes from Sfax and the Kerkennah Islands. The **end room** has marriage costumes and jewellery. The **room on the right** has embroidered shawls, many of the finest of which are from Kerkennah Islands. Steps lead up to the **second floor** where there is a collection of Arabic calligraphy.

Bab Jebli gates

Return back along Rue de la Driba to the crossroads with Rue Mongi Slim and turn right. Keep going until meeting **Rue des Forgerons**, just inside the north wall. Turn left and follow Rue des Forgerons along the walls to ****Bab Jebli**, which is the oldest gate in the medina walls, being more or less unchanged since the 9C. The clay with which it was originally built is still visible in places as are the chunks of Roman masonry which went into its construction. The gate leads through to a large **covered market**, with stalls selling fruit, vegetables and spices, with a butcher's hall at the back.

From Bab Jebli, head south along **Rue des Teinturiers**, which runs alongside the Souk des Etoffes where local blankets and textiles are sold. On the corner of Rue des Teinturiers with Rue Abd el Kader, is the squat minaret of **Zaouia Sidi Abd el Kader**. The entrance in the north wall of the zaouia has a finely **carved portal** with an Arabic inscription. Follow Rue des Teinturiers southwards until it meets the walls of the ****GREAT MOSQUE**. The mosque was originally built in 849 by the Aghlabids to resemble that of Kairouan. However, it was totally reconstructed by the Zirids, and then by the Hafsid caliphs, who made the mosque smaller due to the shrinking population of the city, although it was later to be enlarged by the Ottomans. The **mosque interior**, which has nine aisles and twelve bays, is not open to tourists. The **exterior** is largely clad with abutting souks, except on the **east side** where there is a series of blind arches, a Zirid decorative feature, which contain **inscriptions**. Most of the inscriptions are in Arabic or Kufic; one, however, on a slab of marble, is Byzantine in origin and has a pair of **carved peacocks**. The **minaret** stands on the north-west corner. Like that of Kairouan, it is built in diminishing layers, three in all, but is less austere, being decoratively sculpted.

Sfax Medina minaret

Follow **Rue de la Grande Mosque** south towards Bab el Diwan, and turn right just before the gate. Follow the road that traces along inside the walls westwards for 300m to the shady square, used as an open-air theatre in the summer, in front of the kasbah.

The ****kasbah**, built into the south-west corner of the medina walls, dates from the 17C, although part of the fortifications at the east end are 12C. It is the seat of the **Musée de l'Architecture Traditionelle de Sfax** (open Tues–Sun, 09.30–16.30). Inside, there is a large L-shaped **inner courtyard**, part of which holds fragments of Roman masonry. Steps lead up on the left to a **walkway** that encircles the upper walls, taking in the **main**

tower which has been converted to an exhibition room and contains architectural drawings of Sfax.

Return to Bab el Diwan and leave the medina by following **Boulevard de la République**, an attractive tree-lined street of the French colonial era, south for 250m to **Avenue Ali Belhaouane**. On the opposite side of this busy thoroughfare is the grand façade of the ****ARCHAEOLOGICAL MUSEUM** (open Mon–Sat, 08.30–13.00, 15.00–18.00) which contains archaeological finds from Thaene and the local area.

Room 1, the entrance hall, has Byzantine mosaics from a basilica in Sfax, and Islamic funeral stones. **Room 2**, on the right, is dedicated to the Paleo-Christian era with mosaics and frescoes from Sfax, Thaene, and two basilicas excavated at La Skhirra. On the **end wall** is a striking 5–6C mosaic of ****Daniel in the Lion's Den**, from a church in Sfax. There are several good **tomb mosaics**, many of which depict the deceased or have an inscription. Along the **right wall** is a collection of **pagan funerary monuments**, together with small marble sarcophagi from the Kerkennah Islands and terracotta funerary urns.

Room 3, on the left of the entrance hall, has archaeological finds dating from the Roman era. The detached frescoes on the **left wall** date from the 2–3C and were found at Thaene and Acholla. On the **end wall** is a large 3C mosaic of the **Poet Ennus and Nine Muses**, found in Sfax. Along the **right wall** is a collection of ****4C tomb mosaics** found at Thaene. Many of them depict the deceased reclining on their death-bed; one shows a funerary banquet, another a Venus and cupids.

Room 4, the small room at the foot of the marble staircase, on the right, has a collection of mosaic fragments, mainly from Sfax, and some fragments of Roman masonry.

Room 5, to the left of the stairs, has further mosaics, including a large 3C **portrait of Oceanus** and a smaller mosaic of a **cupid astride a dolphin**.

The **first floor** of the building holds the municipality offices. The **large hall** at the top of the stairs, covered by a dome, has a 2C mosaic on the left wall depicting the **triumph of Bacchus**, found at El Jem.

KERKENNAH ISLANDS

Just 20km offshore, the Kerkennah Islands are a popular ferry excursion from Sfax and a pleasant escape from the city. The archipelago, which is totally flat, the highest point being only 13m above sea-level, is made up of two main islands and a number of isolated islets. The western of the two islands, **Gharbi**, measures 15km by 7km; the eastern, **Chergui**, is 42km by 8km. They are interconnected by a causeway, 600m long, built in 1961 on Roman foundations. The population of the Kerkennah Islands numbers 15,000; most of the inhabitants are dependent on fishing, handicrafts and tourism; agriculture is limited due to the shortage of water.

History

Known as Kyrranis to the ancient Greeks and Cercina to the Romans, the Kerkennah Islands have played an important role throughout history. They were the place of refuge of the Carthaginian General, Hannibal, in

195 BC, following his defeat at the Battle of Zama (202 BC). Later, during Caesar's campaign of 46 BC, Sallust, Roman Governor of Numidia, brought a detachment of ships here to cut off the Pompeians' supply of grain from the Kerkennah Islands, thus helping to ensure Caesar's eventual victory. In the 16C, the Turkish corsair Draghut established a base here, building a look-out tower to protect his ships from surprise attack. In more recent times, Chergui was the hiding place of Habib Bourguiba, who escaped from here to Libya.

The ferry (see above) docks at **Sidi Youssef** (Gharbi), from where the island's only road heads inland to the village of (5km) **Melita**. From Melita, the road continues to the (8km) **causeway** at the east end of the island which connects Chergui. The first village on Chergui is (2km) **Ouled Yaneg**, from where there is a 2.5km track on the left which leads to the beach and hotel complex of the **Sidi Frej tourist zone**. At 2.5km along the coast from Sidi Frej is the site of Roman Cercina and the broken walls of **Borj el Hissar**, an ancient fortress.

Continuing along the main road, the capital of the Kerkennah Islands, **Remla**, is reached after a further 8km. The town has all the basic facilities and a market every Thursday. There is a small museum dedicated to Habib Bourguiba and his escape from Chergui in 1945.

The main road continues for 11km to the fishing port of **El Ataya** at the eastern end of the island. The fishermen here make V-shape traps from palms which they fix into the sea bed to funnel the fish, mainly squid, into an enclosure. You may wish to negotiate a trip to the deserted offshore islands of Gremdi from here with one of the local fishermen.

Organising a fishing trip may also be possible from here, but be sure to agree on a price before setting out.

The rest of the island can be explored by returning for 4km along the main road and then turning right to (2.5km) **Ech Chergui** where there is a textile centre. The road continues for a further 9km to **Sidi Tebeni**, a fishing hamlet on the northernmost point of the island.

28 · Sfax via El Jem to Mahdia

The main road is followed to El Jem with its magnificent amphitheatre, from where the route heads towards the coast, via Ksour Essaf, to Mahdia, making a total trip of 118km. There are five trains a day from Sfax to El Jem, as well as louages, which also run frequently from El Jem to Mahdia.

The alternative coastal route is 104km direct to Mahdia, with an additional 84km to visit El Jem. The coast has a number of sandy beaches with shallow water suitable for children, although it can be clogged with reed. Of particular interest is the (67km) Rass Kaboudia headland where there are the remains of a 6C tower said to be the site where Count Belisarius landed in 533 when he came to wrest Tunisia from the Vandals for the Byzantine throne.

From Sfax take the GP1 northwards, passing through (29km) **Dokhane** and (15km) **El Hencha**, before reaching the village of (20km) **EL JEM**, at the centre of which is the sixth largest and one of the best-preserved amphitheatres in the Roman world.

EL JEM

As you come into El Jem, the first turning on the right leads to the **AMPHITHEATRE** (open daily, 08.30–18.00) which was once surrounded by the ancient city of Thysdrus, a prosperous centre with a population of 30,000–40,000 inhabitants. The contrast with the humble village today could not be greater. As N. Davies wrote in 1862: 'The houses, the gardens, and the plantations sink into such utter insignificance beside this stupendous pile.'

History

The earliest archaeological evidence shows Thysdrus to have been in Punic hands from the 3C BC until Caesar landed on the Tunisian shores at Monastir, during his campaign of 46 BC. It was not until the 2C, however, that Thysdrus became a place of any importance, flourishing through the cultivation of olives, a valuable export commodity in the Roman world. The 36,000 acres of olive groves surrounding the city brought it immense wealth, but it was short-lived, for in 238, just as the final touches were being made to the amphitheatre, a new tax on olive oil was introduced. Local landowners, taking advantage of the political instability in Rome under Maximinus, organised a revolt, which culminated in the proclamation of Gordion I, a 79-year-old senator from Carthage, as emperor. His son Gordion II succeeded him, but was to remain emperor for only 21 days. He died in battle against the Third Augustan Legion which, lead by the Commander Cappellianus, quashed the revolt and sacked El Jem.

The city was never to recover its former importance. The Byzantines transformed the amphitheatre, which had barely been used, into a fortress in the 6C, and in 699 the fortress is said to have sheltered the Berber Queen El Kahina from the Arabs. After the Arab invasions, the city was abandoned, although the amphitheatre remained in almost pristine condition until 1695 when the Ottoman Mohammed Bey made a breach in the north-west wall in order to evict Berber rebels.

The amphitheatre, tickets to which also give entry to the museum, has fine **outer walls** retaining their original height in most places, three storeys high, with arcades on each level, each decorated with half columns of a different order. The **topmost wall**, crowning the amphitheatre, remains intact only on the south side and the **passages and staircases** inside the walls have mostly disappeared, as has the **seating**. Once accommodating 30,000 spectators (somewhat disproportionate to the actual size of the city the amphitheatre served), the tiers of seats looked down onto the **arena**, which is elliptical and measures 65m by 37m. The arena floor has collapsed, revealing **passageways** beneath for wild animals, gladiators and victims.

Return to the main road and continue a few hundred metres further to the **ARCHAEOLOGICAL MUSEUM** (open daily, 07.00–16.30) on the left.

Built as a reconstruction of a Roman villa which was excavated here, the museum contains an excellent collection of mosaics, found here and in other nearby villas. A horseshoe arch leads into the **entrance hall**, on the left side of which is the ticket desk. The hall precedes a **peristyle**, around which the three rooms of the museum are arranged. The **first room** on the left, on the **left wall** has a fine 2C mosaic of ****Orpheus charming the animals**. Orpheus is depicted in the central medallion, and the animals in those surrounding. In the showcases are finds from tombs, including Roman figurines in terracotta, depicting Venus and Eros amongst others, and fragments of marble statues. On the **right wall** are three good mosaics: a section of a 2C mosaic of the **Nile**; a **Dionysiac procession** where the young god is depicted with satyrs; and a 3C **oval mosaic** from a dining room decorated with curvilinear medallions. The **end wall** has a 3C mosaic of the ****four seasons**, which are allegorically represented by portraits of women.

The **second room**, on the **left wall**, has a vast mosaic in two parts, from the dining room of a villa which adjoins the museum. Dating from the mid 2C, it depicts the ****four seasons**, and has a Dionysiac procession along the borders. On the long wall, **facing the door**, is a vast 3C mosaic of the ****nine muses**, vividly depicted and in excellent condition. Next to it is another large mosaic, dating from the same century, depicting **Silene** at the centre surrounded by vines, symbolising Bacchus, intertwined with cupids. On the same wall is a small but notable mosaic of the ****child Dionysus astride a tigress**, also dating from the 3C. The **end wall**, which has fragments of mosaics depicting hunting scenes, has a doorway which leads through to an extension of the museum and an **area of excavations** where several sumptuous villas have been uncovered, including the **Peacock House** and the **Sollertiana Domus**. The **third room**, on the right side of the peristyle, has a large 3C mosaic on the left wall, which has a fine geometric design incorporating animals in combat. The two other large mosaics in this room both date from the 3C and are medallion compositions.

Back outside the museum, to the right of the façade, there is an **18C fountain** with three arches. In front of the museum, on the opposite side of the road and rail track, there is a hollow in the ground, the site of an earlier and much smaller **amphitheatre**. Built in the 1C, it could hold 6000 spectators, although it was later enlarged to hold an audience of 8000.

From the museum head through the village centre, leaving El Jem by the MC87 in the direction of Ksour Essaf. The road passes through a landscape little changed since Roman times, with the red-earthed plain covered in olive groves. At the small village of (12km) **Essadda**, the MC87 climbs up from the plain and continues through hills to (15km) **Ksour Essaf**. This small town, clustered around an arcaded square, has little to detain the visitor, but it is worth making the short excursion from here to the fishing village of **Salakta**, which is built on the site of ancient **Sullectum**.

To reach Salakta, head straight through Ksour Essaf to the mini-roundabout at the east side of the town. Go straight over, following signs to *Musée*, and follow Rue 837 for 6km.

**SALAKTA is a quiet village surrounding a fishing harbour. Turn left at the harbour and follow the road for a few hundred metres to the

Antiquarium de Salakta (open Tues–Sun, 09.00–13.00, 14.00–18.00), a simple building identified by a single column standing in front. The museum houses finds from the local excavations carried out by a French and British group in 1983. In the **entrance hall** is a copy of the **Sullectum mosaic**, which depicts, in black and white, the principal African ports that supplied Rome. The original mosaic was found in Ostia Antica, outside Rome.

The showpiece of the museum is the large mosaic of a 4.5m long **lion** in the **central room**. Dating from the 3C it was uncovered in the villa of Leontius, a manufacturer of armour. The lion, the symbol of the manufacturing company, may have been inspired by the lions that were shipped here for the amphitheatre in El Jem. The two adjoining rooms have pottery and other finds from the excavations, including a collection of amphorae which is accompanied by good explanations in English as to their use and origins.

Before leaving the museum, you may wish to see the Christian **catacomb** of **Arch Zara**; for this you have to be accompanied by a museum official.

Next to the museum is the site of a Roman necropolis, the source of many of the artefacts in the museum. At the south end of the harbour, 500m from the museum, there are further archaeological remains, thought to be of a **baths**, comprising a series of semicircular basins arranged in niches.

MAHDIA

Mahdia, 13km north of Ksour Essaf, is an attractive, fortified coastal town, unspoilt by tourism. The road enters the town at its fishing port, the third largest in Tunisia, and follows along the quayside, which is lined with palms, to a roundabout. Turn left at the roundabout and follow the road to the walls of the medina, the historic centre of Mahdia.

- **Railway station**. Gare de Mahdia, Ave Farhat Hached, tel. (03) 680177. Eight trains daily to Sousse.

- **Bus station**. Place 1er Mai, tel. (03) 680372. Regular buses to Sousse and Monastir. Less frequent services to Tunis and Kairouan.

- **Louage station**. Opposite the railway station. Frequent services to Monastir, Sousse, El Jem and Sfax.

- **Taxis**. Station Taxis Abou Nawas, tel. (03) 695900.

- **Hotels**. The top hotels are to be found in the *zone touristique*, along the beach to the north of the town. The *El Mahdi*, tel. (03) 681300 and the *Club Cap Mahdia*, tel. (03) 681725, have bungalow-type accommodation and swimming pools. The largest hotel is the *Thapsus*, tel. (03) 694495. The *Sables d'Or*, tel. (03) 681137, is less pricey. Next in the range are the *Corniche*, tel. (03) 694201, and the *Panorama*, tel. (03) 680039, both of which are close to the town centre.

- **Restaurants**. Restaurants around the port grill fish over charcoal. *Le Lido* and *Le Quai*, both near the port on Ave Farhat Hached, have good reputations.

- **Shopping**. Weekly market every Friday. Daily fish market near the port.

- **Tourist information**. Inside medina gate.

- **Festivals**. Nuits de Mahdia, July–August.

History

The origins of Mahdia go back to Phoenician times, although the only evidence of the town's ancient past is a vessel found offshore by sponge divers in 1907. Presumably bound for Mahdia, the ship sank in 86 BC with a cargo of fine art objects from Greece.

The next important period in Mahdia's history is the era of the Fatimid dynasty, when the town was chosen for its easily defended position as the Fatimid capital. The Fatimids were unpopular rulers, not least because they were Shi'ite Muslims. The first in the Fatimid line, Obeid Allah, a self-claimed 'Mahdi' (saviour), laid the foundations of Mahdia in 916. By 921, when the Caliph resided there, the peninsula was heavily fortified with a 10m thick wall across the neck. It enclosed an arsenal, a harbour, the Great Mosque and two palaces.

When the Fatimid dynasty moved their capital to the newly-conquered territories of Cairo, they installed the Zirids as governors of Mahdia. The Zirids were disloyal to the Fatimids and did not survive for long, first coming under attack from the Hilalian invasion unleashed by the irritated Fatimids. A series of sea attacks followed with Crusaders landing on the shore of Mahdia in 1088. The town came under Christian control in 1148 when Mahdia was annexed by Roger of Sicily, but was returned to Islamic rule in 1160. Like so many coastal towns in Tunisia, Mahdia was later to became a corsair base, with the Turkish corsair Draghut taking Mahdia in 1549. However, a year later, he unsuccessfully defended the town against the Spanish, led by Charles V, and the walls and many of the public buildings, including the Great Mosque, were razed to the ground.

The main gate into the **MEDINA** pierces the west walls which once stretched from one side of the peninsula to the other. Known as ****Skifa el Kahla** (Dark Gate), the gate is heavily fortified with large towers at either side. It was built by the Ottomans in 1554, following the Spanish invasion, using masonry from the earlier Fatimid walls. The gate leads into a **vaulted tunnel**, 44m long, which in Fatimid times was guarded by a series of seven iron portcullises, each weighing eight tonnes. Inside the walls, there are steps to the terrace of an **artillery bastion**, from where there is a fine panorama of the town and port.

From the gate, **Rue Obeid Allah el Mahdi** leads through the heart of the medina. Silk is still woven here on upright looms, a skill that was introduced in the 19C by Jews who had emigrated here from Libya. The **Musée du Tissage** (closed indefinitely), at 7 Rue Obeid Allah el Mahdi, on the right, documents the history of silk-weaving and has a collection of local marriage costumes for which the Mahdian silk is woven.

Continuing along Rue Obeid Allah el Mahdi, the road opens out into **Place du Caire**, a charming square shaded by trees. On the **west side**, an old **stone loggia** shelters a coffee house, and on the **south side**, four stone **portals** pierce the walls of the ****Haci Mustafa Haniza Mosque**. Built by the

Ottomans in the 16C, the stones incorporated into the portals are much older. The portal on the right has a stone with a **small cross** carved at the base, which came from a Christian building. The tree of life and rosette motifs, however, are distinctly Ottoman, as are the ceramic tiles. The **minaret**, also Ottoman in style, was added in the 18C. Standing on a square base, the octagonal shaft is crowned by a kiosk balcony ornamented with tile mosaics.

Continuing beyond the Place du Caire, the road ends at a vast paved clearing, on one side of which is the ****GREAT MOSQUE**. Founded in 916 by the Fatimid Caliph, Obeid el Mahdi, the mosque was originally built into the sea-walls. The building as it stands today, separated from the sea by a roadway, is a 1965 reconstruction of the Fatimid design, only the façade of the mosque being original. Here can be seen one of the most important architectural innovations of the Fatimid era, the addition of a **grand portal**. Although such portals had previously been used on palaces, it was the first time that it had been added to a mosque. The portal has striking keyhole-shape niches flanking the horseshoe doorway which leads through to a massive **courtyard**, measuring 42 by 50m. Surrounded by horseshoe arches, the lower ones on the north side are Zirid in origin and have cross-vaulting. Walking around to the **back of the mosque**, the **mihrab** can be seen, projecting from the walls. This was a typical Fatimid feature, designed to deepen the mihrab niche inside. The **interior** is similar to that of the Great Mosque of Kairouan, with a wide central aisle and four narrower ones to either side.

From the Great Mosque, head north along the coast, where the vestiges of the **Fatimid palaces** are passed, before forking left up to the fortress of ****BORJ EL KEBIR** (open daily, 09.00–17.00). Built by the Ottomans in 1595, the fortress had vast bastions added for cannons in the 18C. The entrance today is through one of the bastions, although the original entrance is the small door to the right with an inscription bearing the name of the founder, Abou Abdallah Mohammed Pasha. The **main arch**, attractively carved with rosettes and geometric motifs, leads inside the bastion to a **dog-leg hall**. The hall gives onto the large **inner courtyard**, which now holds a stage used for spectacles during the summer festival, and a collection of Corinthian columns and capitals. A row of small **cells**, one of which was an oratory, with pointed arches open onto the courtyard. Steps on the right lead up onto the **walls** from where there are excellent **views**. **To the east** is the tip of the peninsula, known as the Cap Afrique, where there is an extensive cemetery. Many of the tombs here belong to Shi'ites and date back to the 10C. **To the west** is the port and the town.

X THE UPPER SAHEL AND TUNIS BASIN

29 · Mahdia to Monastir

It is 47km from Mahdia via Moknine to Monastir, on a busy coastal road through a densely cultivated and built-up region. There are regular buses and louages from Mahdia to Monastir. The eight daily trains from Mahdia to Sousse also stop at Monastir.

From Mahdia follow the MC82 northwards along the coast for 12km to **Bekalta**. Bekalta, a sprawling town, lies 6km inland from ancient **Thapsus**, the site of the Battle of Thapsus which was a turning point in the history of both Rome and North Africa. Caesar, seeking to bring to an end the long running civil war, caught the Pompeians off guard at Thapsus in 46 BC and massacred 10,000 of the enemy around the town. Scant **archaeological remains** are spread along a sandy beach, but the only discernible structures are the **baths** and traces of the **harbour wall**.

The MC82 continues through Bekalta to (1km) **Teboulba**, from where the region is built up all the way to (7km) Moknine. Set on the shores of a salt lake, **MOKNINE** is a busy and unattractive agricultural town with a large market every Wednesday. The town was once well-known for its crafts, and now has a **Museum of Local Art and Folklore** (open summer, Tues–Sun, 09.00–12.00, 14.30–18.00, winter, Tues–Sun, 09.00–12.00, 14.00–17.30), which is housed in the ex-mosque of Sidi Babana. The main **prayer hall** has a collection of jewellery, costumes, musical instruments, furniture, tools, culinary utensils, red and black Berber pottery and agricultural equipment, including goats' horns used to thresh the olive trees. In the **archaeological collection** there are Roman and Ottoman coins, and Husainid and Hafsid manuscripts.

From Moknine, continue northwards on the MC82 into (2km) **Ksar Hellal**, and then take the MC92, a well-surfaced road, along the coast to (5km) **LAMTA**. This small village marks the site of ancient **Leptis Minor** which once stood at the sea edge. There are no significant archaeological remains, but the ****MUSÉE DE LAMTA** (open Tues–Sun, 09.00–13.00, 14.00–18.00), just outside the village on the right, houses the well-documented (in English) finds from the Tuniso–American excavation project carried out here in 1990–92. The museum is surrounded by a neatly kept **garden** which contains masonry fragments and parts of mosaics found during the excavations. At the **museum entrance** is a **doliman**, a large, round storage jar used to conserve food in the hold of a ship. The entrance leads through to an **arcaded courtyard**, around which the three rooms of the museum are arranged. In an anti-clockwise direction, the **first room** has finds from the necropolis, including a ****wooden sarcophagus** dating from the 3C BC, and good explanations as to the burial procedure. The **second room** is dedicated to life in Roman Leptis Minor with explanations on the economy, amenities, traditions, and also on techniques of fresco, mosaic, heating and roofing. The **amphora collection**, also in this room, has been arranged to show the origins of different shapes of amphorae throughout the Mediterranean. The **third room** has a fine 3C mosaic of the **four seasons** and a beautifully carved **marble sarcophagus** of the 4C.

The MC92 continues to head north along the coast, much of which is badly littered, passing by the towns of (2.5km) **Ksibet el Mediouni** and (3km) **Khniss**. The latter lies on the banks of the Oued Khniss, to the north of which are **salt pans**.

MONASTIR

Monastir, a further 6.5km north, derives part of its income from the extraction of salt, although tourism is fast becoming a major part of its economy, with the development of resorts to the north of the town. Probably due to its well-nourished economy, Monastir is a lively town with a good holiday atmosphere and a Mediterranean feel. The road into the centre of Monastir, signed *centre ville*, leads along the crenellated walls of the medina to the Ribat, the town's most impressive monument, and the large palm-filled square, **Place des Palmiers**, in front of it.

- **Airport**. International Airport Habib Bourguiba di Skanes, Monastir, 8km from centre, tel. (03) 661314.

- **Airline company**. Tunis Air, Rue de l'Indépendance, tel. (03) 661922.

- **Railway station**. Gare Habib Bourguiba, Rue Salem B'Chir, tel. (03) 660755. Frequent services to Sousse and Mahdia.

- **Bus station**. Gare Routière, Ave de la République, tel. (03) 661059. Regular services to Gabès, Mahdia, Sfax, Sousse and Tunis. Shuttle service to the airport.

- **Louage station**. In the bus station. Frequent services to Sousse and Mahdia.

- **Taxis**. Airport and bus station.

- **Hotels**. Most of the hotels in Monastir are to be found along the coast, particularly at Skanes, north of the town. Hotels closer to Monastir range from the five-star *Club Med*, east of the ribat, to the one-star *Yasmin*, 1.5km north of the ribat.

- **Restaurants**. There are a number of seafood restaurants around Marina Cap Monastir, east of the ribat. Cheaper eating places are to be found along Ave Habib Bourguiba and in the medina.

- **Shopping**. Weekly market held every Saturday. ONAT, Quartier Chraga, tel. (03) 662290. Marché Centrale, Les Arcades, Ave Habib Bourguiba. Monoprix, Ave Habib Bourguiba. Magasin Générale, Place de l'Indépendance.

- **Post office**. Ave Habib Bourguiba, tel. (03) 660176.

- **Tourist information**. Office du Tourisme, Rue de l'Indépendance, tel. (03) 681098. Commissariat Regional, Skanes–Dkhila, tel. (03) 661205.

- **Medical care**. Hôpital Universitaire, Ave Farhat Hached, tel. (03) 661143.

- **Festivals**. Son et Lumière festival, summer.

- **Entertainment**. Nightlife in the big hotels at Skanes.

- **Children**. Camel rides on the beach at Skanes. Toy-train rides along the coast road, Route de la Falaise, which service the tourist hotels.

- **Sport**. Boat excursions and deep sea diving are organised by Monastir Plongées et Loisirs, Marina Cap Monastir, tel. (03) 662509. Sailing facilities are available at Tunisie Yachting et Loisirs, Marina Cap Monastir, tel. (03) 663831. There are two golf clubs: Golf de Monastir, Route de Ouardanine, tel. (03) 661120; Golf Palm Links, Skanes–Dkhila–Monastir, tel. (03) 631266.

History

The Phoenicians are the earliest recorded settlers on the Monastir headland, founding a port known as Rous Penna. It was renamed Ruspina by the Romans and served as Caesar's headquarters in 46 BC. The Roman defences were replaced in the 7C by the ribat, one of a chain of Arab

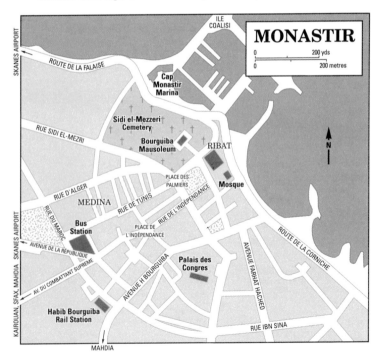

fortresses built along the coast from Morocco to Egypt, to protect Ifriqiya against the Christian crusades. Under the protection of Islamic warriors, Monastir acquired a reputation for holiness and became a centre of pilgrimage. It was said that three nights' stay in the ribat promised a place in Paradise. The town reached its pinnacle of religious importance in the 11C when nearby Mahdia was the seat of the Fatimids. However, following the transferral of the Fatimid capital to Cairo, the town declined. In the 16C, the town became important again when the Ottomans defeated the Spanish and established a powerful stronghold here. In more recent history, Monastir has become famous as the birthplace of ex-president Habib Bourguiba. Bourguiba was born here in 1903 and after rising to power endowed his town with many new buildings, including a family mausoleum and a palace to the north of the town where he now resides.

The ****RIBAT** (open daily, 08.00–19.00), Monastir's fortress, was originally founded in 796 by Harthama Ben Ayam. It was part of a chain of coastal fortresses that gave warning of enemy approach by using signal beacons on towers which could transmit a message along the entire north coast of Tunisia in the space of one day. The original building, centred on a tower, was only 32.8 square metres, but fortifications were added in the 9C and again in the 11C. During the 16C, the Ottomans modified the fortress once more, and further changes were made in subsequent centuries, the most recent alterations taking place in the 19C.

Ribats were manned by Islamic warriors, known as *Murabtin* who engaged in holy warfare. Possibly a prototype for the Crusaders, when not at war the *Murabtin* lived as monks, using the ribat as a monastery.

The entrance into the fortress is in the west walls, at the foot of a **polygonal tower** which is decorated with a series of blind arches. Inside, there is a ticket office and shop selling cards from where a narrow **dog-leg hall**, covered by vaults and with guard rooms along either side, leads into the inner courtyard. The **courtyard**, surrounded by the monastic **cells**, has a collection of Islamic tombstones and inscriptions dating from the 12C. On the right of the courtyard, steps lead up to a **small museum** which is housed in the former prayer hall. The collection includes manuscripts, some ancient Copt woven cloth dating from the 4–8C, Fatimid glassware, Aghlabid pottery, an 11C woodcarved mimber from Kairouan, an astrolabe of 927 from Cordoba and 10C Fatimid coins. There is also a diagram of the fortress showing the different phases of its construction.

A **ramp** leads up from the museum towards the **Nador Tower**, a tall, circular tower that was added to the south-east corner of the fortress in the 18C. The tower, climbed by 90 steps, offers a fine **panorama**, although care should be taken as there is no fencing between the crenellations. The view takes in the yacht marina on the south side, the cemetery and the Bourguiba Mausoleum on the north side, and the Great Mosque to the west.

Back outside the fortress, alongside the west wall is the **Great Mosque**, a simple sandstone building. It was originally built in the 9C, but was enlarged by

Great Mosque

the Zirids in the 11C, at the time they modified the ribat. A simple **portal** leads into the **prayer hall** which is covered by cross-vaults that rest on columns, some of which are Roman.

Heading to the waterfront behind the ribat, to the west, near the *Hotel Splendid*, are the ruins of the **Mosque of Saida**. This small sandstone building (10m by 7m) is named after a Zirid princess and once stood inside a second ribat.

Back at Place des Palmiers, to the north-west is the **Bourguiba Mausoleum**. It is approached by a processional avenue, carved through the **Sidi el Mezzeri cemetery**. Built in 1963 as the ex-President's place of burial, it is flanked by two minarets that were added in 1986, each 25m high, made of Italian marble. The **President's tomb** rests under the central 18-carat **gold-plated dome**, while the green domes to either side mark the burial place of Bourguiba's parents and his first wife who was French. The surrounding cemetery has long been a popular burial ground as among the hundreds of white gravestones are a number of **koubba** (small mausoleums belonging to marabouts). The 12C **koubba of Sidi el Mazzeri**, after whom the cemetery is named, is particularly revered and is decorated with a Kufic inscription and faience tiles. The **octagonal mausoleums** at the entrance to the cemetery, one of which is dedicated to Second World War victims, are more recent additions.

The **medina**, south-west of Place des Palmiers, has retained much of its surrounding wall and entrance gates, but the profusion of souvenir shops inside has left little of its original character intact.

30 · Monastir to Sousse

Sousse is 24km north of Monastir on dual carriageway. There is an hourly train, the Metro du Sahel, from Monastir to Sousse, as well as regular buses and louages.

The MC92 from Monastir follows the coast, past the (6.5km) airport and golf course at the tourist complex (7km), **Skanes**. After 5km, the road meets the outskirts of the city of Sousse.

SOUSSE

The road continues for a further 5km, past the medina walls, to Place Farhat Hached, the city centre. Sousse has a big city atmosphere and plenty to do. The medina offers a break from the incessant traffic, and pleasant breezes blow off the Mediterranean. It lacks green areas but the nearby beaches and promenades compensate for this.

- **Airport**. International Airport Habib Bourguiba di Skanes, Monastir, 15km south on Monastir road, tel. (03) 661314.

- **Airline company**. Tunis Air, 5 Ave Habib Bourguiba, tel. (03) 227955.

- **Maritime company**. Compagnie Tunisienne de Navigation, Rue Abdallah ibn Zoubeir, tel. (03) 224861.

- **Railway station**. Gare SNCFT, Boulevard Hassouna Ayachi. Regular services to Tunis and Monastir, six daily to Sfax, one daily to Gabès.

- **Bus stations**. Place Bab Jedid, city buses, No. 52 to airport. Gare Routière, Ave Leopold Sengor, buses to destinations throughout Tunisia.

- **Louage Station**. Place Farhat Hached. Regular departures for Kairouan, Kasserine, Mahdia, Monastir, Sfax and Tunis.

- **Taxis**. Place Farhat Hached.

- **Hotels**. Most hotels are to be found in the tourist zone along the coast to the north of the city where there is a wide range in both price and quality from pensions to five-star hotels. In the city itself accommodation tends to be cheaper. The one-star *Claridge Hotel* at 10 Ave Habib Bourguiba, tel. (03) 224759, is reasonable and has a good central position. There are one- and two-star hotels to be found in the medina too. The tourist office provides a comprehensive accommodation list.

- **Restaurants**. There are a number of eating places along Ave Habib Bourguiba and on Place Farhat Hached. Along the coast, north of the centre, there are fish restaurants on Route de la Corniche.

- **Shopping**. SOCOPA (crafts centre affiliated with ONAT), Centre Commercial Abou Nawas Boujaafar, Ave Habib Bourguiba, tel. (03) 229900. Covered fruit and vegetable market on Rue de France, just inside the medina east wall.

- **Post office**. Ave de la République, tel. (03) 224750.

- **Tourist information**. Commissariat Régional, 1 Ave Habib Bourguiba, tel. (03) 225157. Syndicat d'Initiative, Place Farhat Hached, tel. (03) 2222331.

- **Medical care**. Hôpital Universitaire Farhat Hached, Rue Ibn el Jazzar, tel. (03) 221411. Clinique Les Oliviers, Blvd 7 Novembre, Route Touristique, tel. (03) 242711.

- **Festivals**. Festival of Local Popular Arts, March. International Festival of Theatre and Music, July–August. Festival of Sidi el Kantaoui, July. Festival of Baba Aoussou, August.

- **Entertainment**. Sousse has a good reputation for its night-life with two discos on Ave Habib Bourguiba, the Topkapi and the Atlantic. Most night-life, however, takes place on the coast in the big hotels to the north of the city. The modern resort of El Kantaoui, 10km north of Sousse, also offers a range of entertainment at the marina and the surrounding complex of hotels and restaurants.

- **Children**. Recreation park, El Kantaoui 10km north. Calèche rides around the town. Zoo, Rue d'Algerie.

- **Sport**. Eighteen-hole golf course, El Kantaoui, 10km north. Riding Club, Ave du 3 Settembre 1934. Tennis Club, Blvd Abou Hamed el Ghazali. Watersports and tennis are available at larger hotels on the coast to the north of the city and at El Kantaoui.

History

Sousse was founded by the Phoenicians as a trading post in the 9C BC. The settlement, with its population of about 10,000, came under the influence of Carthage in the 6C BC, the date of its earliest archaeological remains: a sanctuary and tophet where milk teeth were found from child sacrifices. Carthaginian traditions and religious beliefs, however, changed with the growing influence of the Greek city states. Coins found in Sousse dating from the 3C BC show the Greek goddess Demeter on the obverse and the Carthaginian palm on the reverse. The nature of the sacrifices changed too, and in excavations from the 3–2C BC the great majority of bones belong to animals.

During the Second Punic War, Sousse was the base of the Carthaginian general, Hannibal, although the city later sided with the eventual victor, Rome, in the third and final Punic War. Hadrumetum, as Sousse was known to the Romans, became one of the most prosperous cities in the province, as testified by the wealth of fine mosaics uncovered here.

The city remained important during the Byzantine era, when it was renamed Justinianopolis and became the capital of the province of Byzacena. It was sacked by the Arabs in the 7C, then rebuilt by the Aghlabids from the Byzantine stones and renamed Susa. The city served as the Aghlabid port for the capital at Kairouan and was the point of departure for the Aghlabid ruler, Ziyadat Allah I, before his conquest of Sicily in 827.

With the fall of the Aghlabids, the city declined and was attacked by invaders, including the Normans of Sicily in the 12C and the Spanish in the 16C; shortly afterwards, the Ottomans were installed. The 16C writer, Leo Africanus, described the city under Ottoman rule: 'The towne of Susa, an exceedingly great and ancient towne...the plaines adjoyning abound with olives and figs... the inhabitants being most liberal and courteous people.'

Bombed by the French and Venetians in the 18C, Sousse was further ravaged by Allied bombing in 1942 during the Second World War. The devastation was described in 1950 by Wilson MacArthur: 'Here were the shattered waterfront, the esplanade of palms torn and disfigured by shell-fire and bombing, and large areas of total destruction beside the harbour.'

Now rebuilt, the city is the third largest in Tunisia and has a rapidly growing population and industry, which has risen from 36,000 in 1950 to 250,000 today.

The **MEDINA**, the historic city centre, covers a slope between the port and the kasbah. The **walls** of the medina, which stretch for 2km, and enclose an area of 700m by 500m, date from 859, although some of the stones with which they are built are from the Roman and Byzantine eras. The following route covers the major monuments within the medina—the Great Mosque, the ribat, and the kasbah, which holds a good mosaic museum—and also explores some of the medina's more remote corners. A visit to the museum requires two to three hours, so allow at least half a day for the major monuments, and an hour or so for the lesser sites.

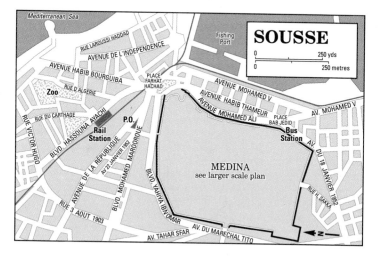

The vast expanse of **Place Farhat Hached**, also known as Place des Martyrs, is criss-crossed by traffic and trains. The area was flattened in 1943 by Allied bombing, which also left a great breach in the medina walls, which lie off the south-west side. Entering the medina through the breach, follow **Rue el Aghalba** for 150m to the **GREAT MOSQUE** (open, 08.30–13.00, except Fri) which is on the left. Commissioned by the Aghlabid Emir, Abou el Abbas Mohammed, the mosque was built in 851 to a design based on the Kairouan mosque. Like the Kairouan mosque, it has **crenellated walls** enclosing a large **courtyard** which is built over a cistern. The courtyard is surrounded on three sides by vaulted arcades that rest on short, square pillars. The fourth side precedes the **prayer hall** (closed to tourists), and is also arcaded, but the arches, which were added in the 17C, are much higher and rest on tall columns. The mosque has never had a minaret; a **squat domed tower**, which was added in the 11C in the north-east corner of the courtyard, is used instead.

Return to Rue el Aghalba and proceed north for less than 100m to the crenellated walls of the **RIBAT** (open summer, daily, 08.00–19.00, winter, daily, 09.00–17.00). It is a unique monument in that it has never been converted into a kasbah and is preserved more or less as it originally stood in Aghlabid times. Forming one of a chain of such fortresses along the coast, to defend against marauding Christians, the ribat was founded, according to an inscription, in 821 by Ziyadat Allah I. It appears, however, that only the south-east tower was built at this time and the remainder was constructed earlier, at least before 796. It is a fortified enclosure, measuring approximately 38m by 38m, defended internally by circular and semicircular turrets on square or rectangular bases set into the walls which are 13.5m high.

The monumental **portal** on the south side of the ribat is flanked by antique columns with weathered Corinthian capitals. Inside the portal there are **grooves** for the portcullis and overhead there are **slits** which allowed boiling oil to be poured on the enemy. The **narrow passageway** leading through the fortress walls, which are 2m thick, is lined with ancient pillars. The pillars support a **vaulted ceiling** which is one of the earliest known examples of the groin vault. The passage emerges at the **central courtyard**, which is surrounded on three sides by the warrior-monks' **cells**, each of which measures 3 square metres and is covered by a barrel-vaulted ceiling. On the fourth side of the courtyard steps lead up to a **mosque** on the first floor. Preceded by a terrace, four square portals lead into the simple interior of the mosque which is two bays deep and has 11 barrel-vaulted aisles.

From the mosque terrace, steps climb up again to the base of the **Nador Tower**, which is 27m high. Inside the tower, a spiral staircase of 74 steps climbs up to the top, from where there is a **panoramic view** over the city, taking in the port, the medina and the kasbah.

From the ribat, before proceeding uphill to the kasbah, a short diversion west takes you to the **Zaouia Zakkak** with its octagonal minaret. The minaret, which is Turkish in style, rises from a colonnaded courtyard, off one side of which is a prayer hall. The prayer hall is covered by a single dome that is constructed from terracotta tubes.

Return to Rue el Aghalba and head westwards to the Mosque of **Abd el Kadar** which is on the right. This small whitewashed mosque has a simple horseshoe portal decorated with ceramic tiles. Continue up Rue el Aghalba to **Bab el Finga**, one of the two gates in the west wall of the medina. Turn left, just before the gate, and follow **Rue Abou Naouas** inside the walls to **Bab el Gharbi**, the second of the gates in the medina's west wall. Head through the simple stone arch of Bab el Gharbi, and turn left onto the busy main road, Avenue Maréchal Tito, for just over 200m to the ****MUSEUM OF ANTIQUI-TIES** (open summer, 09.00–12.00, 15.00–18.30, winter, 09.00–12.00, 14.00–17.30) which occupies the ground floor of the kasbah. The museum is dedicated to mosaics and other archaeological finds from Roman Hadrumetum and Byzantine Justinianopolis.

The **kasbah**, the only parts of which open to the public are those occupied by the museum, stands in the south-west corner of the medina, at the highest point of the city. It was built surrounding a tower, the **Khalef el Fata**, in 859 on the site of a Byzantine fortress. The tower, commanding an extensive view

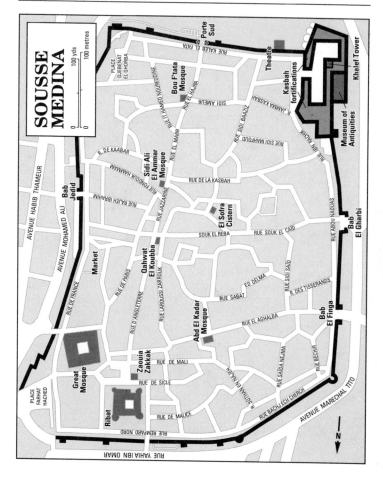

SOUSSE MEDINA

100 yds
100 metres

Porte Sud
RUE KALEB EL FATA
Theatre
Khalef Tower
Kasbah fortifications
R. JAMMA KASBAH
RUE IBN RACHIK
Museum of Antiquities
PLACE DJEBENAT EL GHORBA
Bou F'tata Mosque
RUE EL HAJRA
SIDI AMEUR
RUE ETT HAMED NOUREDDINE
RUE EL MARR
RUE SIDI BAAZIZ
RUE SIDI MAHFOUD
R. DE KAABAR
Sidi Ali El Ammar Mosque
RUE JAZZARINE
RUE FONDOUK HAMMAM
RUE DE LA KASBAH
Bab Jedid
AVENUE HABIB THAMEUR
RUE RALEH IBRAHIM
El Sofra Cistern
Bab El Gharbi
RUE ABOU NAOUAS
SOUK EL REBA
RUE SOUK EL CAID
AVENUE MOHAMED ALI
Market
RUE DE PARIS
Qahwat El Koubba
RUE LARBUISSI ZARROUK
ED DELMA
RUE SIDI SAID
R. DES TISSERANDS
RUE DE FRANCE
RUE D'ANGLETERRE
RUE SABAT
Abd El Kadar Mosque
RUE EL AGHALBA
Bab El Finga
Great Mosque
Zaouia Zakkak
RUE DE MALI
RUE SAIDA NEJMA
RUE BECHIR
PLACE FARHAT HACHED
RUE DE SICLE
R SOTHAN EN NAEH
RUE BACHJ ECH CHERCH
AVENUE MARECHAL TITO
Ribat
RUE DE MALICE
RUE REMPART NORD
RUE YAHIA IBN OMAR

N

of the coast, soon took over from that of the ribat as a lookout-post and light-house. Its design, with a staircase inside the thickness of the wall, and rooms on each floor, was a prototype for many minarets subsequently built in North Africa.

The **museum entrance**, approached by a flight of steps, leads into a **hall** where there is a ticket office on the right and a small shop selling postcards and publications. The hall gives onto a **courtyard** which is surrounded by colonnades.

Room 1, preceded by three steps off the **south colonnade**, has an outstanding 3C mosaic of ****Medusa** that once paved the tepidarium of the baths. The room also contains statues and inscriptions dating from the same era, including a **head of Trajan**, a white marble statue of **Apollo**, and a carved relief showing **Augustus in a triumphal chariot**.

Back in the courtyard, in the pavement of the **west colonnade**, is a 3C mosaic of the **horses of Sorothus**. At the end of the west colonnade is a semicircular mosaic with the head of ****Oceanus**, which once decorated a 2C pool. The **north colonnade** has **tomb mosaics** found in local Christian catacombs and also a collection of **terracotta tiles** with moulded reliefs depicting Adam and Eve amongst other biblical subjects.

Room 2 opens off the north colonnade and contains some of the finest mosaics in the museum collection. Above the door is a 4C ****Venus at her toilet**, found at El Jem, with the four seasons at each corner. Proceeding in a clockwise direction along the **south wall**, there is a 2C ****satyrs and bacchantes** richly interwoven with a surrounding vine. Next to it is the ****triumph of Bacchus**, showing the young god on a chariot drawn by four tigers. The 3C **marine scene** alongside was taken from a pool. On the **west wall** there are some large 3C geometric mosaics taken from the baths. Along the **north wall** is the early 3C ****rape of Ganymede**, with Zeus in the guise of an eagle, surrounded by eight medallions, each of which contains a wild animal. Next is the 2C ****triumph of Neptune**, which is in almost pristine condition. On the **east wall** is a 1C mosaic of the ****Nile**, which was found at El Alia, near Mahdia, depicting pigmies in combat, and boats and aquatic life on the river. Back at the south wall again, the ****legend of Attic** shows a winged victory with Athena on the left and Poseidon on the right. Lastly, the grand composition of ****Apollo and the nine muses** which is particularly finely detailed due to the very small size of the mosaic pieces.

Returning to the courtyard, off the **east colonnade** is **Room 3**, which has finds from the 6C BC **tophet** uncovered near the Great Mosque. The tophet, dedicated to Baal and Tanit, was a sacrificial burial ground and has yielded numerous burial urns and stelae, some of which are carved with the symbol of Tanit.

Back at the **east colonnade**, there is a **passageway** on the left which leads through to the Grand Courtyard. Before reaching the Grand Courtyard, however, turn off right into a small **hallway** which contains further mosaics, including a mid 3C ****nereid riding a dolphin**. The hallway leads through to a series of three interconnected rooms. The first, **Room 4**, has a Punic tomb, found during the construction work on the museum, and finds from the Punic necropolis, including lamps and pottery. **Room 5** has further finds from the necropolis, including 1–3C Roman oil lamps and statuettes, and mosaic fragments, including the 3C **Diana, the hunter**. **Room 6** is dedicated to ceramics and other finds from the Christian catacombs of Hermes which holds 2500 tombs, De Severe which has 5000 tombs and Bon Pasteur, the largest, with 6000 tombs. The latter, which has 105 galleries, amounting to a total 1557.5m, can be visited by applying to the museum authorities.

Return to the passage and proceed to the **Grand Courtyard** which is overlooked by the **Khalef el Fata** tower. The courtyard holds a collection of lapidary fragments and there are steps up from the north-east corner to a **terrace** from where there are good views of the medina and city. Along the east side of the courtyard is a café and the last three rooms of the museum. **Room 7** has a vast ****triclinium mosaic** taken from a 3C villa at El Jem, depicting a dining scene. Amongst the mosaics mounted on the walls in this room is the 3C **tragic poet**, found in a nearby villa. **Room 8** has some 2–3C fresco fragments depicting mythological scenes, large geometric mosaics, and a **marine life**. **Room 9** has a viewing platform from which to look down on the showpiece of the room, a triclinium mosaic of **preparations for a gladiatorial contest**. Dating from the 3C, the mosaic shows four hunters, and animals to be used in the amphitheatre. On the wall to the left of the entrance is the **mosaic of Smirat**, which shows the four gladiators of Telegenii along with their names and those of their victims. In a niche on the opposite wall is a 3C phallic statue of **Priape** with fruits and vegetables, symbolic of his role as protector of the garden.

From the museum, return to Bab el Gharbi and either retrace your steps back to Place Farhat Hached, or take the following itinerary which explores the more remote areas of the medina. From Bab el Gharbi, follow **Rue Souk el Caid** downhill through an area of weaving workshops onto Souk Er Reba. Where the two roads meet, turn right to the **El Sofra Cistern** which is on the right. Dating from the Roman period, the cistern was restored in the 11C and consists of a vast underground chamber with a capacity of 3000 cubic metres. Return to **Souk Er Reba** and continue to **Qahwat el Koubba**, which is on the left, just before meeting Rue d'Angleterre. This historic building of unknown origin surrounds a courtyard which contains a café and carpet shop. It is believed to date back to the 10C when it formed part of a baths or was possibly the audience hall of a palace.

At the junction with Rue d'Angleterre, turn right. After 120m the **Mosque of Sidi Ali el Ammar** is passed on the left. Now hemmed in by buildings, this small mosque dates back to the 11C and has niches and blind arcades decorating its façade. 100m further south is another small mosque, **Bou F'tata**, which has a carved inscription in Kufic script, recording that the building was founded in 838 by the Aghlabid sovereign, Abou Iqual.

Retrace your steps back to **Rue d'Angleterre** which eventually emerges at the square in front of the ribat.

31 · Sousse via Zaghouan to Tunis

It is 158km from Sousse to Tunis, on minor roads, except for a short stretch of motorway. The route passes the Berber village of Takrouna, the baths at Zriba Hammam and a Roman spring at Zaghouan, where there is a hotel that could be used to break the journey. Onward from Zaghouan, there are short excursions to the extensive Roman ruins of Thuburbo Maius, the baths of El Oust, and Uthina.

Public transport is limited and involves changing at Enfidaville, Zaghouan and El Fahs. It is important to take into consideration that places of interest are invariably a few kilometres off the road.

Leave Sousse by following signs to Tunis along the coast for 8km on the dual carriageway before taking a sharp left for 3km onto the GP1. Follow the GP1 for 11km before forking right, onto the A1 in the direction of Tunis.

Hergla, a small town crammed onto a headland, is passed on the left after 8km. Built on the site of ancient Horraca Caelia, in the 2C it was a border town dividing the provinces of Byzacena and Zeugitania. There are no ancient remains, but the town's 18C mosque holds the tomb of Sidi Bou Mendil, a 10C marabout who is said to have sailed home from Mecca on his handkerchief.

After a further 18km, take the Enfidaville exit and follow the MC133 in the direction of Zaghouan. After 3km the road crosses the Oued Abdallah river, 2km beyond which, on the left, is the turning for Takrouna.

Takrouna, a Berber village built on a rocky spur at an altitude of 195m, is popular with tourists, but has retained its rural charm. The road ends at the foot of the oldest part of the village which is reached by winding paths and steps carved in the rock. The focus here is the **Zaouia Sidi Abd Kader**, a small whitewashed mausoleum, which contains the tomb of the marabout, Sidi Abd Kader. The views from the small terrace in front of the zaouia take in a fine panorama of the surrounding region.

Continuing on the MC133, which is narrow and tortuous in places, the road enters the Zaghouan government district after 13km, an area that is heavily mined and quarried for stone, used to make cement. The prairie-like landscape, scarred by slag heaps and dotted with mining villages, is also the source of numerous natural springs. **Zriba Hammam** which is on the left, 17km further on the MC133, is built over just one such spring. The **baths** (open 24 hours daily), after which this small village is named, lie less than 2km from the main road, in a cleft in the rocky hills. The natural hot water that rises here is rich in minerals and is said to have curative properties for skin disorders, although there are no medical facilities. Local holidaymakers rent the nearby apartments, which are currently being extended and developed along with a hotel complex, and spend the day at the baths and the nearby cafés and shops which are well-stocked with toiletries.

The MC133 continues between the red-earthed Zaghouan hills, where olive groves cover the lower slopes, for 5km to Zaghouan itself, the centre of which is reached by forking left.

ZAGHOUAN

Zaghouan, positioned on the foothills of Mt Zaghouan (1295m), is a small town with steep, narrow streets, and modern outskirts that spread into the plain below. Untouched by tourism, the facilities here are basic, but the Roman fountain on the hillside above the town makes Zaghouan worth a visit.

- **Bus station**. Ave Habib Bourguiba. Two buses daily to Tunis. Other destinations include Kairouan.

- **Louage station**. Ave Habib Bourguiba. Regular services to El Fahs and Tunis.

- **Hotels**. *Les Nymphes*, tel. (02) 675094, attractively set in forest on the slopes above the town, offers two-star bungalow-type accomodation. There is also a youth hostel in the town, *Maison des Jeunes*, tel. (02) 675265.

- **Restaurants**. The only restaurant of any note is that at *Les Nymphes* hotel.

- **Shopping**. Small stores in the town.

- **Children**. Small playground below the monumental fountain.

History

Zaghouan stands on ancient Ziqua, which in 82 BC was populated by inhabitants from Chiusi in mainland Italy. The town rose to importance in the reign of Hadrian (117–138), who oversaw the building of the great aqueduct which ran from Ziqua to Carthage. With the fall of Rome, the settlement was more or less abandoned, and did not not revive until the 17C when it was populated by immigrants from Andalucia.

One of the surviving monuments of ancient Zicqua is the 2C **triumphal arch** which you pass as you come into the town. Continuing into the the town centre there is a small **zaouia** with an enamel-tiled dome, belonging to the marabout, Sidi Ali Azous, who is the patron saint of Tunisia. The narrow cobbled streets of the **medina**, which lead off from here in all directions, have small shops and simple fountains.

The other surviving monument of ancient Zicqua is the ****monumental fountain** up on the hill above the town. It is signposted from the town to '*temple des eaux*'. The road winds up for less than a kilometre to the Club de Chasse (hunting club). Take the unsigned right fork here, Avenue des Martyrs, for a further kilometre, following signs to the Pizzeria Temple des Eaux, which is the name of the café next to the fountain.

The fountain, or nympheum, which was built during the 2C is dramatically positioned in the shadow of the rocky peak of Mt Zaghouan. It is preceded by a flight of steps, with pieces of the original stone-carved gutters acting as a banister, and other masonry fragments strewn about. The large pool below the steps, shaped like a figure of eight, filtered the water before it was chanelled along the aqueduct for the 70km to Carthage. At the top of the steps, there is a semicircular structure with 12 niches that once held statues of water nymphs. The central niche once formed part of a temple, and would have held a statue of the fountain's protecting divinity, with a fountain playing in front of it.

From Zaghouan, the MC133 continues to head westwards, through olive groves. The terrain is flat and becomes increasingly barren as the village of (12km) **Bir Halima** is approached. The village is clustered around a mosque, the whitewashed façade of which has a cross, indicating that a Christian community lived here at one time. From Bir Halima, continue west on the MC28 for a further 13km, to **El Fahs**, which lies on the junction with the GP3. The centre of El Fahs, reached by turning left at the junction, has a few basic eating places, but unless you are in need of provisions is not worth visiting.

The ruins of Thuburbo Maius are reached by turning right at the GP3 in the direction of Tunis. After 1km turn left onto the Mejez el Bab road, then right after less than a kilometre onto Rue 627, a narrow road lined with hedges of prickly pear cactus. After a further 1km the ruins are on the right.

THUBURBO MAIUS

Thuburbo Maius (open summer, daily, 08.00–19.00, winter, daily, 08.00–17.00) is amongst the better-preserved archaeological sites in Tunisia and has many impressive monuments. Tickets are available from the office block which also contains a shop selling publications and toilets on the right of the car park.

History

Little is known of the early history of Thuburbo Maius, although the name 'Thuburbo' suggests Berber origins. The first recorded settlement here was established by Roman veterans in 27 BC. It grew rapidly, being granted the status of a municipality in AD 128 when Hadrian visited the city, and was finally made a colony in AD 188, under the Emperor Commodus.

The reign of Commodus (178–193) and the half century following saw the city expand to cover an area of 40 hectares. The inhabitants, who numbered 7000–12,000, prospered from agriculture and were never troubled by war (the city has no fortifications). The city flourished during the 4C when many churches were built and restoration work was carried out, but religious disagreements between Catholics and Donatists coincided with the city's decline, exacerbated by the 5C Vandal invasions. By the 7C the city had been totally abandoned. The site was discovered by Charles Tissit in 1857, although it was not until the First World War that serious restoration began, using prisoners of war as labour.

From the car park, a footpath leads up to the **forum**, the centre of the Roman city. Now a vast dusty expanse, the forum, measuring 49m by 49m, was originally paved and had Corinthian colonnades along three of its sides, with the capitol temple making up the fourth side. Inscriptions found during excavations indicate that the forum was laid between 161 and 192, with major restoration work being carried out in 376.

The ****Capitoline Temple**, built in AD 168, was dedicated to the Roman emperors, Commodus and Marcus Aurelius. A grand flight of white stone steps precedes the raised podium where there are the remains of a portico. Carved from Carrara marble, four of the former six fluted columns have been restored with their Corinthian capitals, standing to their original height of 8.5m. The columns are raised on a vaulted substructure which once housed the treasury but in the years of the city's decline was used as an oil press. It was in these vaulted chambers that the segments of the giant statue of Jupiter, now in the Bardo Museum, were found. Jupiter, along with Juno and Minerva, were the protecting divinities of the temple during Roman times.

The **curia**, or Temple of Peace, as it is often referred to, is reached by five worn stone steps off the north-east corner of the forum. Built during the reign of Antoninus (138–161), it has a small courtyard, measuring 12.3m by 9.25m, which was once surrounded by columns, the bases of which remain in places, as does the beautiful veined marble paving. On one side of the courtyard is a relief of the winged horse, Pegasus, who was the mascot of the Third Augustan Legion. A single chamber leads off from the courtyard and contains a pedestal with a long inscription, which would once have held a statue.

Off the south-west side of the forum is the **Temple of Mercury**, built between 118 and 138, in the style typical of North Africa. This time the preceding courtyard is circular, surrounded by eight columns, some of which are still standing, connected by a passage to the barely discernible cella.

The complex of courtyards off the south corner of the forum were **market-places**, built in the 2C, the main one of which measures 19m by 19m and was once colonnaded. To the south-east of the market-places are the remains of the **winter baths**, which, according to an inscription found here, were totally reconstructed between 395 and 408. The entrance hall, at the north-east end

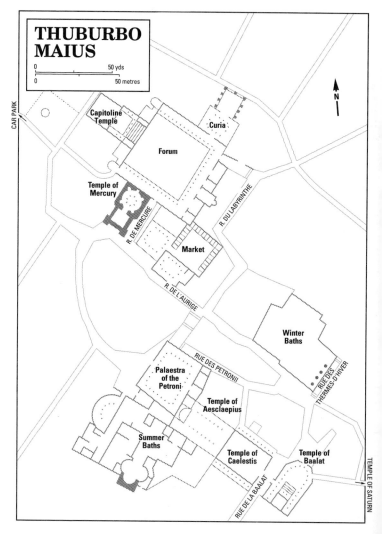

of the building, has three of its original four columns at the centre, stone benches along the walls and remnants of its mosaic paving. A passageway leads through to a large frigidarium with two pools and a series of adjoining rooms which were heated. The southern end of the building opens out into a portico, with two of its original four Corinthian columns of grey stone still standing.

From the winter baths, the Rue des Thermes d'Hiver, leads south-east for 100m to the **Temple of Saturn**. This temple, dedicated to the Roman equivalent of the Carthaginian god Baal Hammon, is built on the highest point of the site. It dates from the late 2C, but was converted to a church in Christian times, testimony to which is the wide central aisle lined with nine grey columns at either side, and an altar that rests on a pair of Corinthian capitals. There is also a cruciform baptistery font set into the ground.

Head back towards the baths, but fork left before reaching them, following the footpath to the **Temple of Baalat**. The temple takes its name from the fragments of a seated goddess found here. A flight of ten white stone steps lead up to the sanctuary, the stones of which lie mostly tumbled to the ground. From the north-west side of the temple, a doorway leads through to a courtyard which once held the U-shaped **Temple of Caelestis**. A paved road runs through the centre of the courtyard to another **sacred area**, dedicated to Aesculapius, the Roman god of medicine, whose Punic equivalent was Eshmoun. An inscription found on the site describes that ritual purity for three days was needed to enter; no hair-cuts, no bath, no sex, no pork or beans. Unfortunately, the ruins of the sanctuary are scant and difficult to distinguish from the market-place that was later built on top.

The **Palaestra of the Petroni** to the north-west is in much better condition. It is named after Petronius Felix and his sons, who, as the long inscription along the north-west side of the courtyard tells us, dedicated the monument to the city in 225. Along the south-east side, the marble portico has been re-erected, complete with its Corinthian capitals which are carved from sandstone, with grapes, pomegranates, pine cones, and acanthus sprays on the abacus. The palaestra served as a meeting place where people exercised before going on to the **summer baths**, which are to the south-west. They were probably used when the source of the winter baths dried up in the hot summer months.

Extensively restored in 361, the summer baths are entered from the west corner of the palaestra. They are considerably larger than the winter baths and consist of a frigidarium, once clad in marble, which has two pools lined with monochrome mosaics, and a caldarium where there are three semicircular pools. Off the north-west side of the baths is a semicircular portico which once contained latrines.

From Thuburbo Maius, continue along Rue 627 which after 1km rejoins the GP3. Heading northwards in the direction of Tunis, the GP3 follows the course of the Miliana river between barren hills and straggly olive groves. After 18km, a lonesome Roman tomb, a single block with a doorway, is passed on the left of the road. A further 8.5km along the GP3, the Roman baths of **Jebel Oust** are off on the right, 4km along the Zaghouan road, the MC133. Still in use, the thermal waters are now piped into a hotel and medical centre, on the hill above the Roman ruins. Inside the complex gates, the first left leads to the **Thermes Romaines**, where some fine mosaics, dating from the 3–5C, have been preserved. The main hall, which has an apse at one end, has a fine geometric mosaic floor. Leading off from the main room are small chambers, numbering some 200 in all, which would have served as rooms for guests who came to the baths for medical treatment. Most of the rooms have mosaic floors and some are paved with a dark violet stone, quarried locally. The baths themselves are up a level from the main hall. The largest pool, which is rectangular, has four very worn steps leading down into it, and the remnants of the colonnades that once surrounded it. The smaller circular pool, which was also originally surrounded by columns, is completely encircled by a row of four steps in very good condition. The other rooms in the baths have fine marble floors, and the **Room of the Four Seasons** is named after its mosaic with a composition based on four medallions. Other ruins in the vicinity date from Byzantine times, including a basilica which was built next to the spring source, where in Roman times there was a temple dedicated to the god Aesculapius.

From El Oust, return to the GP3, which after 6km runs alongside the remains of the great aqueduct, built by Hadrian from Zaghouan to Carthage. After a further 2.5km, there is a right turn, signposted to Oudna station, on the MC36E, which leads to the small archaeological site of **UTHINA**. To get to the ruins, follow the MC36E for 1km before turning left under the aqueduct. Keep straight ahead for 2.5km, and then turn right, just after Oudna station, where a mock Roman column has been erected. A narrow road climbs up for 1km to the farmstead which occupies the site of a Byzantine fort at the centre of the ruins.

History

The site of Uthina was probably Berber in origin, although the ruins seen today are of the Roman city that was founded here as a colony by Emperor Augustus. The colony soon became a wealthy city, prospering on the cultivation of grain. Excavators have uncovered numerous luxurious villas with fine mosaic floors and sculptures, and also a good number of Christian buildings, dating from 256 when Uthina was the seat of a bishop.

The ruins, still under excavation, include a fine **amphitheatre**, which is oval in shape, and has enough of its surrounding arches to make it possible to imagine how it might once have looked. Opposite the amphitheatre are the low-lying ruins of one of the largest of the eleven villas so far uncovered at the site. Known as the **Laberii Villa**, it covers an area of 40m by 40m, and has a courtyard which measures 20m by 14m, around which the 40 rooms of the villa are arranged. Many mosaics have been revealed, including that in the atrium which depicts agricultural life. Nearby are the scant remnants of the **Laberii Baths**. Other ruins include **cisterns** and **storage rooms**. There are also some fine pieces of tumbled masonry surrounding the **fort**, which was built by the Byzantines using Roman stones.

Back on the GP3, the road continues alongside the aqueduct which, to compensate for the gradient in the land, is in places up to 20m high. After

4km, the town of **Mohammedia** sprawls ahead which is only of interest for the ruins of the Ottoman palaces which can be seen on the hill to the left. Founded by Mohammed Bey (1756–59), the **palace** complex was rebuilt by Ahmed Bey in 1842–47, with the intention of making it as magnificent as Versailles. The mud-coloured ruins seen today are a far cry from the original intention, although the interior has some very fine ceramic tile work.

The GP3 continues northwards, through the busy town of (4km) Fouchana from where the suburbs of Tunis can be seen on the slopes ahead, a further 6km away.

A NOTE ON BLUE GUIDES

The Blue Guide series began in 1915 when Muirhead Guide-Books Limited published 'Blue Guide London and its Environs'. Findlay and James Muirhead already had extensive experience of guidebook publishing: before the First World War they had been the editors of the English editions of the German Baedekers, and by 1915 they had acquired the copyright of most of the famous 'Red' Handbooks from John Murray.

An agreement made with the French publishing house Hachette et Cie in 1917 led to the translation of Muirhead's London guide, which became the first 'Guide Bleu' – Hachette had previously published the blue covered 'Guides Joannes'. Subsequently, Hachette's 'Guide Bleu Paris et ses Environs' was adapted and published in London by Muirhead. The collaboration between the two publishing houses continued until 1933.

In 1933 Ernest Benn Limited took over the Blue Guides, appointing Russel Muirhead, Findlay Muirhead's son, editor in1934. The Muirhead's connection with the Blue Guides ended in 1963 when Stuart Rossiter, who had been working on the Guides since 1954, became house editor, revising and compiling several of the books himself.

The Blue Guides are now published by A & C Black, who aquired Ernest Benn in 1984, so continuing the tradition of guidebook publishing which began in 1826 with 'Black's Economical Tourist of Scotland'. The Blue Guides series continues to grow: there are now more than 50 titles in print with revised editions appearing regularly and many new Blue Guides in preparation.

'Blue Guides' is a registered trade mark.

INDEX

Topographical names and subjects are printed in roman type. Names of people, dynasties and religious movements appear in *italic*.

If you would like more information about Blue Guides please complete the form below and return it to

Blue Guides
A&C Black (Publishers) Ltd
Freepost
Eaton Socon
Huntingdon
Cambridgeshire
PE19 3BR
or fax it to us on
0171-831 8478

Name. . . . .
. . . .
Address. . . . .
. . . .
. . . .
. . . .
. . . .
. . . .